The States of the Earth

An Ecological and Racial History of Secularization

Mohamed Amer Meziane

Translated by Jonathan Adjemian

VERSO

London • New York

This work received support for excellence in publication and translation from Albertine Translation, formerly French Voices, a program created by Villa Albertine

This English-language edition first published by Verso 2024
Translation © Jonathan Adjemian 2024
First published as *Des empires sous la terre. Histoire écologique et raciale de la sécularisation*
© La Découverte 2021

The moral rights of the author and translator have been asserted

1 3 5 7 9 10 8 6 4 2

Verso
UK: 6 Meard Street, London W1F 0EG
US: 388 Atlantic Avenue, Brooklyn, NY 11217
versobooks.com

Verso is the imprint of New Left Books

ISBN-13: 978-1-80429-177-1
ISBN-13: 978-1-83929-178-8 (UK EBK)
ISBN-13: 978-1-83929-179-5 (US EBK)

British Library Cataloguing in Publication Data
A catalogue record for this book is available from the British Library

Library of Congress Cataloging-in-Publication Data

Names: Amer Meziane, Mohamed, author. | Adjemian, Jonathan, translator.
Title: The states of the Earth : an ecological and racial history of secularization / Mohamed Amer Meziane ; translated by Jonathan Adjemian.
Other titles: Des empires sous la terre. English
Description: London ; New York : Verso, [2024] | Translation of: Des empires sous la terre. | Includes bibliographical references and index.
Identifiers: LCCN 2023044076 (print) | LCCN 2023044077 (ebook) | ISBN 9781804291771 (trade paperback) | ISBN 9781804291795 (US EBK) | ISBN 9781839291788 (UK EBK)
Subjects: LCSH: Colonization—History. | Colonization—Social aspects. | Imperialism—History. | Civilization, Secular. | Secularization. | Developing countries—Civilization—Western influences. | Environmental degradation.
Classification: LCC JV105 .A6713 2024 (print) | LCC JV105 (ebook) | DDC 909.8--dc23/eng/20231227
LC record available at https://lccn.loc.gov/2023044076
LC ebook record available at https://lccn.loc.gov/2023044077

Typeset in Minion Pro by Hewer Text UK Ltd, Edinburgh
Printed and bound by CPI Group (UK) Ltd, Croydon CR0 4YY

Contents

Preface to the English-Language Edition

Not so long ago, European miners still thought that demons inhabited the underground world. They thus anticipated dreadful encounters with such demons each time they worked in those subterranean labyrinths called mines. The story indicates that massive extraction of underground resources on a global scale would not have been possible without a disenchantment of the soils and the subsoils. Hence, a new question about our troubled times: If modernity is the Anthropocene, and if modernity is secular, is there a Secularocene? To answer this question, one needs to write the history of colonial modernity anew, the history of what I call the states of the earth.

What are the states of the earth? This expression encapsulates a web of intertwined meanings. Each of them captures an aspect of the book and the argument. The states of the earth first refers to the *climate crisis*. The earth is in a state of upheaval. Fires, floods, shortages of water, rising temperatures: these phenomena are now part of our common experience of global warming. But the states of the earth also refer to modern imperial states governing the planet by dividing the earth into multiple territories called *nations*. This book is a history of these political entities that rule the earth through colonial and capitalistic expansions. It asks: What if the states which now unequally rule the earth were responsible for the current state of the earth, namely for climatic upheaval?

Describing the historical roots of climate change requires a history of these states and of their violence. This history begins before the birth of either colonialism or capitalism. In Euro-America at least, the modern nation-state is the heir of medieval Christendom, more precisely of its *imperiality*. On 25 December of the year 800 CE, Western Christendom revitalized the figure of empire through the coronation of Charles the Great as the emperor of the West. Through this imperial tradition, the sovereign constantly claims to be the successor of the Roman emperor while representing God on Earth. The imperiality of power sustains the so-called theologico-political knot. The intertwinement of Christian theology and politics is thus mediated by the Roman language of imperial sovereignty. The empire is the typical mediator between heaven and Earth, deploying violence in this world in the name of a divine power who is himself imagined as a lord or a king.

Imperiality, however, is not a monolith but a battlefield between oppositional forces claiming absolute power against each other. Imperiality first refers to the *title* of empire that each power – the emperor but also the pope and the kings – claims in alliance with or in opposition to other Christian powers. *This realm is an empire* is a typical expression of state sovereignty's absolute claim over a territory. The Crusades are foundational to the making of imperiality. During the Crusades, popes began to see themselves as direct political – and not only spiritual – representatives of God on Earth. As a result, the imperial expansion of the Roman Church was intensified by the Crusaders' wars against Muslims. Defined as the enemies of Christ, the 'Saracens' were understood as the worshippers of a devilish idol known as 'Mahomet'. This specific imperial-Christian discourse is the matrix of what would later become Orientalism. Muslim scholars such as Al-Bakri responded to this discourse in a less theological way than one would expect. 'Their guidelines for ideal conduct' were not 'derived from revelation or from the pronouncements of a prophet', wrote Al-Bakri, since all of them came 'from their kings'.[1] By pointing to the submission of Christians to their kings and the pope, Al-Bakri deployed an early critique of what I propose to call 'imperiality'.

The Crusaders' submission to the imperialities of popes and kings can also be considered as one matrix of modern colonial racism in the Americas. Since the late fifteenth century, missionary and colonial

---

1   Paul M. Cobb, *The Race for Paradise: An Islamic History of the Crusades*, Oxford: Oxford University Press, 2014, p. 12. Al-Bakri's proto-anthropology of the West points to the profound Roman heritage of Christians; see p. 11. This anthropology of Roman imperiality is not a critique of Christianity. The critique of Crusaders by Al-Bakri is not primarily theological, thus dissolving modern fantasies of religious difference as the main source of conflicts.

expansion in the Americas obeyed the 'sacred instructions' commanded by Pope Alexander VI in the bull *Inter Caetera*. The aim was crystal clear: overthrow paganism and establish Christian faith. But this bull was preceded by *Dum Diversas* (1452) and *Romanus Pontifex* (1455). By the middle of the fifteenth century, the pope had given the kings of Portugal the right to 'invade, conquer, expel and fight Saracens, pagans, and other enemies of Christ' (*saracenos ac paganos, aliosque Christi inimicos*) wherever they may have been. Christian kings were thus allowed by the Roman Church to dispossess and perpetually enslave them.

These bulls are the founding act of what I call colonial imperiality, namely the dissemination of a not strictly colonial imperiality through colonial rule. Against postcolonial theory, decolonial scholars have rightly emphasized the central role of the colonization of the Americas since 1492 and thus argued that the racialization of indigenous lives predated Orientalism in the making of colonial modernity. But the two bulls of 1452 and 1455 tell us a different story. The so-called *Saracens* – a word which referred to North African and Arab populations of the Mediterranean – were defined as 'enemies of Christ' long before the conquest of the Americas. In other words, the discourse which invented the so-called *Orient* was the beating heart of imperiality before modern colonialism even emerged. There is no doubt that the genocide of indigenous people and the enslavement of Black people were decisive in the making of the capitalist world. But one needs to connect the history of Orientalism and the colonization of Afro-Asia to this well-known history of violence that constituted the Americas. Connecting histories requires a pluralization of chronologies. In the bulls of 1452 and 1455, Saracens – or Muslims – are considered enemies of Christ, *among all other pagans*, including Jewish and Black people. The Church argued that they deserved to be dispossessed of their land and enslaved. Colonialism was thus born as a mutation of imperiality, during the Reconquista and before the conquest of the Americas. And one should not forget that Christopher Columbus was, in his own mind, a Crusader continuing the war against Saracens who had invaded Spain from North Africa.

By trying to pluralize chronology, I argue against the possibility of assigning a single origin to colonial modernity. This gesture might lead us to reproduce a hierarchy between different experiences of racism and colonialism by claiming that some experiences are more central and paradigmatic than others. But why not begin with the colonization of the Americas, one might ask? And why start this ecological and racial history of secularization during the eighteenth century? I agree with decolonial scholars that 1492 is a crucial moment in world history that connects the *Reconquista* – the destruction of Al-Andalus in Spain by Christian armies – and the conquest of the Americas. I simply argue that colonialism has been in a state of permanent transformation since then. Colonialism, therefore, is not a stable essence whose knowledge would be exhausted by its beginning. The history of colonialism's metamorphosis is not reducible to the study of one of its multiple matrices surreptitiously defined as a single origin. During the nineteenth century, colonialism expanded and accelerated. *The States of the Earth* describes these transformations. Secularization, colonialism, and fossil fuels, dug from mines penetrating deep into the underground world, overlap in this history.

The history first explores the expansion of colonialism which started with the British colonization of India and the French expedition to Egypt during the second half of the eighteenth century. The conquest of Algiers in 1830 was truly historic in that it was the first province of the Ottoman Empire to be colonized by a European power. Second, empires were secularized because, for strategic reasons described in the book, they could not easily and effectively convert these new 'natives' who also were Muslims to Christianity. Conversion to Christianity never disappeared. It coexisted with and was often marginalized by another kind of conversion: the *civilizing mission*. Third, the economies of these capitalistic empires were industrialized. They increasingly depended on fossil fuels to power their steam engines. European hegemony was not globally achieved before the nineteenth century. And the use of fossil fuels, among other industrial weapons, was central to this domination. Africa, Asia, and Oceania were now under European control after centuries of European colonialism in the Americas. Simultaneously, the colonization of the territory of North America was progressively achieved by White settlers. The secularization of empires during the nineteenth century led to the current climatic upheaval; this was an acceleration of the logic of colonial imperiality that had begun long before, during the fifteenth century.

The States of the Earth emphasizes the role of state violence in the making of this climatic upheaval. If fossil capitalism nurtures fossil empires, it is because it depends on the existence of fossil states. The imperial fossil state is what makes capitalism and colonialism work hand in hand against the planet itself. Because states are imperial, they are in permanent competition with one another. Inter-imperial competitions engender a state of globalized warfare which sustains the climatic upheaval. Excavating the subterranean dimensions of imperial sovereignty, this is a material history with metaphysical consequences. While capitalist states were attempting to sacrifice heaven on Earth, they delved beneath the earth. Both institutional religions and state secularisms participated in this process of secularization, attempting to achieve heaven on Earth by destroying Earth itself. The earthly paradise promised by industrialists is increasingly resembling hell, thus indicating that the earth will never bear the burden of heaven.

Banzart, Tunisia, July 2023

Acknowledgements

I would first like to thank my family for who we are: Yamina, Saadi, Iman, and Yacine. This book is first and foremost a trace of our displacements. I was born in London to Algerian parents. We left London when I was six months old to move to the Middle East, more precisely to Kuwait, where I spent my early childhood. During the summer of 1990, while we were on holiday in Algeria, Iraq invaded Kuwait. We thus lost our home and virtually everything we had. We never went back. The early nineties were not an easy time in Algeria either. It was the beginning of what has come to be known as the 'black decade'. This is when we left Algeria for France. This book bears the traces of these experiences and of my ancestors' resilience. My voice is not mine alone.

I would like to thank my editors for believing in this project. Sebastian Budgen and the Verso Books team; Rémy Toulouse, my French editor, as well as the team of La Découverte. I want to thank the translator of this book, Jonathan Adjemian, and Villa Albertine for granting this book its non-fiction prize. Étienne Balibar has been a long-time political support since our first encounter during a debate on secularism in January 2016 at the Sorbonne. Our first disagreement was about violence and monotheism. It gave birth to many discussions during which he became one of my interlocutors. Talal Asad's moral support as well as our continuous discussions on the Upper West Side have nurtured me in ways that I am not fully able to describe yet. Ann Laura Stoler revised the original manuscript with so much depth and insight that I cannot be grateful enough to her. Souleymane Bachir Diagne has been a great colleague from whom I have learnt a great deal. I thank them all for being such great human beings, and for their knowledge and wisdom. And I would like to thank Philippe Büttgen for his precious help during the research process that, while considerably transformed, eventually led to this book.

I want to thank anthropologists Matthew Engelke and Katherine Pratt Ewing for their institutional support during the last part of the research and writing process at the Institute for Religion, Culture and Public Life at Columbia University. Without their generous help, support, and funding over four years, without the seminars I gave and my outstanding students and colleagues, this book would not have become what it is. I would like to thank Mahmood Mamdani for inviting me to present what would become Chapter 3 of the book at the Ifriqiyya seminar in Columbia's Department of Middle Eastern, South Asian, and African Studies. Nadia Abu El Haj, Hent de Vries, Emmanuelle Saada, Todd Shepard, Judith Surkis, Shirin Amir-Moazzami, Meriem Chabani, Elleni Centime Zeleke, Nadia Marzouki, Violaine Huisman, and many of my colleagues at Columbia University have also been great interlocutors. I would like to thank all my outstanding Brown University colleagues and students. The amazing Arab diasporic artistic scene of New York shaped the tone of this book and its atmosphere. Last but not least, I thank Anissa for our many encounters and collaborations, her mystical intelligence and creativity.

Prologue

What is the ecological underside of 'disenchantment'? What took place below our feet when Western powers proclaimed they had liberated us from divine commandments and illusions of transcendence? What were the environmental and planetary consequences of this metaphysical crisis that seems to have struck industrialized Europe during the nineteenth century? *The States of the Earth* responds to these questions by revisiting the racial and colonial elements that upheld – like a subterranean and thus invisible architecture – the event that has been called the 'death of God': that very European will to abolish every remnant of transcendence in the name of Christ, whose most eminent heralds have been philosophers.[1] What Western sociological thought would later call the 'secularization' of the West is nothing other than a belief in the existence of *this world* as the only real one: the certainty that it is here below, on the earth, that salvation can be realized, through *unlimited* enjoyment ensured by a continual growth of riches.

At the dawn of the nineteenth century, European empires called for a reform of the religions whose adherents they had given up on trying to convert. This call was an act of secularization, an order to abandon the mass conversion of 'infidels' to Christianity so that, for a new generation of colonizers, the spirit of Christ could be better disseminated under the

---

1   G. W. F. Hegel, *The Phenomenology of Spirit*, trans. Terry Pinkard, Cambridge: Cambridge University Press, 2018, pp. 450–5.

profane and secular forms of industrial modernity. They thus created a new order. The word *order* designates how space is reorganized by the imperative to modernize, through hierarchy and exclusion. This order – which is commonly described as a 'political project' – was born from a drive to delineate the borders of politics and its religious 'other', until then unstable, in order to demand their separation. In this way, the great critiques of religion tried to ward off the spectres of the divine by abolishing the traces of His so-called Law, or to realize a dream of terrestrial immortality in this world through the infinite progress of the human race – an immortality that religions would have projected into an imaginary heaven.

But secularization is not only a phantasm, as Nietzsche argued in a posthumous fragment of 1881.[2] It is the materiality of the revolutions and reforms through which an order attempted to recreate the world in the image of Europe by dominating it industrially. It manifested geographically in drawing the racial borders of the world, hierarchically dividing the Orient and the West, the Souths and Norths, the Blackness and Whiteness it claimed to want to reunite. But it has also expressed itself geologically, through the exploitation of fossil fuels by states that govern populations while destroying their lives. This book's aim is to write the history of secularization as a prelude to a subterranean history of the state and of capital, and to grasp its enunciation as an order calling for the fulfilment of religion in this world by transforming nature through industry. In wanting to bring down the heavens, the empires beneath the earth put the earth itself into upheaval, decimating the lives of those who oppose their rule. Secularization is not the decline of religion, but the birth of a new climatic order. Secularization is the advent of a Secularocene.

The command to secularize sounded forth in the voice of a ghost that haunts the body of the modern state – a sort of living dead, a hybrid being whose violence condemns its indigenous and Black victims to

---

2   Friedrich Nietzsche, *Unpublished Fragments*, 1881, notebook 11, §163 in *The Complete Works of Friedrich Nietzsche*, vol. 13, *Unpublished Fragments from the Period of Dawn*, trans. J. M. Baker Jr and Christiane Hertel, Stanford, CA: Stanford University Press, 2023: 'The political phantasm that makes me smile as much as my contemporaries smile at the religious fantasies of primitive times, is above all secularization – the belief in the world and the exclusion from consciousness of any idea of a "beyond" and an "other world".'

existence only within a space situated between life and death. This body, fundamentally *deaf* to those who contest it, is that of *Empire*, first animated by a struggle to the death with a rival it calls 'Islam'. It has been obsessed with Jews and Muslims, just as strongly as White civilization is still terrorized by Blackness. Although treated as an intruder, the Euro-Christian signifier of 'Islam' exposes the spectral body of Empire, which implants itself onto the state's organs to weave its flesh. From its meta-morphosis was born what Marx called the critique of heaven: the discourse that calls on men to renounce the consolations of the afterlife but to have faith in the marvels of science and technology, to aspire to salvation here and now and aim to become divine and eternal in *this* world.[3]

The sacrifice of heaven has overturned the earth. This argument organizes the different strata of this book. By no longer turning to the heavens, empires colonized subterranean worlds. Proclaiming the order to realize our salvation in this world by exploiting the globe, they transformed capital into a fossil beast and contributed to bringing about what some call the Anthropocene and consider as a new geological age. This order is secularization. Its history began under our feet. While cracking the heavens, empires were born beneath the earth. Climatic upheaval is not a consequence of humanity's actions; it is the geological sedimentation of the imperiality of the modern West (the way that *imperial logic* remained at work within the West after the end of the eighteenth century), of its sacrifice of heaven. Capitalism did not become a key actor in the extraction of fossil fuels by virtue of its immanent logic or its essence. Only the secular violence of the imperial state converted capital into an extractive machine. Secularization gave birth to *fossil* capital. The index of its reality is neither the absence of God in the city nor the loss of the sacred, but climatic upheaval itself. The Anthropocene is a Secularocene.

Therefore, an ecological critique of what the West has called its secularization cannot be summed up simply by calculating the excess quantities of CO_2 disseminated into the atmosphere by burning fossil fuels. It must perform a critique of the reason that governs industry, of which an obsession with calculation is itself a figure. This reason, forged between the eighteenth and nineteenth centuries, commanded that the bowels of

---

3   Karl Marx, *Einleitung, Marx-Engels Werke*, Band I, Berlin: Dietz Verlag, p. 378.

the earth be probed by geological exploratory missions, that populations be forced to descend into the mines and to work land subjected to
bank credit and chemical fertilizers, so that man could finally be liberated from the 'primitive' state that had led him to invent gods. The great
theme of the critique of heaven – the conquest of man by the murder of
God – is thus the reverse side of another conquest: the conquest of the
world by Europe.

To rewrite the history of secularization as a directive addressed to
African and Asian worlds, but also to all indigenous worlds, is to see in
it something other than its Christian dimension. We must hear a voice
more spectral than the voice of Christ, listen to the sacred spectre instead
of the Holy Spirit – the voice of a body that speaks only on condition of
dying. The critique of imperiality consists in grasping the state's exercise
of violence and its policing of lives. While this book focuses on the
particular relation of the West to Muslim and Jewish traditions, it
deploys a critique of the absolute and quasi-divine sovereignty the
modern state claimed for itself in expressing the order of secularization.
It thus analyses the *institution* that has ceaselessly produced race by
exercising a violence that characterizes the modern state. This state
violence, which hierarchizes lives by conferring death and ceaselessly
brutalizes bodies in its policing, is an effect of its imperiality. Imperiality,
a radical deafness to any form of dialogue, is the essence of the 'violence
in its natural state' that Fanon speaks of which every act of decolonization must confront.[4] What follows is the history of this deafness, which
some call 'Whiteness', and of which racism is only one face.

---

4   Frantz Fanon, *The Wretched of the Earth*, New York: Grove, 1963, p. 61.

Introduction

As the story goes: the West secularized itself, while the East failed to. By separating politics and religion, which non-Western worlds, and Islamic civilizations more particularly, constantly confused, Christianity made us modern. This discourse has been at the heart of Orientalism and its contemporary mutations. Since the nineteenth century, the delineation of the border between politics and religion has presented both Muslim and Jewish communities under the racialized narrative of an inability to secularize. Judaism was seen as an egoistic religion, a law-obsessed fossil that had been made anachronistic by the rise of Christianity. Islam was defined as a religion of the One and of violence, whose incapacity to reform gave birth to liberticide as a sacred law. A central component of Western modernity was born from this delineation, which allowed the industrial West to present itself as the realization on Earth of the promises of Christianity. Throughout the nineteenth century, the racialization of Islam and the colonization of African and Asian worlds made it possible for secularization to be imposed as an order. Long before it came to designate the process by which modern societies emerged through a supposed decline or departure of religions, the order to secularize was itself an actor in the industrialization and colonization of the world. It was by seizing onto Islam – not only as the Antichrist, like the Crusaders did, but as a conquering proselytism armed with a sort of civil code – that the industrial West claimed to dissolve the heavens by exploiting the earth. Along with 'the Orient', 'Islam' thus designates a racial border through which the

West defines itself, by expressing the concept of secularization as an imperative. And as long as the delineation of this border is imperial, the order of secularization that follows from it must also be imperial.

Secularization is an imperial order

Secularization does not mean the death of religions. But neither is it a simple myth through which the modern West thought, wrongly, to have rid itself of religion. For those who, since Nietzsche at least, have held that secularization is a myth, the European Moderns failed to realize that Christianity was at work all the while behind profane masks, working in secret and under borrowed names. This book tries to tell a different story from this usual critique of Christianity as secretly running through the veins of modernity. Secularization is neither the end nor the perpetuation of Christianity by other means. To deploy an alternative perspective, we will need to begin from the way it was enunciated by actors. How, when, and by whom was secularization formulated? The order of secularization that was formulated during the first half of the nineteenth century declared that the French Revolution and Western modernity were meant to *realize Christianity on Earth*. This formulation only became possible once modern figures began to want to reconstruct Christianity as the origin of the Revolution and the essence of political modernity. We should thus examine the process of secularization by studying the ways in which secular or Christian actors in the nineteenth century believed they were fulfilling religion in the profane world, outside of churches and traditions. This gesture is not meant to de-realize secularization by declaring that it never took place. Rather, it aims to grasp it as a set of genuinely real orders, which demanded that humans reform themselves and that the earth deliver up its fruits. Instead of presupposing a definition of secularization as decline, we need to examine when and how this concept has been enunciated and to analyse the forces and transformations occurring at the same time.

How can we rethink secularization as something other than an absence of religion or the continuation of Christianity under profane masks? What powers are affirmed once God no longer speaks within the city? The history of modernity coincides not only with the emergence of the nation-state from the Reformation and the wars of religion; it is the colonial process of disseminating empire as formulated by

Western Christendom. Rather than declaring that modernity *is* Christianity, as Nietzsche did, or that it has ceased to be Christian, we should look elsewhere and pose other questions: How was the imperial confrontation between Western-Christian and Islamic powers during the Crusades globalized through the colonies, beginning in the fifteenth century? How did the colonization of America, Africa, and Asia and the racialization of their populations in the nineteenth century transform Europe's relation to Muslim worlds, and eventually generate secularizing effects?

Answering these questions implies performing a critique of colonial imperiality. Imperiality associates terrestrial power with God and God with a terrestrial power, giving the power that governs humans a divine or quasi-divine status. It deploys violence in the name of God or metaphysical entities such as heaven and claims to be its image, its representative or its son on Earth. It represents the monarch as God and God as a monarch. In a particular form we will examine further, this imperial gesture structures the history of Western colonization, and so is at the heart of the theologico-political dimensions of sovereignty, of the state and of capital.[1] The concept of imperiality makes it possible to analyse the multiple faces of the modern state, showing that there could never be a political theology of sovereignty separate from the questions of empire, of race, and of the colonies. While, in itself, this imperial claim to absolute power is not the prerogative of the West, the singularity of its Western trajectory has to do with how colonialism, from the fifteenth century on, took on the task of realizing empire, this wish for world domination. Without reducing empire to the possession of colonies, my theoretical hypothesis proposes to articulate imperiality in relation to coloniality, while not confounding the two. I call this dialectic colonial imperiality. Grasped historically, imperiality in its Western form appears as the function by which sovereigns have tried to erect themselves as representatives of the divine on the earth, masters of the world, and successors of Rome. What the famous biography of the German emperor Frederick II by Ernst Kantorowicz shows is precisely that the system of

---

1 Carl Schmitt, *Political Theology*, Cambridge, MA: MIT Press, 1986 [1922], p. 36. 'All significant concepts of the modern theory of the State are secularized theological concepts.' I argue, in response, that theological concepts are imperialized before they can be secularized. In other words, all significant concepts of the modern theory of the state are imperialized theological concepts. The secularization of theology in modern politics is the result of the colonial becoming of imperiality.

doubling the sovereign's body, which Kantorowicz puts at the heart of the theologico-political complex in *The King's Two Bodies*, is an effect of the imperialization of Christianity. Imperiality serves here as the language that allows the terrestrial representation of God by the king, pope, or emperor to be enunciated. It thus determines the processes by which Christianity structures the realm of the political *in the West*.[2] After the Western Christian empire was fragmented in the reign of Charles V, during the Renaissance, imperiality was transferred to the colonies, thus giving birth to what would later be known as metropoles. This book examines how this becoming-colonial of imperiality led to what we call secularization. My thesis is that the medieval Christian empire that unified the kingdoms of the West was made impossible by the Reformation. The 'end' of empire in Europe led to its fragmentation *outside of Europe*. Each monarchy claimed to be an empire in its kingdom, as signalled by the English expression 'This realm is an empire.' It was through colonial expansion and slavery that competing European monarchies tried to realize the imperial dream. The result was a phenomenon of imperial dissemination, a phenomenon situated at the foundations of modern racism and secularizing dynamics in Europe and its colonies.

The resulting secularization was neither the simple continuation of Christianity, nor the pure and simple abolition of the residues of a medieval Christian world. It was dependent on the Western process of Christianity's imperialization, which, in turn, is inseparable from its relation to non-European worlds. But, before it decimated indigenous lives in the Americas, Christendom already saw the Islamic civilizations of Africa and Asia as its main political rivals. The representation of Islam as the Antichrist was a theological description of an inter-imperial enmity. However, words such as *Islam* and the *Orient* refer to a multiplicity of worlds which are disseminated in Africa, Asia, and Europe. And, despite the cultural and religious plurality of societies where Jewish, Muslim, and Christian traditions could coexist, they were seen as Oriental and dominated by the alleged 'intolerance of Islam'.[3]

---

2   Ernst Kantorowicz, *Frederick the Second: 1194–1250*, trans. E. O. Lorimer, London: Constable & Co., 1931, pp. 216, 223, 230. It goes without saying that Kantorowicz did not theorize the becoming-colonial of imperiality, leaving aside the metamorphoses of the Roman-Christian language of empire by colonization and globalization.

3   While these worlds were culturally Muslim and politically ruled by ethico-juridical cultures drawn from the Qur'an and Islamic traditions, it was not only Arabs

Orientalism, therefore, started as Islamology, as a discourse on Islam which was then transformed and expanded to refer to other places and traditions considered 'Oriental'.[4] In the discourse of Islamological Orientalism, Islam is thus a theme that can be read as both a signifier and a symptom. It is a symptom not of the West in general or colonialism in particular, but, more specifically, of Western colonial imperiality.[5]

After the critique of Orientalism: race and the imperiality of secularization

During the British conquest of India during the second half of the eighteenth century and the Napoleonic Egyptian Expedition in 1798, European colonialism took up the language of an imperial tradition that preceded the colonization of the Americas and goes back to the Roman Empire. Using this language, Western sovereigns continuously presented themselves as both the inheritors of Rome and the representatives of the divine on Earth. This tradition formed the heart of sovereignty in the West. It was already expressed during the Crusades, but only in the fifteenth century – with the Reconquista, the colonization of the Americas, and Charles V's unsuccessful attempts at imperial reunification of Christendom – did this imperial tradition begin to emerge as a properly colonial language. The imperiality of power, which, in Christendom, had until then been the prerogative of the pope or the emperor, was claimed

---

and Muslims who lived in these societies. For example, Amazigh people ('indigenous' North Africans), Black people, and Jewish communities were part of Al-Andalus.

4   I use the word 'Islamology' to distinguish between the Western scholarly discourse on Islam and the broader discourse of Orientalism to which it nonetheless belongs. *Islamologie* is more common in French than it is in English. I use it to describe the French and more generally Western scholarly production on Islam as an object of study. The main feature of Islamology is the idea that Islam cannot separate religion from politics and thus immediately presupposes secularization as a concept and a norm to which non-Western civilizations should adapt.

5   Western imperiality is not reducible, of course, to the West as a cultural entity. I do not argue that there is a coherent cultural entity called the West or the non-West. 'The West' refers to an unstable political network of competing territorial powers we usually call 'nation-states' whose ideologies bear the trace of a multilayered imperial language. As such, the West has been globalized via the globalization of capital and of the state. This globalization is not a totalization or exact reproduction of the West abroad. It is a dissemination and a fragmentation.

by European monarchs who declared that their kingdoms were empires. The materialization of this empire implied the possession of colonies. Thus, the medieval imperial tradition was transformed, during the Classical Age, into a language of Western coloniality. This imperiality does not designate an invariant, a substance that remains identical to itself throughout history, but, rather, a process of disseminating Empire through the colonies, a dissemination of *the imperial by the colonial*. At the heart of this book is the history of the secularization effects provoked by the colonial transformation of empire in the nineteenth century. Throughout this process of secularization, monarchical and missionary practices of evangelization became civilizing missions, transforming Muslim 'infidels' into colonized subjects. Secularization refers to these particular transformations linked to the colonial dissemination of imperiality throughout the nineteenth century. By becoming colonial, the Western Christian empire metamorphosed to the point that it gave rise to an imperiality liberated from the sustainment of transcendent heavens.[6]

Imperiality is what subjugated the colonies to the metropoles and connected colonialism to state sovereignty. It has been recognized neither by postcolonial critique and its decolonial successors, nor by the classic critiques of modernity and Christianity. Imperiality is what remained of the Holy Roman Empire after its fragmentation. It is what Christendom – the imperial unity of Christian princes – bequeathed to modernity after the emergence of nation-states. The European colonies were the sites where this imperiality was manifested, the imperiality of sovereign states born from the rubble of the Western Christian empire. From there, the unity of the West came to correspond to the unity of the imperiality that haunted the multitude of European and American states and empires.

To make a historical critique of this imperiality presupposes that we re-examine the chronologies according to which the only matrices of modernity are Christianity, the Reformation, or the colonization of the Americas. Its history does not begin in Europe and does not follow a linear narrative that runs from its Roman or Christian origins to its end today. While the Crusades may have provided its point of departure, the history of imperiality underwent a decisive mutation during the Egyptian Expedition in 1798. This book thus examines the way in

---

6 For a description of this process, see the final section of Chapter 1, as well as Chapter 6, 'A Circle of Returns'.

which the expedition's project, even by virtue of its failure, was taken up in Africa through the colonization of Algeria after 1830. One of the premises that guide this study's methodology is that the failure of empires structures history by inaugurating the circle of their dissemination.[7] Imperiality is a result of this failure. Proposing an analysis of its metamorphoses over time, this book specifically examines how the colonization of North Africa in the nineteenth century contributed to the secularization of Europe. What appears if we start from this (North) African site is nothing other than the blind spot of most existing theories of colonialism: the imperiality of the sovereign powers that dominated the whole of the globe. This imperiality corresponds neither to coloniality nor to Christianity itself. The beating heart of secularization, it appears in all its singularity only through the history of the irreducible conflicts between European colonial empires and particular Muslim traditions, conflicts that took place in Africa and Asia during the nineteenth century.

Imperiality was thus manifested through Western discourse about the Orient and, more specifically, about Muslims. But the West did not, for all this, simply continue to pursue its crusade against Muslim worlds, as is often wrongly said. The imperiality that the Roman Church constructed over the course of its 'holy wars' was generalized to the entirety of the world by its *becoming colonial*. Then, in return, the colonial transformation of empire won out over the Christian heaven itself. By following this hypothesis, this book aims to re-examine the foundations of postcolonial theory and its decolonial successors, rewriting an overlooked part of the critical history of imperial Orientalism laid out by Edward Said.[8] If Orientalism has been one of the languages through which empires racialize colonial populations, it is neither a simple ideology of colonialism, nor a discourse by which the West has constructed the Orient in its own image, ever since Ancient Greece. Orientalism is an effect of the *imperiality of knowledge* that defined

7 The inaugural moment of its history is described in the final chapter, which can be read as an alternative introduction to a cyclically structured work.

8 Edward Said, *Orientalism*, New York: Pantheon Books, 1978. This text is recognized as founding postcolonial studies. The critique of Orientalism and of colonial representations of what is not Europe has numerous precursors. One of the unacknowledged matrices of postcolonial and decolonial theory is the internal critique of the 'coloniality' of anthropology formulated by Talal Asad, beginning in the early 1970s. See Asad, 'Two European Images of Non-European Rule', in *Anthropology and the Colonial Encounter*, London: Ithaca Press, 1973, pp. 103–21.

Islam as the enemy during the Crusades, before it structured the knowledge the West has produced about the non-European world. As Cedric Robinson shows in *Black Marxism*, imperial representations of Islam as Antichrist, of its supposed violence and sexual licence, were at the heart of the birth of racism.[9] Orientalism and colonial knowledge were born from the way that Christians, during the Crusades, demonized the Prophet Muhammad as a false prophet, denying Islam any truth while reducing it to a diabolical heresy. Meanwhile, the institution of scholarly Orientalism established during the nineteenth century in the wake of the Egyptian Expedition was a subversion of this Christian imperiality by the Enlightenment, in which Muhammad passed in the European Orientalist imagery from the status of Antichrist to that of great man and conquering legislator.[10] Orientalism then became an operator of secularization, through its key historical role in the criticism of the Bible and other sacred texts. While acknowledging this transformation, Said never deployed a theory of secularization.[11] But one cannot understand the colonial spread of Orientalism without understanding the secularization of empire. Conversely, a theory of empire should examine how the Western construction of the Orient helped to usher in the secularization of the West itself. And, while considering 1492 as the starting point of what they call 'colonial modernity', decolonial scholars also presuppose a theory of secularization, as they inevitably need to describe the transformations of colonialism happening during the nineteenth century.[12]

The secularization of Orientalism was contemporaneous with a new racial geography that generated the European division of Africa and the

9 Cedric Robinson, *Black Marxism*, Chapel Hill: University of North Carolina Press, 2000 [1983], pp. 67, 89, 95. Fanon's analyses seem strangely to pass over this 'genealogy' of anti-Black racism in silence. Robinson also shows that the perception of Islam by Western Christians is inseparable from their vision of the Moors and Blacks who inhabited Andalusia.

10 This complex transformation, performed by those whom historiographic convention calls the 'Lumières', is described in Chapter 1.

11 On secularization as a key structure of modern Orientalism, see Said, *Orientalism*, pp. 113–22. Said defines secularization as naturalized Christian supernaturalism, thus using an expression inspired by Thomas Carlyle. He doesn't provide a theory of secularization that would clarify its connection with colonial empires. I argue, instead, that one needs to understand how the imperiality of secularization has determined the spread of Orientalism since the nineteenth century.

12 See Walter Mignolo, *Local Histories/Global Designs*, Princeton, NJ: Princeton University Press, 2000, pp. 57–9.

Arab world into two distinct geographical regions. Scholarly Orientalism
was one of the mechanisms by which Africa was defined as a 'black continent', by the characterization of Egypt and the Maghreb as 'European' or
'Oriental'.[13] Orientalism was one of the operators of the process by which
most colonial subjects deemed 'Oriental' were racialized via their religion. The congenital violence that colonial racism attributed to the North
African and the Arab emerged from the nineteenth-century characterization of Islam as fanatical. The supposed 'violence of Islam' was thus
naturalized, inscribed into the body of the indigenous subject by colonial
racism. European Islamology and discourse on religion gave institutional
force and legitimacy to colonial racism by making the Muslim body into
the incarnation of a politico-religious violence that never fails to provoke
horror and indignation in secular societies. Thus, the Western *colonial*
relation to Arabs and Muslims, established in the aftermath of the 1798
expedition, was a key mechanism not only of racism but of secularization
itself. Nonetheless, it was *not the only mechanism*: the birth of the industrial world also presupposed the parallel transformation of freed Black
slaves into a subaltern labour force, submitted to the salariat of misery by
a capitalism that had abolished slavery the better to maintain colonial
order through the principle of free labour. To the extent that imperial
secularization corresponded to the moment of false, White abolition –
led by figures such as Victor Schoelcher and William Wilberforce – it was
among the conditions for the transformation of racial capitalism by nineteenth-century liberalism.

After the critique of secularism: faith without rituals and rituals without faith

To redefine the concept of secularization, it is necessary to clarify that of
religion. Religion is a European concept that does not refer to any
universal essence, any anthropological reality that could be observed in
every society. If nothing is 'religious' in itself, then, the boundaries of
what is religious and what is not must themselves be seen as political
decisions and effects of the exercise of sovereign power. If it did not

---

13   One of the inventors of this divide is Général Faidherbe, *Le Sénégal: La France
dans l'Afrique occidentale*, Paris: Librairie Hachette, 1889, pp. 14–16, 165.

define what is religious, the West could not define itself as secular. The more the West seems to have liberated itself from God, the more, paradoxically, it makes religion an object of discourse. The varying discourse on religion can thus be analysed as an index of secularization, as it has determined empire, race, and Orientalism since the late eighteenth century. Rather than trying to determine what religion is by attributing a problematic universality to it, other questions present themselves: Who defines religion? Who wields the power to define others' religion? What effects does this act of definition have on those who speak it and on those they claim to define? Secularization is an order because its expression depends on a definition of the essence of the religions whose alleged contents it aims to realize on Earth. Its history can thus be written by looking at the variations in the concept of religion that have followed from its many uses. In examining 'secularization', therefore, this book does not describe any supposed decline of religion, as earlier and now-contested theories of secularization have done. Indeed, religion has not become private or marginal. On the contrary, a social intensification of piety in the public sphere and the expansion of Christian missionary activity have been the corollary to the secularization of institutions in the nineteenth century.

Nor has religion been reduced to individual belief under the reign of modern, liberal, and Protestant norms, as is assumed by critiques of secularism.[14] The secularization of the state led to the invention of what the French call *cultes*: the organization of non-Christian ritual practices according to vertical and hierarchical structures, while believers are subject to surveillance from a constant policing. By separating faith and ritual, modernity did not give way to a primacy of beliefs over practices. Rather, it opened two possibilities: the development of faith without practice, and that of practice without faith. Secularization unfolds as the double birth of beliefs abstracted from all ethical or ritual practice, and

---

14 See Talal Asad, *Genealogies of Religion: Discipline and Reasons of Power in Christianity and Islam*, Baltimore, MD: Johns Hopkins University Press, 1993, pp. 28–30. While I agree with Asad that religion is not a universal anthropological concept, I argue against the idea that secular modernity defines religion solely in terms of private belief. I do not argue, as Asad does, that secularism problematically defines religion as belief. I argue that secularization is a set of contradictory processes by which religion can be privatized or politicized in distinctive ways once it increasingly becomes an object of study, thus exceeding the boundaries of Christian theology.

also formal rites stripped of faith and ethics.[15] The proliferation of ortho-praxies and religious formalisms is thus itself one face, not of archaism or of an oppressive essence of religions, but of secularization itself.

Contrary to many anthropologists of secularism, I do not claim that a liberal but still Christian colonialism exported secularism and religious freedom throughout the world. Rather, I am trying to grasp how *imperiality* has been deployed through colonialism while producing secularization effects *internal to religions* in Europe and beyond. From here, it is neither the paradoxes of secularism and *laïcité*, nor the essence of Christianity, but rather *the process of secularization in its double link to empire and to capital* that can be analysed in terms of the historical transformations of Western discourse on 'the Orient' and non-Western worlds.[16]

Towards an ecology of secularization

But the consequences of secularization go beyond the question of imperialism. What has been missing from analyses of the interdependence between colonialism and secularization is an ecological perspective. In trying to effect a transfer of sacredness from the heavens to the earth, secularization made the latter (and its administration) the only possible site for empires to be

15   During the nineteenth century, Orientalist and pan-Germanist author Paul Anton de Lagarde criticized the liberal definition of religion in terms of private belief and emphasized the role of practice. See Chapter 5.

16   This method can be distinguished in several ways from both Asad's anthropology of secularism and the works of its critics, such as Étienne Balibar's. First, the majority of anthropologists of the secular or of Christianity – because they substitute for the concept of secularization an analysis in terms of secularism, secularity, or the globalization of Christianity – only rarely describe the processes of secularization that took place in Europe and the colonized world in the nineteenth century. Where Talal Asad does mobilize the concept of secularization, he tends to reduce it to the emergence of the modern nation-state. While he does forcefully analyse certain *colonial* aspects of secularization, Asad does not conceptualize the way in which these were articulated with race, gender, capitalism or with what I call the imperiality of power, of which state sovereignty is only one manifestation. Asad's and Balibar's critiques of secularism and universalism both share the same presupposition about the nation-state as the 'last instance' in the explanation of their exclusionary potential, which results from the absence of a theory of imperiality. See Étienne Balibar, *Secularism and Cosmopolitism*, New York: Columbia University Press, 2018, pp. 34–42, 48–56. This absence of imperiality as a specific problem also characterizes, in my view, the majority of theoretical works belonging to postcolonial and decolonial currents.

legitimated, thus opening an era of predation on nature, of resource extraction and the unlimited exploitation of the subsoil in search of fossil energy during the first half of the nineteenth century. These transformations provided the material basis for the expansion of industrial capitalism, initiating the conditions of production responsible for the ecological upheaval whose effects we are experiencing today. Secularization can be understood as the order of empires beneath the earth, and so as the common language of state and capital that have overturned the climate since the nineteenth century. From this point of view, the colonization of Africa, Asia, and the Middle East helped to usher the world into a new, unprecedented state of upheaval, by plunging into the entrails of the earth and expanding the extraction of fossil fuels across the planet. The analysis of what I call the fossil state shows that the inter-imperial rivalry born from the death of medieval empire led to global warming. What unifies these histories of race and on climate is nothing other than secularization, of which I claim imperiality is constitutive. From here, the indices of the secularization initiated in the nineteenth century can be found in the air we breathe and the food we eat, rather than in the study of attendance rates at churches and other places of worship. What is needed is an ecological critique of secularization, to retrace the climatic and racial effects of the so-called disenchantment of the world.

It is not only to the side of capital that we must turn our gaze to understand the ongoing destruction of nature and the threat of the extinction of life that weighs on the planet. We should also look to the history of the imperial and racial violence through which capitalism was born and is ceaselessly reborn, to the history of a process of which capitalism is not the parent, but rather the child. We know that the birth of capital in its fossil form was closely connected to the emergence of new techniques of ruling racialized populations during the nineteenth century. Beyond this legitimate criticism of colonialism's central role in causing climate change, I also argue that imperial secularization sustained the accumulation of *fossil* capital. We therefore need another critique of heaven and Earth, a new history of state and capital through the lenses of their shared imperiality. We will begin this history in Egypt, with a declaration by which, during the Egyptian Expedition, the secular republic announced itself to be Muslim.

1

The Republic Converts to Islam: The French Expedition to Egypt and Its Afterlives

While still in the throes of the Revolution, the French Republic launched an expeditionary project to Egypt. Its goal was straightforward: to destroy British hegemony over the Indian trade, and to build an empire able to rival the British. This imperial 'expedition' was led by a Republican army composed of atheist, deist, and agnostic revolutionaries. But upon arriving on Egyptian soil in 1798, its commander, Napoleon Bonaparte, declared: 'Qadi, Shaykh, Shorbagi, tell the people that we are true Muslims. Did we not defeat the Pope who had preached war against Muslims? Did we not destroy the Knights of Malta, because those fools believed God wanted them to make war against Muslims?'[1]

Why did the world's first secular army proclaim itself to be Muslim? How did Islam suddenly become the publicly professed doctrine of a revolution engaged in struggle with the Church? Did something at the heart of the Republic's declared anticlericalism endow it with a secret desire to convert to Islam? The proclamation of a 'Muslim France' was much more than simple opportunism. By presenting a dimension of Orientalism overlooked by postcolonial critique, these questions help us to reorient the critique of imperial knowledge. By approaching the

---

1   Napoleon, quoted in Henry Laurens, *L'Expédition d'Égypte (1798–1801)*, Paris: Seuil, 1997, pp. 108–9. For an examination of the expedition in the broader context of Egyptian history, see Afaf Lutfi al-Sayyid Marsot, *A Short Story of Modern Egypt*, Cambridge: Cambridge University Press, 1985, p. 50.

imperiality of Orientalism through different questions, this chapter aims to rewrite an aspect of its history that has remained a blind spot for its critics.[2] The imperiality that the French Revolution invented in Egypt was a claim to absolute knowledge and power, as unattainable as it is constitutive of the West. Its secularity appeared in the drive to produce signifiers that looked 'Islamic' while not belonging to Muslim tradition. Without ever being or becoming Muslim, the army and its Orientalists *claimed* to be 'true Muslims'.

Is Orientalism an 'Islamic' power?

While its seminal status and political importance are unquestionable, Said's critique of Orientalism tends to reduce practices of governing Islam to mechanisms for dominating Arabs and 'Orientals'. But Bonaparte's proclamation has nothing to say about the Orient. It is concerned with the Prophet and the Qur'an, Muslim authorities and judges: in a word, with the sources and institutions of Islamic tradition. While highly strategic and devoid of sincerity, this declaration still cannot be reduced to the typical mechanisms of domination used by Orientalist discourse. It does not merely speak for Muslims; it *addresses itself to their supposed representatives* in an attempt to induce their consent. This is why France proclaimed its supposed Islamic belonging in an address to Muslim authorities. In order to speak *in the name of Muslims*, the Republic needed to nurture the ambition – troubling and cavalier, but also impossible – of speaking *as Muslim*. But, for France to profess Islam, it would have to cease being Catholic. The solemn proclamation that 'we are true Muslims' could only mean: 'We are no longer Catholics.' The Islamic signifiers professed by the Republic can therefore

---

2 Edward Said, *Orientalism*, New York: Pantheon Books, 1978, pp. 82–3. Orientalism cannot be understood only as an anachronistic betrayal of the humanist and Enlightenment heritage. See Samira Haj, *Reconfiguring Islamic Tradition*, Stanford, CA: Stanford University Press, 2004, pp. 1–3; Wael Hallaq, *Restating Orientalism*, New York: Columbia University Press, 2018. On the continuity between the Enlightenment project and the expedition, see Laurens's remarks in *Orientales I: Autour de l'expédition d'Égypte*, Paris: Éditions du CNRS, 2004, pp. 15–29. For a critique of Said that discusses the distinction between Orientalism and a sociology of Islam based on ethnographic fieldwork, see Edmund Burke III, *The Ethnographic State*, Princeton, NJ: Princeton University Press, 2014, pp. 24–8.

be analysed as an index of the empire's secularization. Something was born during the expedition that had not existed in the time of the Crusades, the conquest of the Americas, or the transatlantic slave trade: a way for subjects liberated from God to proclaim themselves 'true Muslims', by which they meant that they lived in a secular way.

The following pages analyse imperial knowledge's pseudo-Islamic professions of faith. They read the expedition as an exposure of the imperial trajectory of secularization, which would lead to the establishment of the modern state in its Bonapartist form. This trajectory can be seen in the French state's attempts, still ongoing today, to reorganize Islam as a *culte*, or organized ritual practice, and to centralize its institutions. The following chapters will examine how, despite its failure, what Bonaparte started in Egypt came to be disseminated and fragmented through the colonization of Africa and Asia.

While I choose the expedition as a historical beginning of this history, its significance in Egyptian history should not be overstated. I do not argue that the French expedition was the opening of the modern era in Egypt and the Arab world, despite the influence of Napoleon on Muhammad Ali of Egypt. What I try to examine is, rather, how the expedition in Egypt contributed to the establishment of secular modernity *in France and Europe*. Nonetheless, the institutions that Bonaparte created in France, particularly the civil code, undeniably played a decisive role in the transformation undergone by many Muslim-majority countries from the nineteenth century on. Napoleonic law was a model for modern reforms of 'Islamic law' in the Ottoman Empire and his former provinces. It was at the heart of the secularization processes by which religious law was confined to family law. Islamic law thus became qualitatively different for at least two reasons. On the one hand, it became law in the modern sense of the term, as opposed to ethico-juridical practices, to the extent that it was now reformed – sometimes even *codified* – in keeping with the model of the Napoleonic Civil Code. On the other, it was closely connected with a related transformation of the family itself, as *'usra* came to designate a nuclear and monogamous unit, following a European model that had previously been foreign to Muslim worlds.[3]

---

3 On the reform of Islamic law and the family in Egypt, see Talal Asad, *Formations of the Secular: Christianity, Islam, Modernity*, Stanford, CA: Stanford University Press,

One therefore needs to unpack the concept of modernity to describe the Napoleonic institutions which served as models for reforming Islamic law from the nineteenth century on. I argue that this Napoleonic model of imperial secularity was created after the expedition to Egypt, as part of the entangled histories between Europe and North Africa. By using concepts such as secularization or imperiality instead of modernity, I want to understand the hegemonic norm imposed by Europe by creating other concepts and using other methods than the ones deployed by Europe itself.

Conversion in reverse

Several years before the expedition, the Comte de Volney, an Orientalist and Enlightenment philosopher who had visited Egypt and Syria, had predicted that the Muslim population would present an obstacle to any conquest of Egypt. The lesson Napoleon took from this prediction was that if he wanted to 'escape the Prophet's curses' and 'not be included among the enemies of Islamism', he would need to make himself a friend to the Muslims. He would thus need to 'convince and win over the muftis, the ulama, the cherifs, and the imams, so that they would [interpret] the Qur'an in the army's favour'.[4] As we have seen, the proclamation of an imperial tie of friendship with Muslims was not only about the construction of the Orient by the West; it resulted from a strange drive to *produce Islamic signifiers without being Muslim*. As an expression of anticlericalism, the proclamation was neither sincere nor an outright lie. The empire that could call itself Muslim was one that no longer converted infidels to Christianity but aimed, instead, to civilize them by strategically converting to their religion. The Republic thus inverted the conversion pattern of the Ancien Régime by presenting itself as a power that appeared to convert to Islam.

In abandoning conversion to Christianity, the revolutionary mission was transformed into a machine that devoured knowledge of the countries it conquered. From now on, it would conduct ethnography on

---

2003, pp. 228–41. On the way in which Sharia was reconstituted through codification, see Wael Hallaq, *Sharīʿa: Theory, Practice, Transformations*, Cambridge: Cambridge University Press, 2000, pp. 367–70; on the centrality of the French model, and thus of its empire, in the history of the colonization of the Arab and Muslim world, see ibid., pp. 433–8.

4   Napoleon, cited in Laurens, *L'Expédition d'Égypte*, p. 131.

colonized peoples and tribes, observe their morals and religion, and classify them however it could in a grand table of civilizations drawn with the full confidence of its Enlightenment. The deployment of this knowledge meant not only that Muslims would be put under surveillance, but also, and above all, that they would be made to profess fidelity to the Republic without being required to renounce their faith. At the same time, Napoleon imposed a code of conduct on his soldiers that was in conformity with the Egyptian majority's religion. He even seriously considered having his army strategically convert to Islam, speaking not in terms of faith but of practicality.[5] This 'change of religion' would have taken place 'only for sound reasons', according to Napoleon, and it would be justified by its 'immense political results'. 'The empire of the Orient, and perhaps the subjection of all Asia' was 'worth a turban and a pair of pantaloons', which 'all this could be reduced to'.[6] In these circumstances, therefore, conversion meant nothing more than conforming to rules as part of a strategy to produce external signs of belonging. The army's conversion would take place only after it had advanced to the Euphrates, into the heart of the contemporary Middle East. The *game* of conversion to Islam was thus a strategy to be employed only after the threshold of conquest had been crossed. Only the expedition's territorial advance could justify the French army becoming Muslim. As long as the conquest had not advanced sufficiently, the possibility of becoming emperor in France and in Europe needed to be kept open. In Napoleon's eyes, the soldiers' aversion to the plan was not a serious obstacle: 'The army, disposed as it was, would surely have taken to it, seeing in it no more than laughter and pleasantry.'[7]

Underneath the question of Orientalism, then, is the question of the particular relations between politics and religion that characterize imperiality. No one would seriously maintain that Bonaparte's address to the Muslims of Egypt was sincere. But it is important to stress that his discourse was *epochal* only because it fitted into an ideological environment that conditioned what is so often called his 'opportunism' through and through. Bonaparte was no more sincere in embracing Islam than

---

5   Laurens, *Orientales I*, p. 155. A French officer, Menou, did indeed convert to Islam for strategic reasons.

6   Napoleon, cited in Laurens, *Orientales I*, p. 156.

7   Cited in Laurens, *Orientales I*, p. 156.

he was when, on his return to France, he declared himself a *Catholic*. His strategic use of power played out through an approach to religion that was itself an effect of the Enlightenment. Napoleon's opportunism would certainly not have taken the same form – he would never have expressed his charlatanism this way – if he had not been at the head of a revolutionary army. It was the secularization of imperial violence that led Bonaparte to approach Islam in Egypt and Catholicism in France as majoritarian religions, to which he took necessary recourse only in the name of good governance.

Expressing himself as he did in Egypt, Bonaparte was not merely producing a representation of the Orient. He combined the attempt to secularize the empire with an attempt to make himself the Prophet's secular successor. The new imperial construction of the readability of indigenous life was able to subvert and replace missionary logic only by borrowing the pseudo-Islamic language of conversion, feigned for 'sound reasons'. The Revolution would need to speak *as if* it were secular and Muslim, if it was to extend beyond Europe to the whole world. The revolutionary army would need to cease to be Christian, and in the exclusive service of one language and tradition. This meant that new practices of controlling indigenous authorities would have to be elaborated.[8] And, as long as Muslim elites needed to be transformed into the strategic allies of this new imperiality, Napoleon called on his soldiers to tolerate and respect Islam: 'Do not contradict them . . . work with them as we worked with the Jews and the Italians; show respect for their muftis and imams, as you did for the rabbis and bishops. Show *the same tolerance* for mosques and the ceremonies prescribed by the Qur'an that you did for convents and synagogues, for the religions of Moses or Jesus Christ.'[9] We could ask what meaning the word *tolerance* has within the military economy of an imperial expedition. If in times of peace tolerance might mean suspicious condescension from the police, as an arm of colonial war it could easily become a technique of counter-insurgency.

The wording of Bonaparte's address to the Muslims expresses its anticlerical nature. Napoleon called himself a friend of Muslims insofar as he presented himself as an enemy of Islam's centuries-old enemy: the

---

8   Laurens, *L'Expédition d'Égypte*, p. 111.
9   Ibid. (emphasis added).

Church, with its popes and crusades. The Republic thus called on Egyptian Muslim authorities to interpret the Qur'an to the army's advantage, establishing an Islamic theology of the Revolution that conformed to its wishes.[10] The beast announced in apocalyptic prophecies, the Antichrist – 'Mahomet' in the eyes of the crusaders – was no longer to be exterminated. Islam would now be 'pacified', with Muslims waving the Tricolor and allying themselves with the Republic under pain of death.[11] Even their prayers would be prescribed: 'Glory to the Sultan, and glory to his friend, the French army.'[12] The proclamation, by their future emperor, that the French were 'true Muslims' was the assassination of the heavens by a terrestrial army preparing its imperial metamorphosis. By secularizing its violence, the empire implied that it was tolerant, but also that it contained all religions within itself and could make use of them as it saw fit. The empire would translate its principles into each religion, testing the universality of the revolutionary watchwords of 'liberty, equality, fraternity'. This empire of translation, of which Orientalism is only an effect, aimed to produce Muslim consent to French domination, and so to constrain the enemy to a 'friendship' that was devoid of meaning. Napoleon could then dictate prayers to believers, while claiming he was restoring their rights.[13] In the name of God, the Revolution proclaimed that 'the renewal of the century' had arrived amid the ruins of the old religions, and prophesied the rebirth of nations and of Egypt's ancient splendour.

The French Revolution's pseudo-Qur'an

In the name of God, the Merciful, the Compassionate, there is no god but God, he has no son nor any partner in his reign. On behalf of the French Republic, founded on liberty and equality, General Bonaparte, head of the French army, informs the people of Egypt that for too long the Beys who govern Egypt have insulted the French nation and treated its negotiators with disdain; the hour of punishment has arrived. For too long, this collection of slaves bought in the Caucasus

---

10   Ibid., p. 131.
11   Ibid., p. 109.
12   Ibid.
13   Ibid.

and Georgia have tyrannized the most beautiful part of the world; but the Lord of the worlds, God the Almighty, has ordained that their empire should end.[14]

Here, the Republic speaks in the name of Allah and of Islam. It displays its power by invoking the name of the One God against tyrants, professing a pseudo-Islamic theology of revolution. The languages of the revolutionary, the legislator, and the prophet are hybridized within the body of its still-nascent imperiality. By declaring that the 'Lord of the worlds' had ordained an end to the reign of the Beys, the oppressors of the Egyptian people, this secular imperiality made God the imaginary name of the Republic announcing the end of the old theocratic empires. God's judgement becomes *immanent* to the world through the immensity of terrestrial empire. This empire claims to represent God on Earth, to be His image. It functions by translating the quranic statement according to which, as 'sustainer of all the worlds' (*rabb al 'ālamīn*), God causes them to *grow*, into the imperial language of the *Lord* of the worlds.[15] *Allah* is the sustainer of infinite pluriverses, not the imperial or royal sovereign of a single and finite world. While *Rabb al'ālamīn* does denote the idea of an ultimate reality, it also, incidentally, emphasizes the dynamism of a cosmology consisting of multiple and transforming worlds.

Why did the imperial state attempt to speak a pseudo-quranic language to which it seemed, at the same time, deliberately deaf? Was the goal to present itself as the fulfilment of the world's historical religions, bringing their heavens down to the earth and fulfilling prophecies that would now seem to have been only predictions of an uncertain future? Speaking a pseudo-Islamic language invented from whole cloth, this nascent imperiality drew on a type of knowledge that, far from being monolithic, allowed it to speak a plurality of languages and to show a multitude of faces in service of its various interests. This type of knowledge was deployed by the horde of Arabic-speaking counsellors whose names fill the colonial archives. It was also mobilized by

---

14   Ibid.
15   Muhammad Asad, *The Message of the Qur'an*, Gibraltar: Dar Al-Andalus, 1984, pp. 1–2, note 2. In this translation, Asad proposes a translation of *rabb* not as 'Lord' but as 'Sustainer'.

Orientalists who, beyond the frame of the Middle East, continuously hoped to revive the peoples of an Orient that had supposedly been strangled and buried by the domination of an intolerant Islam. The theme of the 'resurrection of the Orient', inherent to Orientalism, assumed that the peoples of Asia and Africa were half-dead, living only like fossils. The empire of the Revolution was itself already a subterranean empire – not because it sought to exploit carbon as a fuel, but because it employed archaeological domination by means of systematic excavation. This imperial archaeology let Europe speak in the name of the buried pasts of the peoples it ruled, while claiming to resuscitate the civilizations that, in its view, had been reduced to ruins by the intolerance of Islam.

To show this, we will need to investigate the history of the concepts that informed the imperial language of the Republic's expedition to Egypt. This will lead us, first, to reread the diplomatic and anthropological works of one of the expedition's principal inspirations: Volney, whose works Napoleon read and annotated.[16] It was through his work, in part, that the expedition's discourse was constituted.[17]

Calling for the resurrection of peoples

The imperiality that was born during the Egyptian Expedition inherited Volney's transformation of the critique of religion, derived from Spinoza, into a new imperial ideology. Although he never preached conquest, and he defended the principle of the self-determination of peoples during the Revolution, Volney still contributed to the invention of the colonial idea of the civilizing mission.[18] In the wake of Rousseau and the European Enlightenment, he was the founder of an anticlerical language of imperiality. His contribution was to establish a secular morality, presented as a catechism for the French citizen and founded on natural

---

16 Thierry Lentz, *Le Grand Consulat, 1799–1804*, Paris: Fayard, 1999, p. 43. Napoleon had read and annotated Volney's *Ruines* and *Voyage en Égypte et en Syrie*. The two men first met in Corsica before the expedition, in 1792, the same year as Turkey's second defeat by Russia in a conflict that began in 1787. The first Ottoman defeat had taken place in 1774. See Hallaq, *Sharīʿa*, pp. 396–7.

17 Laurens, *L'Expédition d'Égypte*, pp. 21, 34; Laurens, *Les Origines intellectuelles de l'expédition d'Égypte: L'Orientalisme islamisant en France (1698–1798)*, Istanbul: Isis, 1987, pp. 67–79; Said, *Orientalism*, p. 81.

18 Laurens, *Les Origines intellectuelles*, pp. 77–8.

science and the physical study of man as a simple natural phenomenon.[19] It was indeed to Volney's writings that French revolutionaries turned when they sought to outline a secular morality said to be 'scientific'. Volney thus extended the work of Spinoza, who had declared, in his *Ethics*, that the gods were only effects of human projection. Their origin could be found in the incapacity of still-'primitive' man to understand the causes that determine natural phenomena; the gods were the sanctuary of his ignorance. This discourse, which would be imposed by a whole scholarly institution in the name of emancipation, found its imperial translation in Volney and then Napoleon.

Volney's naturalism is a secularism. His *Voyages* constantly bemoan the noxious influence of the power of priests and religions. He continuously includes religion among the primary causes for the inertia of individuals and nations. He defines religion as neither more nor less than a constant of underdeveloped societies.[20] While free thinking had been associated with ethnology since the Renaissance, Volney helped to tip Enlightenment free thinking into a critique of all taboos, of all past priests and religions.[21] The founding of the science of man is thus indissociable from the critique of heaven, and from a history of religions seen as so many inventions of human consciousness. Volney, and others after him, would call this critique of heaven *ideology*: the secular science of religious ideas.

The prophecy of a legislator who would destroy the priests and so inaugurate a new people came to be expressed as ideology, giving form to a new imperiality. This empire of museum-like resurrection, contemporary with the first cultural museums, saw the emergence of Islam and the Islamic conquests as the primary actors in the death of civilizations, with only ruins left behind. The argument was that fanaticism had tried to destroy all the great civilizations that preceded it: the critique of religion thus helped to establish the language of the colonial imperiality that invaded Egypt, and it was Volney and the French ideologues of the late eighteenth century who made this critique's imperial transformation

---

19   His theories were taken as authoritative by the ideologues of the period. See Martin S. Staum, *Minerva's Message: Stabilizing the French Revolution*, Montreal: McGill-Queen's University Press, 1996, pp. 121–2.

20   Ibid., pp. 157–8.

21   Michèle Duchet, *Anthropologie et histoire au siècle des Lumières*, Paris: Albin Michel, 1995, pp. 9–10.

possible. Bonaparte's imperial profession of faith should be seen not as a remnant of religion, but as an effect of his atheism.

Volney's imperial ideology can be seen in the basic outlines of the 'Eastern Question', an expression used in the nineteenth century to refer to the geopolitical events that resulted from the Ottoman Empire's military and economic decline between the end of the eighteenth century and the First World War. The national borders separating the countries of Eastern Europe and the Middle East would result from this 'question'. Volney's *Considerations on the War with the Turks*, written in 1788, was an attempt to prophesy this change in the diplomatic balance. He predicted nothing less than the imminent and inevitable destruction of the Ottoman Empire, and a new Russian hegemony in Eastern Europe.[22] Working from this prediction, he presents his book as a critique of French diplomacy towards the Ottoman Empire, whose strategy at the time was based on alliance with the Ottomans to counter Russian hegemonic pretentions. Against this, Volney argued that France should support Russia against Turkey, which was now in decline and so unworthy of support.

In this text, we can also read the matrix of a new imperiality, whose racial and ecological trajectories are traced in the following chapters. It was after reading Volney that Napoleon would promote France to the title of imperial power, giving himself the mission of replacing the Ottoman Empire in its Arab and African provinces. France would thus carry out the mission Volney had given to Russia. But Volney also invented another crucial theme, one we have already encountered and that would persist throughout the nineteenth century: the *resurrection of the dead Orient by the living West*. Like a grammar, this idea would structure the relations between imperiality and Orientalism across the nineteenth century.

The project of resurrecting nations, in Volney's words 'so truly capable of inflaming the imagination' of Europe, involved 'conquering Greece and Asia' and 'banishing from those delightful countries [the] barbarous invaders'.[23] The location for this new empire was not only the Orient

---

22 This Russian hegemony would only become a real threat after 1827, but there were signs of a shift in relations of force in Russia's favour as early as the late eighteenth century. See, on this, Chapters 4 and 5.

23 Volney, *Considerations on the War with the Turks*, London: J. Debrett, 1788, pp. 31–2.

but also *the other Rome* – Constantinople, or Istanbul – through whose reconquest imperiality would found a global empire uniting West and East, Occident and Orient. In Orientalist reason, this region was reconstructed as the origin of civilization. The empire would count 'among [its] domains the most celebrated quarters of the East', 'reigning at once over Byzantium and Babylon, over Athens and Eckbatana, over Jerusalem, Tyre, and Palmyra'. As an emancipatory power, it would abolish slavery, produced by the supposed tyranny of Islam, and so fulfil the 'noble purposes of ambition': to 'emancipate so many nations from the odious yoke of fanaticism and tyranny'. This project of liberation would 'restore the arts and sciences to their native soil' and so open 'a new career to legislation, to commerce, and industry'. Resurrection by empire, in short, implied the effacement, 'if possible, [of] the glory of the *ancient* East by that of the new', the resurrected Orient.[24]

From here on, secularism would be the keystone of the imperiality that was destined to spread over the ruins of the Ottoman Empire. If 'the power that occupies Constantinople' could ensure that 'a strict impartiality be observed between the various sects, and that universal toleration, of which the Emperor has given the first example, established', with religious ideas denied civil effects, and 'if the legislature is committed to skilful and pure hands, that enter into the spirit of the Orientals; acting upon such principles, this power will soon outstrip all the old Governments'.[25] To free enslaved peoples by destroying Islamic law meant to neutralize all civil effects of religion, denying it the least influence on collective life. The secular empire that Volney imagined is thus presented as the sole possible resolution of religious conflict. By forcibly imposing what he calls 'tolerance', it prescribes a necessary secularization to the Oriental minorities in Europe still subject to the yoke of the Turks' fanatical Islam. This prescription is the condition for their future integration into the empire as subjects. If, Volney writes, 'the government grants the tolerance of sects prescribed by politics and reason, which religion itself ordains, these same Armenians, Greeks, and Jews who today are foreigners will tomorrow become subjects'.[26]

---

24 Ibid., p. 32.
25 Ibid., p. 84.
26 Volney, *Considerations*, p. 71 [translation modified].

What Volney describes as emancipation is indissociable from the emergence of a discourse whose full importance will be measured only at the end of this book. This discourse defined the Ottoman Empire as a state founded on the negation of religious freedom and human rights.[27] The block to a great peaceful reunion of peoples was 'Islamic fanaticism', supposedly the foundation of this empire, which is thus illegitimate because it is religious, intolerant, and reactionary. Declaring that Islam does not allow the coexistence of religions, and subjects non-Muslims to tyranny, Volney announced the necessary disappearance of the Ottoman Empire, leaving its territories in Europe and Asia to a liberating and emancipating domination. Islam is disqualified, defined as fundamentally incapable of religious tolerance and pluralism. Secular civility will now found the right to empire, promoting new emperors to the Roman title by expelling the Muslims. The resurrection of peoples is an effect of the domination of subjects finally liberated from Islamic oppression.

According to Volney, as we have seen, the ideal territory for the reign of liberty was not in Europe and the West. As early as 1788, Volney declared that a new Near East could be born from the ruins of the Ottoman Empire, liberated from Islam and the Turks by a European Empire. This dream of an empire uniting East and West was the first ideal territory of secularism, before the Revolution proclaimed it as an order. It was formulated in the midst of ruins, like the ones Volney described in his scholarly presentation of an Ottoman Empire reduced to the gloomy image of fanatic and intolerant rule over religious minorities. The idea of empire invented in this scenario appears as the body of the secular, following Volney's own wishes, to finally authorize that the Turkish Muslims be chased out of Europe.[28]

The workings of fanaticism

This discourse of the radical exclusion of Islam is inscribed within the long history of imperiality. In the prophecies of the Renaissance, vanquishing the Muslims had once conferred the 'right to Empire'.[29] On the eve of the Revolution, chasing the Muslim Turks from Europe and

---

27   Ibid.
28   Volney, *Considerations*, pp. 64–5.
29   Laurent Gerbier, *Les Raisons de l'empire*, Paris: Vrin, 2016, p. 43.

retaking Constantinople was still the double condition for the legitimate exercise of imperial function. But what now promoted a power to the imperial title was no longer the defence, with swords raised, of the Christian religion from the infidels, but, instead, the imposition of tolerance and, subsequently, the dissolution of fanaticism. The function and goal of this war of conquest, rather than of conversion, was to reintegrate the ancient capital of the Eastern Roman Empire into a new empire freed from fanaticism. But, according to Volney, this Empire of Enlightenment would still need to make use of religious fanaticism, as an instrument that was both provisional and strategic.

Volney understood the geopolitical conflict between Russians and Turks as a war of religion, a war between opposing fanaticisms. The Ottoman Empire represented Muslim fanaticism, and the Russian Empire Christian fanaticism; in some sense the latter played the part not of good savage but of good fanatic in opposition to the former. Good fanaticism was an instrument of civilization because, being itself 'barbaric', it was best positioned to civilize what Volney called the 'Oriental race'. Fanatical violence appeared in a double form: it was a religious figure of political illegitimacy, but also a method of taming, the instrument of an order that would impose 'religious tolerance' on its subjects willingly or by force. Imperial sovereignty is the teleology of peace that controls the potential explosions of violence that religious fanaticism makes possible. The policing of religious communities therefore authorizes a reasonable use of religious conflict. Only a secular empire could reduce religions to the rank of simple 'instruments', because an instrument is necessarily something exterior to the one who uses it. In order for religions, in their plurality, to become strategic resources, the empire would need to refrain from declaring a single dogma to be the only truth. It would then be able to use Christian fanaticism against Muslim fanaticism, confident that Russian fanaticism would evaporate through the process of civilization.

Volney acknowledged that some contested the Russian imperial title by declaring that Russia was not sufficiently civilized to intervene in the Orient. Its people were still in a state of servitude, while the classes that were not were hardly enlightened, and its government was despotic. All these were signs of profound barbarism.[30] But, Volney replied, this was

---

30   Volney, *Considerations*, p. 35.

only because the effects of reforms were not yet visible. The Russians were still far from being true civilized moderns and could rightfully still be termed barbarians. But 'barbarians' are 'the fittest for the conquest we speak of', Volney wrote.[31] In a racial discourse that anticipates the hyper-virilization of Muslim 'fanaticism', Volney declares that the morals of the French and the Europeans, too far removed from the fanaticism of the Crusades, were too civilized to be capable of waging war against the Muslims.[32] The strong arm of civilization, its only means of conquest, must be a fanaticism which, as we have seen, Volney predicted was on a path to extinction.

Volney therefore made the following diplomatic recommendation: France should take the side of the Orthodox Christians, because their fanaticism would be softened by civilizing reforms. Islamic fanaticism, on the other hand, rebels against all forms of light. During the period of latency between barbarism and civilization, violence must be employed as an unavoidable tool to serve the triumph of civilization, industry, and the arts in an Orient at last liberated from the spectres of the one God. Because their fanaticism could never be abolished, the Turks were lost for Europe.

An underlying theory of war identified *civilization* with the supposedly rational use of violence and barbarism. Once civil peace was posited as the goal of every use of violence, Enlightenment reason could validate the unavoidable and beneficent violence of European civilization against the arbitrary violence of religion. *The word* civilization *means nothing other than the right to make appropriate use of* barbarism. Civilization is the end that justifies all means, following a diplomatic reasoning that cannot be reduced to colonialism in the strict sense.[33] While, during the Revolution, Volney used this diplomatic reasoning to support an opposition to French imperialism *in Europe* in the name of the self-determination of peoples, he praised the English colonization of India. And an opposition to direct colonial intervention – a principle expressed in his *Voyage to Egypt* – did not prevent him from believing that it would be in the interest of the Egyptian people for them to be governed by new masters rather than the Mamluks or Ottomans. While the identity of

---

31   Ibid., p. 36.
32   Ibid., pp. 36–7.
33   See Laurens, *Les Origines intellectuelles*, pp. 77–8.

these new masters was undetermined in the *Voyage*, it opened the space of imperiality that Napoleon would actualize.

This imperiality, based on educating peoples and converting them to the principle of their own self-determination, constitutes the matrix of the civilizing mission. Civilization became a mission once it was necessary to make converts to the new world. The critique of religion belongs to the critique of *missionary* colonialism. The imperial critique of Christian colonialism is an ideology in which liberation and private property overlap. It declared that the peasantry, in Europe and elsewhere, could not free itself from the tutelage of priests except by becoming landowners. The critique of the colonial mission made it possible to wrest the mission away from the Christians, from the monopoly of Christ and of heavenly empire. Secular civility took the torch from the Christian mission, which it had defeated and so could employ as a resource.

From Islam as Antichrist to the Prophet-Legislator

How was it possible, as Napoleon did, to derive from a discourse so hostile to Islam a politics of strategically claiming to be Islamic? To answer this, we need to identify another matrix of secular imperiality: the set of discourses through which the Prophet 'Mahomet' (Muhammad) was described as a legislator. The confident declaration that great men *make* religion was in effect what led the empire of the Revolution to profess its Islamic credentials. Something at the very heart of European anticlericalism and its critique of religion led revolutionary discourse down the path to a new imperiality.

Through the workings of the European anticlerical machine, 'Mahomet' went from false prophet to great man. While he may have 'spouted a mass of fables he claimed to have received from heaven', wrote Prophète Condorcet, one of the founding fathers of French *laïcité*, 'he won battles'.[34] With brutal simplicity, this statement shows how Islam went, in the eyes of European reason, from a heresy fomented by the devil to a human invention, the creation of a legislative genius who used

---

34 Condorcet, cited in Henry Laurens, *Le Royaume impossible: La France et la genèse du monde arabe*, Paris: Armand Colin, 1990, pp. 14–15.

religion as a means to govern and conquer.[35] This codification of proph-esy as legislation was presented as an unveiling, revealing the profane reasons hidden behind sacred masks, the human actions surreptitiously disguised as acts of God.

Napoleon's discourse in Egypt transformed this pseudo-scholarly paradigm into an imperial declaration. What the future emperor aimed to occupy was, quite literally, the place of prophetic legislator as config-ured by the critique of heaven. Because the Lumières and ideologists had unveiled the revelation of 'Mahomet' as the work of a great man, Napoleon could paint himself as the Prophet's successor, in opposition to the Turkish and Mamluk Muslims themselves. The figure of the Prophet of Islam was redrawn as a great man ruling over the Arabs, so that the Revolution could become an empire. Under the effect of the Enlightenment, and in the margins of Christian representations of Islam, Bonaparte saw 'Mahomet' as a great man, the legislator of the Arabs, who had used Islam to give his people power over the Orient and Africa. Napoleon wanted to be his successor because he saw him as a conqueror who, like all great men, strategically made *recourse* to reli-gion. 'Recourse to the religious' became an imposture whose interven-tion was a requirement of all greatness.

Through this gesture, the Roman tradition of *translatio imperii* – the transfer of power from one empire to another – was extended outside the Roman and Christian frame to include Islam. We might say that, through this translation, laws came into communication, as revolution-ary law claimed at once to abolish and fulfil Islamic law. The discursive space of the quranic tradition was thus invested with a *strategic plurilin-gualism*. The translation of the revolutionary declaration into an Islamological language served to Orientalize the Revolution, de-West-ernizing liberation and opening it to the world. The transfer of the *khali-fat* to the French army was also a transfer of the pre-Islamic knowledge of the great ancient civilizations that Orientalist scholars said had been 'ruined' by the caliphs, but which could be rediscovered through archae-ological research in Egypt. The *translatio imperii* was thus also a *transla-tio studii*: the transfer of power from one empire to another was also a transfer of knowledge. A vast project was organized to decipher ruins

---

35   Jean-Jacques Rousseau, *The Social Contract*, trans. C. Betts, Oxford: Oxford University Press, 1994, pp. 160–1.

and establish a museum of lost traditions. This gigantic project, reducing traditions to a past that could be appropriated, unfolded through the work of the Egyptian Scientific Institute. This was a founding moment not only for Orientalism and Egyptology, but also for the colonial ethnology of African societies. It provided the model for Louis Faidherbe's foundation of colonial Africanism in Senegal, a colony where the French Empire also sought to impose itself as a Muslim power.[36] The empire established a sort of pseudo-Islamic code which, far from being part of a living tradition, was merely a collection of empty signifiers.

In some sense, it was the Lumières who invented what they called 'religious imposture', by giving birth to a Bonaparte. The empire that was to be established in their name made religion an instrument of power, insofar as it distinguished itself from what it defined as religious. A specific form of what is sometimes denounced as the instrumentalization of religion was put to work: an effect of the reason defended by the Enlightenment, which presupposes that, by its very essence, religion should be exterior to power. It was precisely because Napoleon criticized the heavens that his discourse became pseudo-messianic, and precisely because he was faithful to no god that he claimed to fulfil biblical and quranic prophecy within the immanence of this Earth. An *imperial messianism without transcendence* was articulated, translated into Orientalism's Islamological language. Napoleon erected an imperial and revolutionary system of policing that put Islam under surveillance while claiming to liberate Muslims. This strategic messianism belonged to the 'eschatological atmosphere' that inspired Bonaparte, and gave him the profound conviction that he was truly both the Saviour awaited by some and the Antichrist feared by others.[37]

Because, under the effects of secular criticism, God became one word among others, His name could be used as one resource among others. The birth of these strategic prophecies opened the path for the emergence of imperial theologies of Revolution. By announcing himself as 'Messiah', Bonaparte claimed to fulfil prophecy on Earth, as well as the secret hopes of Egypt. Indeed, the future emperor's

---

36   Jean-Louis Triaud, 'L'Islam au sud du Sahara: une saison orientaliste en Afrique occidentale', *Cahiers d'Études Africaines* 2010, pp. 907–50.
37   Laurens, *Orientales I*, p. 157.

army took the title of *Mahdi*: the Messiah come to liberate Muslims from the yoke of their Mamluk overlords. It was there to *oppress the oppressors*, and could do so only by declaring to the Muslims that it was opposed to the Church. The imperiality of holy war and the Crusades that the Roman Church had once issued against the Muslim world now turned on itself. No quest for converts, but rather strategic conversion to Islam. No more domination by assimilation, but rather by translation and the hybridization of codes. The imperiality that had constantly preached war against an Islam defined as Antichrist was thus reborn by turning against its celestial matrix.

Islam-Antichrist and imperial prophecy

Did imperiality merely cease to be Christian and become revolutionary? The Egyptian Expedition required a mutation of the prophetic and biblical language by which Christians had made themselves prophets of the end times and opponents of the Antichrist. The model for this prophetic language came from an Old Testament scripture, the Book of Daniel. As resignified by Christian theology, the announcement of the arrival of the Son of Man and the end of time became an announcement of the coming of Christ, giving birth to the discourse we call Christian eschatology or messianism. In Egypt, what was repeated was not Christianity itself, but a neo-biblical tradition that was deployed to announce not the end of time and the coming of Christ, but the advent of liberty through regeneration. This prophetic tradition had been constructed by Christians during the Crusades. Joachim of Fiore, a well-known medieval Christian monk, is likely the father of this prophetic tradition, which contemporary philosophies of history have sometimes understood as a secularization.[38] Prophecies of the end of time and the extermination of the Antichrist underwent a decisive mutation with Joachim. They began to identify the apocalyptic ten-horned beast – that, according to the Bible, would appear on the threshold of the end of time – with Islam, and Mahomet with the Antichrist. When Islam became the face of the imperial enemy, this provoked a theological mutation within Christianity itself. The blood of Muslims could now be shed without

---

38 Karl Löwith, *Meaning in History: The Theological Implications of the Philosophy of History*, Chicago: University of Chicago Press, 1949, pp. 1–10.

those responsible needing to confess their violence as a sin in order to be saved.[39]

Throughout the Renaissance and early modernity, this imperial and biblical prophetism was repeatedly directed against the Turks. Through the conquest of Egypt, it also came to haunt revolutionary language. The old prophecies of the Christian empire of heaven had run aground on the lands of Africa and Asia. Through the critique of religion, their profane fragments became the language of an industrial imperialism imposing itself on the earth. 'Scholarly' and literary Orientalism is probably only a surface effect of these mutations of biblical and imperial prophetism, transformed into predictions of revolutionary ideology and strategy. Napoleon said of himself what the papal monarchy had said of Islam during the Crusades: that he was the Antichrist. The theme of Islam as Antichrist was reversed, since now Napoleon declared that he was Muslim because he was the enemy of the pope. The roles the emperor gave himself were equivalent: new Mahomet, Mahdi, and Antichrist. Subverting the words of the Christian empire of heaven and the Church's Crusades, Napoleon spoke the language of his own pseudo-Qur'an. Seeking to take the imaginary place that Orientalism and the critique of religions had attributed to Mahomet – legislator, war chief, and emperor – Napoleon intended to write a new Qur'an in conformity with his interests. Today, France has still not exited this waking dream, which its Lumières ceaselessly revive. Indeed, it was as a 'man of the Enlightenment', an emancipated being and inheritor of Voltaire and Rousseau, that Bonaparte saw himself: as founding a new civil religion and instituting a new people, while turning the Qur'an into a civil code that Mahomet had invented so he could conquer the world. And it was in this role that he carried out lies and assassinations.

39   Francisco Bethencourt, *Racisms: From the Crusades to the Twentieth Century*, Princeton, NJ: Princeton University Press, 2013, pp. 13–73; Jean Flori, *Guerre sainte, Jihad, croisade: violence et religion dans le christianisme et l'islam*, Paris: Seuil, 2002, pp. 159–89.

The first empire

Why does the history of the First French Empire and the secularization of Europe begin in North Africa? If Napoleon secularized France and Europe, he was able to only by occupying the role of the legislator who, according to Volney, would impose tolerance in an empire of the Orient and Africa. As we have seen, he gave this role the imaginary face of 'Mahomet', dressed in the costume of the Antichrist that Christians, for centuries, had identified with Islam.[40] This radical upheaval of Christian prophecy and Orientalism was not solely discursive. While, clearly, Napoleon's discourse did not cause the secularization of the First Empire, it helps us to understand the imperiality of the structure of *policing* that the state imposed on what it called *cultes* or 'religions'. Neither the history of European colonialism nor the emergence of the modern nation-state in Europe can be understood without the Egyptian Expedition.

Did the model of the bureaucratic and administrative state established in France after 1804 incarnate the pseudo-Islamic and 'Oriental' imperiality that Napoleon invented? In other words, how did the Egyptian Expedition contribute to the secularization of the French state and of Europe? It has long been established that the Egyptian Expedition contributed to Napoleon's *coup d'état* by enhancing his popularity in France, opening the plebiscitary tradition that continues to structure the paradoxes of electoral democracy.[41] But Napoleon's individual itinerary was only an index of secularization's non-European trajectories. The fact that the First Empire received its birth certificate in North Africa exposes the imperiality of the language of the French state, the structure of the concepts that still govern its abstract law and policing of religious communities of practice.

The state's principal techniques for organizing, governing, and regulating the new spaces of secularity that family and civil society represented were first tested during the Egyptian Expedition, on North African peoples. What matters, then, is not whether the expedition betrayed the French Revolution, or was its necessary consequence, but a different question: How did the Egyptian Expedition contribute to secularizing Europe? Did it allow the First Empire to institute revolutionary

---

40 After all, did not Nietzsche make Napoleon one of his anti-Christian heroes?
41 Lentz, *Le Grand Consulat*, pp. 50–1.

equality and liberty through state reform? Was the imperial architecture of the state built in Europe on the basis of the attempted but failed conquest of North Africa and the Arab world?

State control of religion

The First Empire reformed law, science, and religion. A law and science without God were born, while the state recognized religions without recognizing God. *Religious pluralism was organized by the state through the reform and surveillance of religious ritual practice.* Priests' and pastors' salaries were paid by the state, under the rule of the abstract principle of equality. Shortly afterwards, under the July Monarchy in 1831, rabbis would also be salaried. The reforms organized religions into identified *cultes*, or organized ritual practices, paving the way for them to be subordinated, controlled, and financed by the state. Religious discourses and ritual practices were simultaneously protected and surveilled.[42] The civil code disregarded confession. Abstracted from their religious affiliations, citizens became equal before the law. This abstract legality saw religion as the paradigm of inequality, obliterating the complexity of concrete reality behind the flattening term *religion*. The regulation of religion was thus crucial in the general process of real abstraction through law. The secular state's blindness in principle to differences of class, race, and sex in the name of abstract equality does not contradict its policing of religion. Religion as produced and organized by state reform of traditions played a crucial role in denying the name of God any meaning whatsoever within the city.

To be secular is to speak less of God than of religion; it is, in some sense, to proliferate the *religious* on the ruins of the divine. The empire no longer recognized the *truth* of Catholic dogma, but, instead, recognized Catholicism as the majority religion. In making a strategic alliance with the Church, after Napoleon in Egypt had declared himself its enemy, the First Empire of the secular no longer aimed for heaven, salvation, or the end of time. It aimed for mastery over its religion and the religions practised on the part of the Earth over which it claimed sovereignty. For this reason, the presence of religion in the public sphere is not an archaic residue but a contemporary production, an effect of the

---

42   Ibid., pp. 20–1.

secularization of institutions. Without speaking and performing the religious, how could these institutions call themselves *secular*?

By codifying religion into the idiom of the nation, the state made it possible for Christians to identify claims of Christian superiority with majority rule. A new grammar permitted a defence of the rights and identity of the nation. This grammar linked religion and family, Christian religion and national identity. From then on, the empire's profession of faith would take the form of statistical fact: 'The Catholic religion is the religion of the vast majority of the French.'[43] Religions could now be described and observed as social facts, approached through the statistical reason that the emperor followed attentively. The Ancien Régime had recognized the *divinity* of the Catholic Church; the modern state recognized only the simple existence of Catholic *religion*, because it no longer recognized the existence of God. The social reality of religion tended to be substituted for any divine or transcendent reality. The certainty of the existence of religion made another certainty – that of faith in God – precarious. Through religion, it was society that came to take the place of God. Once the empire was secularized, religion could become socially useful or superfluous; and it would be judged by this criterion of utility.

The non-recognition of the Catholic Church's divinity was not merely an absence. It was the other side of a transformation in the status of Catholic tradition, the forced conversion of Christianity to the new rules and discourses of public life. Once Christianity became a majoritarian social fact, one simple parameter among a multitude of others that must be taken into account by the government of a given population within a given territory, public reason and state reason became secular. The Catholic faith *had* to be publicly recognized as a religion, out of statistically informed governmental necessity. Religion then could regulate the space of morality, identified with the intimate space of the family, and so be understood as the matrix of nation, society, and moral order.

Secular reason thus gave religion new powers. Far from a privatization of religion, these powers were distributed across both public and private spheres. Its field of action was confined to the domestic space of the family, redefined as the supposed matrix of society and public morals. In

---

43   Cited in Jean Baubérot, *Histoire de la laïcité en France*, Paris: PUF, 2013, p. 20.

addition, the practice of religion was funded, publicly recognized, and regulated by policing. In secular reason, religion was socially useful. Piety was identified as the maintenance of moral order in domestic space and in society, and Christian charity became assistance for the poor. These new spaces for the legitimate exercise of religious practices emerged alongside the formation of the modern nation-state.

The declaration of the empire as Catholic was at once *formally necessary* and *materially contingent*. It was necessary for the empire to have one religion or another; whether this was Catholicism or Islam mattered little. The empire should profess the religion of the *majority*, which it defined by governing the population according to statistical studies. As long as the majority it governed was religious, the empire must profess their religion. The revolutionary Republic declared itself Muslim in Egypt and Catholic in France because this was what the logic of political representation of the sovereignty of the people demanded. From here on, the empire would dissociate the existence of religion and the existence of God. It would separate public recognition of religion as fact from political recognition of its truth. This grammar is imperial not only because it is colonial, but also for reasons connected to the Roman and medieval meaning of the word *empire*: the civility of the state is set up as a mediator of conflicts, a conciliator and defender of the peace.

The monarchical dimension of empire itself is a consequence of the question of *instituting* equality and liberty, within a stable order guaranteed by the state. In order to divert opponents of the Revolution away from loyalty to the Ancien Régime and neutralize the risk of restoration, it was necessary to manipulate the symbols of the monarchy. This meant creating an appearance of continuity between the monarchy and the Revolution – showing that the French Empire could be as monarchical and Catholic as the Ancien Régime – in order to stabilize the Revolution.[44] The reconciliation of order and revolution, clerics and Lumières, and thus of the two Frances, was incarnated in the new empire. The imperiality of hegemonic power corresponds to the creation of a hybrid, a permanent ambiguity that results from a proliferation of strategic alternatives within the art of governing. Napoleon thus made Catholicism and monarchism into two sets of exterior signs that he could

---

44 Louis Bergeron, *L'Épisode napoléonien*, Paris: Seuil, 1972, pp. 24–8.

appropriate and mobilize, the better to manage public opinion. Preventing the restoration of the Ancien Régime required him to appropriate its monarchical symbols into an economy that was both tactical and an expression of his empire. The Church's definitive subjection to the state was a crucial aspect of this.[45] The Concordat with the Church of Rome, signed on 15 July 1801, re-established unity with the Catholic Church by submitting all priests to the power of the state and transforming them into functionaries. For Napoleon, the sacred was not a sacrament.[46] The sacred was merely one religious symbol inscribed within a profane logic of signs, wherein the Catholic Church no longer subjected the emperor to God or to its own spiritual authority. It would now be required to recognize the absolute authority of the administrative state, to accept the compromise introduced by the Concordat. It would cease to protest against the sale of the Church goods that had been looted during the Revolution. Constrained to converting to secularization or reacting against it, it faced the alternative imposed on every political theology: revolution or reaction. The empire attempted to make the clergy civil, after it had failed in its attempt to create a civil clergy recognizing the legitimacy of the revolutionary Republic and professing liberty, equality, and fraternity as so many Christian values.

In articles that Bonaparte appended to the Concordat without consulting Rome, the empire instituted religious pluralism. It converted traditions into *cultes*, and imposed a model of vertical organization onto the religious institutions of all communities. In order to become *cultes*, confessional traditions were required to reform themselves and establish hierarchical representation. The state integrated religious traditions into the capitalist salariat, subsuming them as functionaries. In the name of freedom of religion, priests and pastors became salaried functionaries of the administrative state. Under the First Empire, this system was applied to Catholic priests and Protestant pastors, and it was extended to rabbis by the constitutional monarchy of Louis-Philippe. The parliamentary debates around this expansion show that the foundation for the decision was the empire's organization of the Jewish religion as a *culte*. The First Empire had to organize Jewish representative organizations under state control before the *culte* could

---

45   Lentz, *Le Grand Consulat*, pp. 435–79.
46   Aurélien Lignereux, *L'Empire des Français, 1799–1815*, Paris: Seuil, 2012, p. 64.

be officially recognized in 1831 and rabbis put on salary, like Christian priests and pastors.[47] Attempting to dissolve the communitarian and juridical dimension of Jewish tradition, the French state effected a vertical reform: in the words of the Comte de Clermont-Tonnerre, it refused everything to the Jews as a nation and accorded to them everything as individuals. This reform began in 1806 with the creation of an assembly of Jewish notables whose task was to ensure Jewish organizations' loyalty to the empire, as well as the compatibility of Jewish law and common law.[48] This first act of reform was followed by an attempt to constitute a centralized body by creating the Consistoire Central Israélite (Central Israelite Consistory), an official representative organization of the Jewish community in France. Jewish tradition was thus reformed and transformed to meet the demands of modern life, and then integrated into the body of the imperial state and its administrative mechanisms through the intermediary of a single representative body. The invention of the *culte israélite* by the French state thus ensured its recognition by establishing its supposed representatives. This would then provide the basis for the equal treatment of Jews and Christians in all contexts.

As the *culte* was free and public, the practice of religion was not private; but it was still required to conform to the regulatory policing that limits, in order to protect, the exercise of freedom of conscience. Because the *cultes* owed their liberty to the state, they had to submit to its policing: such were the terms of their contract with the empire. The first secular pact thus contributed to redefining the role of religion in terms set by public and dominant morality. The system of public recognition of *cultes* made it possible to pose a morality presented as natural, universal, and the common foundation of all religions. It was possible to police the different *cultes* because religions were presented as so many forms of a single and unique morality – as Jean-Étienne-Marie Portalis, one of the principal drafters of the civil code, declared. This foundation of religion on morality did not make religions superfluous; rather, it meant that, for reasons of efficiency and pragmatism, the

---

47   Debate, 1 February 1831, in the Chambre des Députés, parliamentary archives (1787–1860), Paris, 1887, vol. LXVI, p. 439.

48   See Mayanthi Fernando, *The Republic Unsettled: Muslim French and the Conditions of Secularism*, Durham, NC: Duke University Press, 2014, pp. 111–13.

government affirmed the social utility of religions in order to give real authority to morality. Supposedly natural morality was socially active in the form of religion; 'a morality without dogma' would therefore be like 'justice without courts'.[49] Within this framework, Catholicism was redefined as the *body that formulated natural morality for the usage of the majority*.

Once the secular state had socialized morality through religious dogma, religion could become the opium of the people. The social function of religious institutions consisted in 'making bearable the dangers and injustices inherent in the state of society'.[50] Religion thus became part of what would soon be called the 'social question'. It was inscribed in the play of public powers not as private belief but as *practice*: as cult and as morality.

The empire that emerged from the Revolution and sought to unify Europe was thus the first of its kind. The universal domination it sought to establish was no longer a restoration of Christendom, but a state that administered religious communities of practice by dividing religion into private belief, public practice, and natural morality. The truth of these beliefs became a matter of indifference. Unbelief remained socially marginal, but in the university and its laboratories irreligion and materialism could be socially embraced. In the same process, Catholicism was nationalized. The state thus organized traditional practices into vertical and representative structures that, by recognizing them, it put under its control. Religion became a mere instrument, one element to which the state could take recourse in order to maintain public order. It was this model of secularization that allowed the state to pacify the religious conflict opened by the Revolution. Napoleon justified these authoritarian and dictatorial policies in the name of the greatest number, and the sovereignty of the people who had elected him.

Catholic in France, Muslim in Africa

My policy is to govern men as the greatest number wish to be governed. This, I believe, is how one recognizes the sovereignty of the people. By becoming Catholic, I ended the war in the Vendée; by

---

49 Portalis, cited in Baubérot, *Histoire de la laïcité*, p. 28.
50 Ibid.

becoming Muslim I established myself in Egypt; and by becoming an
ultra-Montagnard I captured hearts in Italy.[51]

Napoleon transformed Catholicism into a majority religion, just as in
North Africa he attempted to transform Islam into a *culte*. The revolutionary Republic that strategically declared itself Muslim was an empire
of popular sovereignty. By claiming to represent the people, it aimed to
convert the religions within its territory to the true civilization. It was
the practice of the democratic principle in plebiscitary form that transformed the Empire of Revolution into a pseudo-Islamic secularism. In
order to satisfy the people, the future emperor had to play the game of
strategically converting to the great religions. The empire's secularity
was applied through his ability to speak the language of all religions, to
translate himself strategically into each religion so that he could establish a rule that claimed to represent popular sovereignty.

So then, could we say that the Islam of the expedition was the
empire's first religion, in anticipation of what Catholicism would
become in France when it was declared the religion of the French
majority? Napoleon was no more sincere in calling himself a Muslim
in Egypt than when he called himself a Catholic in France. These were
similar techniques, which could be used to subjugate Egyptian
Muslims or the Church in France. Napoleon's goal was not to convert
Muslims, but to master and control the authorities that he wrongly
considered to be guardians of Islam. Pursuing this, he invented the
policing of *cultes* in Egypt before he instituted it in France. Trying to
establish Muslim allies and to organize them into representatives of
Islam, he founded policies for the funding and recognition of a *culte*
he attempted to create from scratch. He fully funded the celebration of
the Prophet's birth, and invested the Shaykh Al-Bakri with juridical
power over all of the *sharifs* of Egypt.[52] Napoleon's goal in subjugating
the Muslim elites was to support strategic allies of his government. He

---

51   Bonaparte to the Conseil d'État, 16 August 1800, cited in Lentz, *Le Grand
Consulat*, p. 435. Napoleon's policy was clearly to the disadvantage of the revolutionaries
who were firmly opposed to the Concordat. He responded with hostility to its opponents,
sometimes using physical violence. He gave Volney a kick to the stomach during an
interview in which the latter had the bad idea of contesting the Concordat. See Lentz, *Le
Grand Consulat*, p. 459.
52   Laurens, *L'Expédition d'Égypte*, p. 111.

thus addressed his declarations not directly to the African peoples, but to intermediaries whom he needed to appease if he was to achieve consent to his rule.

The creation of a cultural centralism, a sort of Muslim clergy, followed from the secularization of imperiality. The policing of the Muslim *culte* and the instrumentalization of religion were the other side of the drive to transform Islam into a unified and hierarchized religion, a drive that is constitutive of modern mechanisms of regulating religious pluralism. But, if Bonaparte wanted to establish control of Islam in Africa, he would also need to define Islam as the foundation of the social life of the Egyptian peoples, in the same way that he would define Catholicism as a majority religion.[53] He declared to his army: 'The people with whom you will be living are Mohammedans; their first article of faith is this: There is no god but God, and Mohammed is his Prophet.'[54] The Shahada, made into an 'article of faith', seems here to appear as a fact to be strategically appropriated by colonial Islamology. The point was not to determine the truth or falsity of the conquered subjects' religion or, like missionaries, to identify them as heretics or idolaters, but to rule a population defined as majority Muslim by 'tolerating' Islam, the principle the future emperor commanded his armies to respect.[55] Respect for Islam meant the tolerance and surveillance of what the Republic named as a *culte*. Islam would be codified as a set of practical prescriptions. Islamological knowledge codified religions as social facts evaluated in terms of their practical effects. The resulting concept of Islam was much more than a two-dimensional image of the other – it was an operator of representation in the political sense. It allowed Islam to be organized as a *culte* that *represented* Muslims in a centralized and governable way. This structure of organizing and surveilling communities organized into *cultes* was at the heart of the secularization of the state that took place under the First Empire.

---

53   Napoleon, cited in ibid., p. 115: 'We are friends to the Muslims and to the religion of the Prophet; we wish to do whatever will please you and favour your religion.' Here Islam is approached as the religion of the Prophet – that is, as Muhammadanism.

54   Cited in ibid., p. 40.

55   Ibid. The passage cited earlier is relevant here: 'Do not contradict them; work with them as we worked with the Jews and the Italians; show respect for their muftis and imams, as you did for the rabbis and bishops. Show *the same tolerance* for mosques and the ceremonies prescribed by the Qur'an that you did for convents and synagogues, for the religions or Moses or Jesus Christ' [emphasis added].

The secularity of the imperial state was thus verified by its ability to translate itself into different religions, to be converted not into living traditions, everyday practices, or virtues, but into signs of religious belonging. By this strategic conversion, imperiality aimed to convert the divine to modernity and human rights. It was not only believers but religions themselves that were converted to civilization, while the latter was translated into the languages of religion. The Napoleonic Grand Sanhedrin was one example: Napoleon and his ministers gathered together the representatives of the Jewish *culte* with the task of condemning anything in the Talmud that was contrary to civilization, and founding a Judaism that had been reformed and modernized by the state. But another illustration is the concept of *Christian civilization* that took shape around 1830. One clue to this new language is that it could be mobilized to oppose what was then called the 'emancipation of the Jews'. What were constituted under the First Empire were so many spaces of secularity, within which debates could take place on the compatibility of different religions with civilization. These debates continue to form an integral part of the public sphere in liberal and secular democracies and contribute to government decision-making in the guise of expert opinion.

The ability to convert through translation presupposes a grammar by which religion is established as social fact and the moral foundation of peoples. The first example of this strategy was the Muslim Napoleon of Africa and the Orient. When the European and Western Napoleon ordered the Roman Church to consecrate him as emperor at Notre-Dame de Paris, he 'Catholicized' an imperial strategy that had first, in Africa, been pseudo-Islamic. The act by which the Napoleonic Empire declared itself Catholic in France was the same act by which it declared itself Muslim in Egypt: imposing a truth translated into the multitude of religions, which became so many languages in which the same equal freedom of men could be spoken. This form of imperiality could colonize traditions from inside, inflecting them, one at a time or all at once, in service of the interests of empire's reason. Napoleon was no more Muslim than he was Catholic, but he seized onto Islamic signifiers in Egypt the same way that he seized onto Catholicism in France in order to nationalize it. He understood this as a civilizing of traditions, regenerating them while leading men towards their own liberty. Irrespective of the substance of the confessions of the peoples it ruled, the empire of the secular relied on the fact of religion for support, because it held as a human truth that religion determines the character of peoples.

Reliance on Catholicism in France and Islam in Egypt thus derived from the same strategic imperiality. Bonaparte transformed Catholicism into a civil religion just as he tried to transform Islam into a *culte*. He dressed himself in the costume of the Mahomet imagined by centuries of racial Orientalism, whose ghost he claimed to reincarnate when he dictated prayers to the Muslims of Egypt in which they would swear fidelity to France. When he constituted Catholicism as civil religion and gave himself the imperium of the Church, he imposed a single Catholic catechism that instructed fidelity to the emperor.[56] It was by representing Muslim authorities as a clergy and attempting to rewrite the Qur'an to support his rule that Napoleon invented the imperial language that allowed him to institutionalize the Revolution as empire. Through this, in part, practices were born by which the secular state could control, recognize, and surveil religious practices – a far cry from any separation of the political and religious. The French law of separation between Church and state, established in 1905, never made a pure and simple break with the properly imperial system of public recognition and control of *cultes*, even if it ceased to finance them. Before we turn to the colonial deployment of this system of control in Algeria, we first need to understand how the universalism at the heart of the French Republic's official discourse functioned during the Egyptian Expedition.

From imperial secularization to the fulfilment of Christianity on Earth

The Egyptian Expedition was a decisive moment because it prefigured the future of the French Empire after its defeat in Europe. Indeed, North and West Africa were the territories where the French imperial spectre would spread after it was broken in Europe by the Treaty of Vienna. It is therefore impossible to argue that the Napoleonic imperial project was defeated, without taking into account its legacy in France's Mediterranean, African, and Oriental policies – that is to say, in its colonial project

---

56   Baubérot, *Histoire de la laïcité*, p. 21.

between the Second Empire and the Fifth Republic. The imperiality of French government that ran aground on the European continent was disseminated overseas by the colonization of Africa. The more the empire retreated in Europe, the more it seemed to be only a dream, and the more colonization took on a decisive importance.

As the spectral rebirth of the Roman Empire through colonial expansion, the secularization of imperial power beginning at the end of the eighteenth century can be analysed as the birth of a *new formation of empire*. The threshold of 1800 marks a sort of historical leap that precludes reducing the secular empire and its colonies to the medieval Christian empire or earlier colonial empires.[57] Secularization unfolded through the ways in which the empire of Christendom, which died with Charles V and the Reformation and was then fragmented and diffracted through colonialism and slavery, produced irreducible and secular effects in its dissemination. The imperiality of the secular state was *renascent* before it was revolutionary. The first reason for this is that its initial fragmentation took place during the Renaissance. The second is that its historicity consists of a cycle of permanent rebirths. Imperiality is the fruit of an upheaval in the imperial idea produced by the crisis of medieval Christianity and the emergence of a *first globalization*. The colonization of the Americas coincided not with the disappearance of the imperial idea but with its redefinition, by Mercurino di Gattinara and Charles V, but also by Bartolomé de Las Casas and Juan Ginés de Sepúlveda.[58]

For Las Casas the imperial idea served to resolve an intrinsic contradiction, allowing him to criticize colonial violence, in opposition to Sepúlveda, while still calling for the conversion of the natives. In his anticolonialism, the violence of real colonization, which he condemned, was contrasted with an ideal colonization, whose goal would be to educate the 'Indians' of the Americas and transform them, through peaceful and humanitarian means, into free subjects. In their criticism of the violence of military colonialism, Saint-Simonism and a certain strand of Marxism invoke the phantom of Las Casas. From this point of

---

57   The chronology is not self-evident. The empire did not end in 1800; but its imperiality was secularized.

58   On the modern metamorphosis of the imperial idea in Gattinara, see Gerbier, *Les Raisons de l'empire*, pp. 44–5 (see also the imperial idea as expressed by Hernán Cortés, ibid., p. 49).

view, Las Casas's idea of empire expresses a new structure of imperiality through its becoming colonial.[59]

Imperial ghosts, therefore, do not challenge but rather confirm the death of the empire. The immense reappearance of the old imperial spectre with Napoleon seems, at the same time, to be the most blatant confirmation of its unavoidable death, through the failure of the Napoleonic conquests. But this failure was nonetheless *inaugural*. Napoleon's failure to constitute a European empire was accompanied by a sort of dissemination of the imperial project outside Europe, carried within a new colonial project.[60] Because the Republic was colonial, and its colonization was founded on the defeat of the empire, its universalism could only be imperial. This universalism, haunted by imperiality, is a form of secularization. A theme common to the history of empires and of philosophy is indeed expressed in the legacy of the Egyptian Expedition: the earthly fulfilment of Christianity within profane history. This invention, which was properly revolutionary before it became Hegelian, leads us to the relation between the history of European philosophy and French colonization in North Africa. To a reader who might object that, at root, imperial secularization is nothing but Christianity, I would respond with another question: how did the empire come to define modernity as the fulfilment of Christianity? How is it that the common certitude that we are still Christian, albeit in a disguised form, was in fact expressed by the ideologues of *laïcité* and the French colonial empire? Asking these questions, we follow the thread of an often ignored aspect of the history of republican universalism and secularism – the role of its German and Hegelian heritage – in order to grasp its imperial dimensions. My hypothesis is that imperiality determined how the concept of secularization was expressed. The order of the fulfilment of Christianity through secular modernity was endlessly reformulated by the ideologues of colonial empire.

---

59   For the transformations of the imperial idea in Las Casas, see Nestor Capdevila, *Las Casas: une politique de l'humanité*, Paris: Le Cerf, 1998, pp. 93–6.

60   See Chapter 6.

2

Giving Birth to the Universal: How the Colonization of Africa Secularized Europe

Bonaparte's imperial establishment of a modern and bureaucratic state is indissociable from the invention of a key theme in European thought: the fulfilment of Christianity by the French Revolution. Declaring that the revolutionary event had realized the kingdom of God on Earth, the ideologues of the triumph of the modern West aimed to convert Christians themselves to industrial civilization. This chapter examines the colonial mechanisms and implications of the definition of the West as the secularization of Christianity. It shows that this theme went hand in hand with the foundation of a new universalism, freed from all theological limitations. The order to secularize the empire coincided with a will to secularize the universal. This led to a legitimization of the colonization of Algeria as the first moment of the expansion of the Republic on the African continent. From 1830 on, the colonization of Algeria played a determining role in the intersecting formations of French Republicanism and social Catholicism.

The theme of the secularization of Christianity was invented somewhere between 1820 and 1830. According to this thesis, the modern age was the realization of Christianity on Earth. Its most systematic expression can be found between the lines of Hegel's philosophy of history, but its dissemination contributed to the invention of a new language, inseparably theological, revolutionary, and colonial. French Republicanism itself was constituted through an appropriation of this Hegelian language, which it deployed as a weapon against the centuries-old alliance between the Roman Church and the absolute monarchy. Mobilizing this language to construct the Republic's colonial ideology, founders of *laïcité* such as Edgar Quinet and Ferdinand Buisson designated France, or what Jules Michelet called the 'Republic of the world', as the site *par excellence* for the fulfilment of Christianity on Earth. Christianity had to be redefined as the religion of the exit from religion, the only religion in the world able to transport an entire civilization beyond the limits of religion itself, in order for something like Republicanism to become possible.[1] But, for the industrial West to be set up as the revelation of Christianity, beyond the narrow confines of Christians themselves, the very concept of Christianity had to be reformed from top to bottom. It could then appear as the only religion that, by engendering its own displacement, could carry away with it every form of transcendence. In this way, secular universalism presupposed the myth of Christian exceptionalism.

Naming the universal in imperial philosophies of history

It was just before his death that Hegel formulated this theme, by understanding the French Revolution as the continuation of the Reformation. In his 1831 lecture course in Berlin, the Revolution appears as the dawn of the modern era, an unprecedented moment where man, for the first time, made himself sole legislator of the world.[2] Hegel conceptualized this event as the fulfilment of Christianity by the advent of the modern rule of law in Europe. This state, he maintained, was the divine on Earth. 'God has become man,' he declared; 'such is the liberation offered in the

---

1   Jean Walch, *Les Maîtres de l'histoire 1815–1850: Augustin Thierry, Mignet, Guizot, Thiers, Michelet, Edgar Quinet*, Paris: Champion-Slatkine, 1986, pp. 9–13. By way of Jules Michelet, Hegelianism thus contributed to structuring practices of national and global history, securing its positivist and scientific legacy. The philosophy of history is not an archaic and theological residue to which we could oppose the scientific seriousness of historical practice: it is one of the places where the modern practice of history was born, and it led to the emergence of historical positivism by shifting historical analysis away from simple literary narrative.

2   G. W. F. Hegel, seminar from 28 March to 1 April 1831, in *La Philosophie de l'Histoire*, Paris: Librairie Générale Française, 2009, pp. 559–64. (This seminar will appear in Volume 2 of Hegel, *Lectures on the Philosophy of World History*, forthcoming from Oxford University Press.)

Christian religion.'[3] Christianity thus, although in a still-religious and limited form, anticipated what Europe would achieve in reality, in this world, through the combined actions of the Reformation and the French Revolution. Hegelian ontology posed revolutionary universalism as Christ fulfilled. Secular universalism declared it was realizing the Christian universal, and secularism presented itself as Christianity. But, for the fulfilment of Christianity in the world to be identified with the very meaning of history, Islam had to be staged as the appearance of a different religious universalism. Islam became the religion of the Orient, while Christianity became the religion of the West.[4] Through this double gesture, Hegel identified Islam as evidence of the Orient's death, while justifying the triumph of the West. This 'other revolution' that Islam represented failed because of the too radical and abstract transcendence of its God, which gave rise to a historical void whose manifestation was a drive to destruction. Thus, the fact that Islam did not engender modernity was a result of its inability to establish the freedom it proclaimed abstractly, and which it fanatically identified with submission to the one God. This failure, Hegel declared, had excluded Islam from the scene of history. Vainly pushing against time in its attempt at the rebirth and liberation of the peoples of the Orient, Islam, according to Hegel, was destined for failure and a retreat into a reactionary attitude. This act of Orientalizing Islam was thus also a gesture through which Christianity was Westernized.

The imperial philosophy born in the nineteenth century could only declare that the modern West was destined to secularization at the cost of reducing Islam to theocratic law. The naming of Islam as a civil code and social order in a state of confusion with the religious took place only in tandem with the articulation of the concept and order of secularization. The separation of Islam and the West organizes the geography of secularization, and so forms part of its coordinates. The theme of the secularization of Christianity thus cannot be understood in isolation from the quarrel of Western thought with what it recognized in the image of Islam.

How did a theocratic Islam come to be opposed to a secularized West? The question contains its own answer: it was only once the order

---

3   Ibid., p. 468.
4   Ibid.

of secularization came to define the destiny of the West that Islam could appear as theocracy. The history of the idea of the secularization of Christianity, its fulfilment within the world, is indissociable from Orientalist constructions of Islam as theocracy. This geography of global religions determined the invention of secularization by causing the essence of Christianity to be redefined in comparative terms. Was Christianity invested with the power to secularize only once other religions were disinvested of it? How did we come to judge the value of religions in terms of their capacity to be secularized? The history of the concept of the secularization of Christianity should thus be approached by looking at the hierarchical construction of religions deemed unable to secularize.

It was only when it became possible to define religion as a scientific object and to give it an evolutionary history that secularization, understood as the fulfilment of Christianity on Earth, could become a key aspect of the industrial project. It was within such a progressive and comparative history of religions that the concept of secularization was articulated as a command thrown in the face of the world. The order of secularization was expressed by its imperial defenders as the consummation of the history of human religions, culminating in the profane fulfilment of a Christianity that simultaneously announced its own coming death within a higher communion. Without an analysis of how the concept of religion was constructed and spatialized within a philosophy of progress, the articulation of secularization, whether as political project or philosophical concept, will remain incomprehensible. How was the hierarchization of religions in terms of their ability to secularize substituted for, while it transformed, older distinctions between orthodoxy and heresy, true religion and false prophets?

The declaration of the secularization of Christianity is the effect of a geography of global religions that defines and compares, but also hierarchizes. Secularization could be defined as the fulfilment of Christianity by defining the latter as the last religion, the religion of the exit from religion.[5] Historical religions became so many steps in the progressive

5 Marcel Gauchet is one of the last representatives of this old French and neo-Hegelian tradition, which is situated at the heart of Republicanism and owes much more to Germany than the nationalist epistemology that opposes laïcité to Protestant secularism would like to admit. See, for example, Marcel Gauchet, *The Disenchantment of the World: A Political History of Religion*, trans. Oscar Burge, Princeton, NJ: Princeton

development of humanity, of which secular modernity and industrial civilization are the culmination, the fulfilment on Earth. Christianity could be declared to have historical superiority over other religions: valued as the civil religion of modern freedom rather than as the one true religion. The imposition of a hierarchical geography of religions and civilizations by the philosophy of history thus determined the invention of secularization as the secret truth of religions, and the resolution of conflicts between them. This geography's beating heart was the declaration of a conflict between two religious universalisms, symbolized by Christianity and Islam. The domination of the industrial West was then imposed as the only possible peaceful resolution of the historical struggle of religions for world domination. In this way, secularization became the legitimation of a new empire that claimed to take up the mantle of the bygone empire of universal religions. It expressed itself as an act by which the Orient and Africa would be resurrected, through the regeneration of Islam.

Republican prophetism

What the West calls its secularization is thus inseparable from the formation of new colonial empires. The concept of the secularization of Christianity presupposed an approach to peoples in terms of their religions, which then legitimated an empire that allowed them to coexist by regenerating the nations they belonged to. The empire's secularity became the condition for its universal legitimacy and supposed neutrality. It was through the work of Jules Michelet and Edgar Quinet that the theme of the fulfilment of Christianity on Earth became a key mechanism of French colonialism and laïcité.[6]

Republicanism, inheritor of the expedition to Egypt, intended to reopen the history of the Muslim Orient and to regenerate Islam by

---

University Press, 1999. Most of Gauchet's favourite themes are already found in Hegel, Quinet, and Michelet. French laïcité is in truth as Protestant and German as it is imperial.

6 Gauchet, Disenchantment of the World, pp. 173–6. Michelet's Hegelian lineage passes through Victor Cousin, who he knew and who also introduced him to Giambattista Vico. French Republicanism was constructed in a dissident posture that contested the bourgeois liberalism of the so-called July Monarchy, while, at the same time, opposing the Second Empire. Despite this fundamental difference between Republicanism and the social liberalism of the Saint-Simonians, Michelet had numerous Saint-Simonian friends, with whom he met particularly at the Ethnological Society of Paris.

colonizing Algeria. What Michelet called universal history was described as the journey of an abstract and collective entity, the human race, to which individuals belonged and in which they participated. But the history of the world was not only human. It was also a cosmic and magnetic history through which nature and spirit sealed their alliance. Man's gradual separation from nature appeared as the history of the globe itself. The human race spread out across the earth following the globe's magnetic currents, which travelled from the Orient to the West. This account of the Oriental beginnings of world history seems to be drawn from Hegel. The Indian, fundamentally alienated, never ceases praying and, prostrate before his God, forgets his own humanity by divinizing all-powerful nature. The path to liberation thus begins in Persia, whose history is reduced, as in Hegel, to the human establishment of a religion of Light that anticipates the advent of Abrahamic monotheism.[7]

At the end of this journey, the Republic, secular and liberated from God, is positioned as the only real and social Church. The French Revolution appears as a sort of second revelation, taking place through history. Christianity, Michelet declared, was a first revelation, the dawning of a process that 'delivered man by shattering the city' and 'liberated God by shattering idols'. Christianity thus 'constructed moral man'; 'in the concept of equality before God it established a principle that would later find fruitful application in the secular world' in the form of equality before the law.[8] Christianity was thus the revolutionary principle of the history of a world called to fulfil itself in Republican equality and freedom. *Heaven could be realized on Earth only if Christianity became redefined as a revolutionary event.*

'What about the universal and divine city of which Christian charity gave you a presentiment and which you promised to realize here on Earth?' Michelet addressed this question to the imperial prophets of the Christian West who had promised to realize heaven here below, to identify the empire that would at last make the prophetic dreams of the Bible into reality. What was needed was the ability to decipher God's

---

7   Jules Michelet, 'Introduction to World History', in Edward Kaplan, Lionel Gossman, and Jules Michelet, eds, *On History: Introduction to World History*, Cambridge: Open Book Publishers, 2013, pp. 26–7.

8   Ibid., p. 60.

revelation, an interpreter who could not only understand its meaning but realize it in practice, and so effect a full passage from Christian to secular. 'If a social sense is to lead us back to religion, then the organ of that new revelation, the interpreter between God and man, should be the most social of all peoples.' This chosen people were the French: 'The moral world received its Word in Christianity, the child of Judea and of Greece'; but only 'France will explain the Word of the social world that we now see beginning.'[9] Elected to the imperial title, France's task would be to secularize Christianity, to fulfil it on Earth.

Imperial theology was both revolutionary and social. The divine on Earth is no longer the state; it is the people themselves who will realize Christianity on Earth. The social community, as incarnation of the new Word, is destined to become the empire. The transposition of heaven onto Earth is no longer the translation of God himself. This is not empire as clergy of a transcendent God who stays in heaven, but humanity recognizing itself as self-creating and creating its history, contemplating its divinity as it becomes real through an infinite progress. Earth can welcome heaven only on the condition that it fulfil Christianity within a *society divinized by the ongoing dissolution of the illusory transcendence of God.* After the death of religious alienation, humanity will at last know that it is divine, because it is freed from God. France's mission was to reveal the divine in man within a new society. The colonial Republic spoke a neo-scriptural language in which the Bible was reduced to a collection of symbols that it secularized and reappropriated in order to declare itself absolute.

Michelet's academic history described a progressive mixing of races: 'At the point of the most perfect mix of the European races, the social Word rings out in the form of equality in liberty.'[10] France is to the other European nations what Greece was to mute Asia. With its national rivals Orientalized, France was chosen to carry the imperial title and to represent by itself the essence of the European West. 'This last step away from natural, fatal order, away from the God of the East, is a step toward the social God who is to reveal himself little by little in our very liberty.'[11] God no longer designated nature, as in Spinoza. The divine was grasped

---

9   Ibid., p. 61.
10   Ibid., p. 61.
11   Ibid., p. 59.

as humanity's own progressive liberation on Earth. The imperial nation Michelet appointed to reconcile heaven and Earth was 'the republic of the world'.[12] The empire announced by the apocalyptic prophecies of the European Middle Ages was transformed into a republic; the imminence of the end of the world became the infinite space of progress.

The revolutionary Christ and the colonial Republic in Africa

'Great revolutions,' Michelet wrote, 'are preceded by their prophetic symbols,' thereby describing the indebtedness of his colonialism to the imperial language of the Christian West.[13] In it, Charlemagne and Bonaparte appeared as figures announcing the coming of the future empire. The Christian empire of the West appeared as an anticipation of the Napoleonic Empire, but even more so as its civilizational continuation by the Republic. If a colonial ideology exists, it was elaborated here, in the language of the Book of Daniel combined with that of the *translatio imperii*. Through this combination the secular Republic was presented as the one true and Catholic Church, and secular humanism as being more truly Christian than Christians themselves.

Secularism was thus presented as Christianity fulfilled, as revelation made reality, in this world, by the Revolution. But, if the Republic claimed to have realized the secularization of Christianity on Earth, the test of its universality would be expansion to Europe and Africa. Republican universalism therefore first wanted to free Spain from the rule of monks, before it colonized Africa while posing as the continuation of what would be called 'Islamism'.[14] French expansion on the African continent was understood as the continuation of the process of secularizing Christianity, realizing divine freedom and unifying the world. Christianity and the French Revolution made the union of Africa and Europe into the sign of the concretization of universalism.

For his part, Quinet, one of the founding fathers of the French Republic, developed the imperial theme while he defended the colonization of Algeria, and more generally of Africa and Asia, in the name of a regeneration of Islam. If Volney's Orientalism had intended to revive

---

12   Ibid., p. 60.
13   Ibid., p. 63.
14   Ibid., p. 62.

civilizations destroyed by Islamic expansion, Quinet's presented a project of secularizing the universal that was intimately linked with a project of regenerating Islam. Colonization would make Islam rise from its ashes by fulfilling its aims on Earth. Imperialism could then say it was more Islamic than Islam, more Muslim than Muslims, and portray its expansion as the concrete fulfilment of religious dreams. In keeping with the Egyptian Expedition's pseudo-Islamic strategies, Quinet's universalism declared that, by the Republic ceasing to be religiously Christian, universal Christianity would be realized through the most profane of actions. In a pastiche of Hegel's philosophy, Republican colonialism announced the death of God and of religious alienation.[15] It declared that the Republic would realize Christianity outside of any religion, and that, by struggling against Catholic tradition and the monarchical residues of Christendom, it would be more truly Christian than Christians themselves.

Formulating this thesis required a theory of colonial modernity. The modern era began, Quinet declared, with the 'discovery' of America. A 'new religious idea' had led Christopher Columbus to America: a prophetic presentiment of the overcoming of religious differences within a higher spiritual unity.

> The soul of Joan of Arc and the soul of Galileo were both within him . . . Columbus was the first crusader of the modern world. Carried over the oceans by the combined breath of all churches, he crossed the expanse on the winged griffons of Isaiah and Ezekiel. This was a new orthodoxy that mixed together what Catholicism loved and what it cursed, the Gospels, the Talmud, the Qur'an.[16]

Quinet declared that colonialism was an empire of spirit, which 'before it sets out, gathers its forces . . . opens,' and 'spreads its wings to their full extent, to cross the abyss'. This spirit was the union of religions into one single faith. Before Columbus, 'no one had deployed within himself a faith so vast, or so to speak, with such a large wingspan', Quinet

15 François Furet, *La Gauche et la révolution au milieu du XIXè siècle. Edgar Quinet et la question du jacobinisme, 1867–1870*, Paris: Hachette, 1986, pp. 18–19.

16 Edgar Quinet, *Le Christianisme et la Révolution française*, 11th lecture, Paris: Fayard, 1984, pp. 189–90.

continued. This was a faith in humanity that dissolved particularities, or universalism as such. 'In Christopher Columbus, the thought of one people, one race of men, one sect, or one particular communion vanished in the face of humanity'; indeed, Quinet declared that *colonial* evangelism surpassed 'Christianity itself'. He interpreted secularism as the truth of Christianity, revealed in its colonial future. 'Standing high above the accumulated Churches', Quinet sees Columbus looking, 'with the eyes of the soul, as from the top of a tower, [at] the new world across the abyss'. 'Unity, solidarity, the moral indivisibility of the world': 'this sentiment' was breathed forth by 'the least of his words'. Quinet added a note: 'I say that the Holy Spirit works within Christians, Jews, Moors, and all other sects. For the execution of the trade of the Indies, neither mathematics nor world map suffice for me; but the word of Isaiah can do it.' The founder of Republicanism called on the colonial project to launch secular universalism by going beyond the quarrels of the Churches. Columbus's supposed ecumenicalism called for a universalism that could exceed the limits of Christianity itself. Colonization would become the site of the fulfilment for biblical prophecies, through an association of all religions that the conquest of the Americas had been unable to realize:

> If one thing is evident, it is that the Church of the Middle Ages, at the time of the discovery of America, failed in the greatest mission of the modern era. It put a curse on innocent earth that had known no defilement but the dew of Eden; it struck to death races who had left the abyss and were requesting the baptism of the future.[17]

For Quinet, the colonial past was still to come, because colonialism should revive races rather than exterminating them. He condemned the extermination of the American Indians as a consequence of Catholic fanaticism. Against the Catholic Church, guilty of this crime against humanity, Quinet set North America: a 'powerful empire rising from the earth', thanks to which the Carpenter would 'become the world's teacher'.[18] North America appeared as the fruit of a colonizing genius fed by the very essence of Protestantism. But, despite its supposed

---

17   Ibid., p. 192.
18   Ibid., p. 203.

'beauty', the spectacle of American democracy did not satisfy Quinet, who was looking for a secularism as *the reconciliation of Protestantism and Catholicism in a higher unity*. Quinet defined this unity as Christ, realized beyond the limits of Christianity. The universalism incarnated by the Republic was, thus, the fulfilment of religion's promises in the world. The task of upholding these promises fell to colonization. If Catholicism had betrayed its mission, to take its place would mean to resume the imperial project and to fulfil Christianity by colonizing a new earth. 'Christianity's first explosion reconciled the Germanic and the Roman race' and 'had given them a shared consciousness'. Today, 'the task is to reconcile worlds still more separate: the Arab, Persian, and Indian world, and Europe'.[19] It was thus to the Orient, and no longer to the West, that colonialism should turn in order to fulfil the Empire of Christ, beyond Christianity itself.

According to Quinet, the empire could only be secularized if it colonized the Muslim world. The colonization of Algeria was the continuation of a larger process of the colonization of the Orient by the West. 'At root, this sacred task speaks to the genius of all Western peoples'; 'this is why the Moscow peasant wants to reach Constantinople, why England is in Pondicherry, why we were yesterday in Egypt, and are today in Algiers'. From here, he posed the question of how to attribute the imperial title. 'In this vast gathering, it seems that these three peoples, like the Three Kings, go before a great unknown, the cradle of a new law that will bring peace to all.' 'Who', Quinet asked, 'will see the first star?' Because no pope was needed to consecrate the Republican emperor, the answer to this pseudo-prophetic question would be something other than an ecclesiastical decision. From now on, it would be decided by the immanence of history. 'Whoever can first lift themselves above the ideal of the past', the theocratic ideal of the Church of Rome, Quinet tells us, would become the true visionary empire.[20] This is why the founding of a secular order would be the touchstone for the universality of a new imperial law. The new empire would succeed where Roman Catholicism had failed, by definitively substituting the colonial mission for the logic of the Crusades. The failure of the Crusades, Quinet declared, could be explained by the fact that Catholicism was not a fully realized

---

19   Ibid., p. 148.
20   Ibid.

universalism, but rather a limited one. Their failure had shown that the Church was unable to realize this Christian universalism on Earth. Through the colonization of Muslims, conflicting universalisms would be made to test their universality. 'Catholic terror could do nothing against Muslim terror', because it was still religious. Thus 'the inferno of the West threw itself against the inferno of the Orient' and 'each had disarmed the other'.[21]

Quinet defined Islam as a Christian heresy that had developed from the theology of Arius, as 'the Arianism of Mahomet'.[22] Arianism is a doctrine that declares that God is not a Trinity but only a Father. Islam was thus presented as a religion of the Father, a denial of the divinity of the Christ and Son of Man. To bring the Spirit of Christ down to Earth required colonizing the lands of Islam, because only a power that dominated Muslims could proclaim itself secular and thus truly Christian. The subjugation of Islamic traditions thus appeared as the touchstone for the universal and for institutional secularization. The true incarnation of God in Man was heaven descending in the form of an empire ruling the earth. By reconciling Christians and Muslims in Algeria, France would prove it had made the globe's religions and races melt together into a new and higher unity. What replaced the Crusades was thus the fulfilment of their empire not by Christianity but by the end of religious divisions and Churches.

'Each epoch, the Qur'an says, has its book', Quinet wrote. 'Show us,' he declared, 'not by dissertations but by actions, that the new book is written every day within social life.'[23] France became this book being realized on Earth: a quranic fulfilment, a new prophecy in keeping with the era. 'Spread France out in the desert, open like a great book, whose every line becomes real – in an action, in a higher justice, in a more powerful creation, in a more splendid glory, in a more holy politic; this is the only way by which, over time, the sparkling letters of the Qur'an will be made to fade.' By its secularization, France would succeed where the Crusades had failed. 'The Crusaders sought only Christ's tomb; because they continued to possess the sepulchre, the Muslims believed themselves still to be masters of God.' To succeed, a different

---

21   Ibid., p. 148.
22   Ibid., p. 74.
23   Ibid., p. 149.

resurrection would be affirmed: 'Show that there is no longer a need for the tomb, because he is resurrected, and returns to sit in spirit at the entrance of the desert.' Then Islam and the whole Orient would submit, Quinet assured. 'You wish to convince the Orient that wisdom from above became flesh some eighteen hundred years ago, but do better: prove to them that this wisdom, this love, this awaited paraclete is incarnated and revealed in the world this very day in the shape of European society.'[24]

The Crusades, thus, would be fulfilled within this world beyond the narrow confessionalism of Christianity, and at last surpassed. From here, the signs of the world would receive a new readability. Deciphering the signs of nature extended to deciphering the signs of religion, not only by secular reason but performatively, through social action. Imperialism was thus called on to decipher the social secret of the universal religions – Christianity through empire, Islam through colonial submission. With the secret of religion unveiled, the fields of society and culture could invent themselves and be used to confront nature. The book of nature, written in the mathematical language of a Galileo, would now describe society itself. The profane readability of the signs of the world, the idea of Creation as a book, moved from one pole to the other, exceeding and determining the distinction of nature and society. The transparency of the world's meaning was not only hermeneutic; it was also performative. It was social action itself that would reveal the new book, a book in conformance with its era.

According to Quinet, what the act of colonization would secularize was nothing other than Islam itself. This implied that the French Empire would be a fulfilment of Islamic prophecies, that the colonial messiah would realize the Islamic idea of Christ's return at the end of time. To conquer Islam, what had to be socialized in the imperial flesh would thus be the Muslims' own prophetic premonition. This meant neither more nor less than making French colonization a divine order in Muslim eyes, and so provoking their consent to the empire. This was what secularization required. The French colonial empire would be effectively *Christian* only if it did not declare itself as such, and no longer professed Catholic doctrine. Only a secular empire, an empire that presented itself as the historical realization of what the Muslims' decadent Islam had

---

24   Ibid., p. 149.

vainly aimed for, could establish itself peacefully and sustainably in an
Asia and Africa populated by Muslim men and woman. Separation from
the Roman Church and the subjugation of Muslims were two paths that
joined into a single road to modernity. Secularizing France and colonizing Islamic lands belonged to one and the same process. So the Egyptian
Expedition was reborn in North Africa:

> Napoleon, recounting the Egyptian campaign, paused on an event
> that in part explains his power over Oriental imagination. One day, at
> the divan of great sheikhs, he was informed that certain Arabs had
> killed a fellah and stolen his herd; he then became indignant and sent
> three hundred cavalrymen to punish the perpetrators. Stunned by his
> sympathy for a stranger, and by the large number of men roused up in
> the cause of a poor man, the sheikh cried: 'Was this fellah your rela-
> tive, that you became so angry?' 'Yes,' replied Napoleon; 'all those I
> command are my children.' 'Ah!' the sheikh said, bending low, 'you
> speak like the Prophet!' In this brief moment, the Muslim genius felt
> itself laid low by the genius of the Gospel. What was it that made these
> men of the desert bend before Europe's representative? A truly reli-
> gious speech, carried through by a strong arm.[25]

What was to be done in Algeria was thus what Napoleon had done in
Egypt: speaking the words of Islam so that a secular empire could fulfil
the Gospel. 'Extend this speech to politics as a whole,' Quinet wrote, 'and
you will have the secret of Europe's future power over the Orient.'[26]
Quinet drew the conclusion from this that neither England nor Russia
could establish themselves deeply in Asia. Their colonization had
remained only material and economic, and so was superficial. 'In these
circumstances,' he concluded, 'only France seems called to a conquest
more intellectual than it is material.'[27] France's imperialism would be a
conquest of Muslim souls, which would allow it to move between Asia
and Africa. The African continent that lay open to France could only be
colonized spiritually, only by an association of material arms and spiritual weapons. 'Africa hears the very sound of our people's dreams,'

---

25 Ibid., pp. 148–9.
26 Ibid., p. 149.
27 Ibid., p. 150.

Quinet wrote.[28] The Christian dreams of secular France resonated in Africa because their prophecies without transcendence were the old medieval prophecies of empire turned colonial. The enemy was no longer the Muhammadan to be exterminated or converted, but was now an enemy racialized through Islam: the Arab, seen as a priest of war.

> This relic of Muslim power derives from what they have sheltered within the idea of God, as within a citadel that cannot be taken. Most often, the West has stopped at the level of priest; let us quickly climb higher. Every Arab is a priest of war; every European must become a priest of alliance.[29]

The West would have to go further than the level of priests if it wanted to strip the Arabs of their remaining power and colonize Africa. It would need to go beyond priests, because priests would not be able to fight the remains of Arab Muslim power in North Africa. But to overcome this remnant of power no longer meant waging brutal war. It was not by preaching war that Islam would be stripped of power, but by preaching a form of association that would win out over war. Only secularism could win out over fanaticism. Buisson, another foundational figure of *laïcité*, said the same thing on his return from Africa. This project was far from isolated. France would try it in Algeria before extending it to Africa and the Middle East. Secularization became the condition for colonial pacification, the legitimacy of the universal itself. The imperial idea of world peace could thus justify the use of violence to fulfil religions on Earth, by secularizing them within the fabric of a profane colony liberated from the spectres of God.

The unfindable Muslim Luther

Quinet saw this project of 'regeneration' by colonization as an act of charity tested by its being addressed to Africa. It would involve a strategic conversion of France to Islam, as a necessary act of translation to prepare Muslims for submission to the republican universal. By this act

---

28   Ibid.
29   Ibid.

of charity, a 'Muslim France' would appear.[30] The conquest that Quinet strongly called for was more than an occupation: the materiality of occupation would merely be a means to another conquest – deemed spiritual and so of a higher order – the shared work of secularizing Islam and the Republic. *Through it, liberty and equality would be universalized by secularizing Islam*, the only way of 'dominating the fray of sacred wars' by means of profane war; in this way, French colonial ideology would make the 'desert races' reborn, conquering the Sahara beginning with Algeria.[31] The theme of the resurrection of the Orient was transformed into the drive to resurrect Africa, passing from Orientalism to colonial Africanism.

Imperial secularization thus approached Islam as a 'revolution of the Orient', an anticipation of revolutionary equality and of the real universalism that, in aborted form, had led to failure. The failure lay in Islam's inability to realize its spiritual content on Earth in a revolutionary fashion, to make itself into a world by organizing a society that was self-founding, no longer based on the invocation of God. In the eyes of this Hegelian colonial ideology, Islam was characterized by the inability to realize the universal outside of a strictly *religious* form. Islam's incapacity to regenerate itself by producing its own dynamic of secularization was what, in Quinet's text, gave Europe and particularly France the new title to empire. Republicanism posed an absolute and moral right to colonize Algeria and the rest of the African continent, legitimating the exercise of violence unleashed against African populations both north and south of the Sahara. The reality of universalism would be proven by its ability to legitimate putting colonized people to death in the name of regenerating the Orient.

The coloniality of this secular universal manifested itself through the theme of a reform of Islam, on the model of Luther. Quinet asked: How could 'this dogma, parched and buried in sand, be brought to life'? If Islam had died, within and at the hand of history, as the ideologues of colonialism had assumed since the Egyptian Expedition, this was so that Islam could be resurrected on Earth. To those, like the Saint-Simonians in Egypt, who 'announced the arrival of a Muslim Luther', Quinet replied that 'by itself, the Orient' could not 'make itself young again'. 'What

---

30 Ibid.
31 Ibid., p. 151.

would a Muslim Protestantism reform? The Church? There is no Church'
in Islam, insisted one of the founding fathers of the French Republic.[32]
Islam could not 'regenerate' itself; it was incapable of effecting its own
reform through its own efforts. For Quinet, the alternative was clear:
either a Muslim Luther would appear, as Saint-Simonians such as Ismaÿl
Urbain were declaring, or Islam must be forced to transform. But,
according to Quinet, because a Muslim Luther never had and never
could exist, the only possibility for a renaissance of Islam was not to
make Islam Protestant, but, rather, for it to submit to colonialism so that
it would become *secular*. This was the reasoning behind Quinet's colonialism. Only a secular and not a Protestant Republic could 'rejuvenate
Islam', because what was needed was not a religious reform on the model
of Protestantism but rather a reform imposed by the imperial state. It
was then a question not of founding a Church, necessarily absent in
Islam, but of constructing an 'Islamic *culte*' through the arbitrary election of Muslim representatives subjugated to French interests. The
double process of colonizing Africa and secularizing Christianity by the
foundation of secular universalization would thus substitute for an
impossible *religious* reform of Islam. Secular universalism took the place
of 'Muslim Protestantism', articulating itself in the place of its constitutive absence. The project that would become Republican *laïcité*, the
radical separation of civil and ecclesiastical society, was formulated by
Quinet as an alternative to the impossibility of reforming society by
reforming religion in France. The thesis that presided over the invention
of *laïcité* was precisely that religions are the foundation of societies.

The theocratization of Islam and the Christianization of democracy

The distinction between a democratic, liberal Christianity and a theocratic Islam goes well beyond Republicanism, and also structured the
work of Alexis de Tocqueville. His reflections on democracy were related
to his sociology of secularization, by which he defined the limits within
which religion should be circumscribed in democratic societies. 'At such
times religions ought, more cautiously than at any other, to confine
themselves within their own precincts; for in seeking to extend their

---

32   Ibid., p. 135.

power beyond religious matters, they incur a risk of not being believed at all.'[33]

Tocqueville's colonial writings on Islam in Algeria can only be understood in light of this norm. In opposition to what the religious should be in itself, and counter to the spirit of democratic societies, Islam – warlike, liberticidal, and theocratic – constantly transgresses the borders of religion. The impossibility of secularizing Islam was doubled by the idea that any liberalism or democracy was impossible in societies where the Qur'an 'is the source of the laws, ideas, and mores of all the Muslim population'.[34] 'Islam' here refers to the civil code to which the indigenous Algerians whom France was planning to colonize were subject. Tocqueville was interested in the Qur'an only as the heart of a power that had to be struck down so that it could be colonized. He understood Islam as the paradigm of confusion between the political and the religious.[35] Tocqueville identified the absence of clergy in Islam with a structural incapacity to distinguish civil and religious spheres. According to him, Islam was a religion of law, a total and religious law to which all other aspects of life were subordinated; the supreme priest was consequently the prince and vice versa. Tocqueville examined this confusion from a sociological rather than a theological perspective, trying to evaluate Islam starting from its social effects as legal religion. What distinguished him from Christian authors who supported the same thesis was that he did not intend to defend the clergy. To the contrary, he showed that the presence of clergy constitutes a social problem, although he did not use this argument to praise the practical and social genius of Islam, as did Orientalists who were close to Emmanuel Joseph Sieyès, such as Konrad Engelbert Oelsner.[36] He considered its confusion of the religious and civil to be the source of an innate incapacity for democracy and change.

33   Alexis de Tocqueville, *Democracy in America*, ed. Isaac Kramnick, New York: W. W. Norton & Co., 2007, p. 392.

34   Alexis de Tocqueville, *Notes sur le Coran et autres textes sur les religions*, introduction and commentary by Jean-Louis Benoît, Paris: Bayard, 2007, pp. 30–1.

35   Ibid., p. 39. The aim of this text is to determine why there is no priesthood and thus no clergy in Islam. 'Mahometism is the religion that has most completely confused and intermixed the two powers, such that the *great priest* is necessary the *prince*, and the prince the great priest, and all acts of *civil* and *political* life are regulated more or less according to religious law.'

36   Ibid., p. 40.

The decline of the Muslim world was defined as the result of this Islamic confusion of the political, civil, and religious. Tocqueville's sociology of religions relied on colonial sociology in Algeria, which invented a comparative approach to Islam and Christianity. Tocqueville's concept of Christianity saw it as a proclamation of the equality of men. 'It was necessary for Jesus Christ to come to Earth to make it known that all members of the human species were naturally similar and equal', Tocqueville wrote, making Christ the founder of universalism.[37] This idea of an elective affinity between Christianity and democracy presupposes the racial definition of Islam as religious law that structured the colonial ideology employed in Algeria.

The transfigured Christ and the imperial Messiah

'France needed only to appear on the threshold of the mosques for that enigma from Oriental popular tradition to become clear, according to which the transfigured Christ would become the last caliph of Islam.'[38] With these words, Quinet performed an appropriation of tradition typical of imperial secularization. He presented the French domination of Muslims as the fulfilment of Islam and tradition, in opposition to the Muslims themselves. Quranic prophecy was translated into the language of imperial prophetism. The realization of Christ on Earth served to designate the arrival of an empire about to reduce the Muslims of Algeria and Africa to colonized subjects. With these words, the empire expressed a colonial theology of liberation for Muslims through the realization of a revolutionary Christianity on Earth. By claiming to fulfil certain Islamic prophecies, colonization merely re-engaged the biblical prophetic language that the Egyptian Expedition's strategic messianism had made profane. The heretical tradition founded on the critique of heaven was the site for the enunciation of secular universalism. Through it, Orientalism would continuously valorize certain historical Muslim 'heresies' against present Muslim orthodoxy, creating

---

37   Ibid., p. 75.
38   Quinet, *Le Christianisme et la Révolution*, p. 136. While quranic tradition does recognize Christ as a prophet, he is never identified with God, or even defined as a divine being. The Qu'ran recognizes Christ but does not recognize a Son of God, because all divine engenderment is presented as impossible. Certain traditions declare that Christ will return at the end of time, but the majority do not say he will be the last caliph.

arbitrary separations between different confessions and schools that it set up as the keystone of its supposed erudition.

According to this German-inspired secularism, the colonization of Africa was destined to bring the universal to Earth by establishing a 'Republic of the world'. Republicanism declared that the secularization of France and of Europe itself implied the colonization of the African continent, with the conquest of Algeria as the first step after the Egyptian failure. The drive to fulfil Christianity on Earth was not merely an imperial theme found in the philosophy of history. The ideology that it helped to found would nourish the practices through which institutions were secularized by its role in organizing their actors' language, both in the metropole and in the colonies. How did the racial distinction between the Muslim Orient and the West – Christian in principle but secular in its effects – participate in secularizing Europe? And how did this distinction allow Christians and secular figures to establish compromises – such as the Church's rallying to the Republic or the law of 1905 – on the basis of excluding Muslims? Was it the idea of the earthly realization of revolutionary Christianity in Africa that let them surpass their religious conflict and seal a secular pact, articulated with the colonial civilizing mission?

Teachers and the secular mission in the colonies

A colonialist text from 1887 treats missionaries in Africa and schools in Tunisia as two sides of the same coin. The text was written by Ferdinand Buisson, one of the inventors of French *laïcité*, who we encountered earlier. His texts unfolds a conception of moral 'preparation' of the indigenous for colonization, a strategy of forming consent to domination: education should 'prepare', Buisson wrote, 'for a reconciliation of races inside the school, in order that it might be possible elsewhere'.[39] The school here was the advance guard of colonization, from which Buisson drew a model of scholastic association, a sort of educational indirect government. There should not only be French schoolmasters, he wrote; indigenous people should also be associated with the scholarly mission. His proposal called for establishing schools with indigenous

---

39   Ferdinand Buisson, 'Nos Pionniers en Afrique', *Revue Pédagogique* 10, no. 6, 11 June 1887, p. 491.

monitors, hybrid teacher-students combining the roles of tribal chief and native informant.[40] 'The central and decisive point, the knot of the question of educating natives in Algeria as well as in Tunisia' was thus 'establishing standard courses for the formation of native personnel'.[41] This technique of scholarly association was at the heart of the model of secular colonial schools that Buisson proposed.

The first means of access to indigenous populations, and the only one that could 'pacify' the colony as Buisson wanted, was to teach them the French language. To change the 'native interior' in effect presupposed changing their language.[42] This policy had already been successful, according to Buisson, because 'even today, more than one French idea has been carried into their minds along with the language'.[43] This policy of Francization would secularize Muslims by reaching their souls. Buisson reported a primary school where the children had condemned the abrogation of the Edict of Nantes and, as Buisson told it, declared that a Muslim prince would have done wrong by abrogating it, since the prince 'does not have the key to hearts'. Buisson cited another example of a school where the children were poor but sang *The Marseillaise*, proclaiming the Republican trinity: 'Liberty, equality, fraternity.'[44]

The function of these set pieces was to establish the secular school as the only effective means of colonization. Religious education and Christian missions were accused of provoking distrust and feeding fanaticism among Muslim children. For as long as 'our public teaching was confessional by law and our schoolmasters taught the catechism, as long Arabs and Kabyles had never seen anyone other than monks and nuns arrive to teach their children, they have noted their devotion, their goodness, their good and admirable conduct; but an uneasiness has remained at the bottom of their Muslim hearts and, as a report to the minister put it frankly a few years ago, "they are still distrustful of the Christian marabouts". Buisson's conclusion was unequivocal: if '*laïcité*' did not exist in France, it would need to be invented in our African

---

40   Ibid., p. 496. 'This is the nursery of the future native teaching corps,' writes Buisson. He also proposed the creation of colonial school manuals specifically intended for indigenous pupils.

41   Ibid., p. 507.

42   Ibid., p. 497.

43   Ibid., p. 505.

44   Ibid., p. 506.

possessions'.[45] A visit of 'several weeks in a Muslim country' would lead one to oppose any idea that the policy of secularization should not be applied in the colonies. According to those views, it was proper to 'secularize in France', but 'in Tunisia, in Egypt, in the colonies' it would be better 'to employ congregants as the initial promoters of French schooling and civilization'. But, Buisson asked, 'is it not there, to the contrary, that we should dedicate ourselves to avoiding all religious passion?'[46]

Buisson's strategy consisted of making colonial *laïcité* an example for the metropole, constructing the colonial school as an avant-garde. The colonial situation, faced with an unconvertible Islam, demanded an even more imperious secularization of the school than in the metropole. It would thus be absurd to maintain Catholic education in the colonies, and the Catholic congregations themselves were proof of this, as they were already practising *laïcité* in the colonies. 'The congregants know this so well themselves that, in a praiseworthy policy, what they do first in these countries is to practise *laïcité*, seeing it as a condition sine qua non for their success', Buisson maintains. Members of the colonial clergy 'professed' and 'practised to the full extent of their ability an absolute respect for diverse beliefs'. Those establishments in the colony where nothing was 'more strictly forbidden' than 'religious proselytism' were treated as exemplary.[47] In other words, the Catholics had been forced to secularize themselves so that they could educate Muslims.

Throughout his construction of the avant-garde exemplarity of the educational mission in the colonies, Buisson addressed himself to both the religious and the anticlerical in the metropole. He ideologically reconstructed colonial space as the site from which the 'two Frances' could be embryonically reconciled, by resolving the longstanding conflict between Catholics and revolutionaries. The great pact that these two parties would seal to create a secular state in the metropole would materialize first in the colonies. Christians and secular figures in the metropole thus ought both to learn from the colony and in some sense let themselves be secularized by it. With a description of a man of the Church explaining a Republican textbook of morality and civics to the indigenous people, Buisson set up the Catholic teacher in service of

---

45   Ibid., pp. 511–12.
46   Ibid.
47   Ibid., p. 512.

the state in its colonies as a great Republican model. He opposed him to 'reactionary' Catholics who protested against the use of textbooks in the school, most likely referring to the scandal caused by a textbook written by Paul Bert, which was banned by the pope.[48] By showing that a reconciliation between Catholics and the Republican order was possible, the colony would teach the European metropole a lesson in secularism. By showing the two sides communing together in the same patriotic work, it would prove that the pact was not a chimera.

Napoleon came back to haunt Ferdinand Buisson's discourse, as it had haunted that of his predecessor, Quinet. 'We know today how to penetrate the Islamic world,' Buisson proclaimed; 'so let us resolutely penetrate, no longer with iron and fire, bringing a war of race or of religion, but bringing the light of those eternal truths that gleam with the same brilliance in every age and under every sky, which belong not to the Jew nor to the Christian, nor to the Muslim, because they belong to humanity.' Like Hegel and Quinet, Buisson professed colonial charity to be the fulfilment of Christianity beyond Christianity itself. The charity directed to Africa and Muslims would thus be pagan to the extent that it would be supported by principles that had preceded the religious divisions that prevented men from unifying at last. The beating heart of this secular and colonial charity was nothing but love for the human race; and colonial humanism declared the extent to which *love of man* was infinitely superior to love of God, and more divine than the God of religion himself. This primary (because original) love was what the Church's Christianity had obscured, and it now had to be restored through secular work, in the colonies as well as in the metropole.

What the Catholics said in Algeria

My argument is not that *laïcité* is colonial, nor that Christians participated in it only inadvertently. Nor am I suggesting that only liberal Catholics were complicit in colonialism. The least liberal and secular Catholics also prophesied using imperial language, from the very start of Algerian colonization. Supported by apocalyptic writings from the Bible, what they announced was neither more nor less than putting

---

48 Ibid.

Islam to death, as depicted in imperial prophecies inspired by the Book of Daniel. 'The last days of Islamism have arrived,' wrote Louis Veuillot, a celebrated Catholic traditionalist and anti-liberal, at the height of the war of conquest. Alongside one of the most violent colonial armies, at the heart of the war raging in North Africa in the 1830s, he triumphantly announced that, 'attacked from all sides, the crescent is breaking and disappearing'. Catholic colonialism hoped to revive the defunct Empire of Christ on Earth by proclaiming a war to the death against 'Islamism'. But Catholics could express this will to resurrection on one condition: understanding profane and industrial colonialism as an *unconscious instrument* of the realization of Christ. For the colonialism that was born after the French Revolution, converting Muslims to *Christianity* was no longer the heart of the mission. The Catholic discourse Veuillot promoted had another goal, which would soon be associated with the 'civilizing mission'.

Veuillot first turned to the calculations made by supporters of Charles V's restoration of Christian empire, initially during the Middle Ages and then in the Renaissance, who methodically calculated the future using clues they found in apocalyptic symbols from the Bible. What colonization would realize on Earth could be defined as a function of these calculations.

> Calculations established from the Apocalypse of Saint John and the prophecies of Daniel give to the reign of Mahomet a duration of thirteen centuries. The thirteenth century is not yet finished, and Byzantium is about to fall back into Christian hands. In twenty years, Algiers *will have no other God than Christ*; in twenty years, Alexandria will be English, and what will England be in twenty years? Where will the cross not go once Alexandria, Algiers, and Constantinople are its points of departure?[49]

From here, the Christian mission in North Africa would be lived as the fulfilment of the Crusades through the intermediary of the

---

49   Louis Veuillot wrote this work on Algeria after he accompanied Thomas Robert Bugeaud to Algiers. He supported a missionary conception of colonization. Veuillot, *Les Français en Algérie: souvenirs d'un voyage fait en 1841*, 2nd edn, Tours: A. Mame & Co., 1847, p. 2. Emphasis added.

secularization of empire. To the claim that the contemporary world was no longer Christian, because the people were indifferent to religion and the princes were infidels, Veuillot responded that all were unconscious instruments of Christ combatting Islam.[50] The old model of exterminating the Islamic Antichrist became an expression of the fulfilment of Christianity by empire:

> The conquests that Europe would not make for faith, it will make for commerce; the missionaries will follow the merchants, as they followed the Crusaders. Believing we have given ourselves over to trade, we complete the Crusades. Our unbelieving merchants will finish the work begun by the fervent Christians of the Middle Ages. No matter what name it is given, here is a civilization beside which Islamism cannot hold.[51]

Secular colonialism here becomes an instrument for the fulfilment of Christ's reign on Earth. The Empire of Christ is no longer realized on Earth in the form of an empire of the faith, but, instead, as an empire of civilization and industry. Imperial and apocalyptic prophecies find their fulfilment at the heart of the colonization that is the most profane, the least Christian in appearance. Despite the industrialists' and merchants' unbelief, despite even their infidelity, Veuillot assured his readers that the great trade circuits were realizing the work of Christianity on Earth. By fulfilling Christian prophecies, secular colonization was destined to open the way for the Catholic mission and restore its universality in Africa and Asia. Imperial language thus allowed the least liberal Christians and the most anticlerical secular figures to deploy the same idea. At the heart of the colonial ideology formulated during the wars of conquest for Algeria, the idea of the realization of Christianity through the domination of Muslims became a shared theme in secular and Christian political theologies.

---

50   Ibid.
51   Ibid.

How the colonization of Africa secularized France

How did this double formation of Christian missionary order and secular scholarly mission contribute to the Republican pact in the metropole? The secular Republic was the fruit of a historic compromise between the Catholic Church and the anticlericalism of the Enlightenment.[52] Because Catholicism had to become *reconcilable* with modernity and liberal democracy in order for such a pact to be sealed, it cannot be assumed that Christianity simply gave birth to secularization. This hypothesis would make the properly colonial mechanisms of the birth of the Republic invisible. The Roman Church's rallying to the French Republic, and the pope's official recognition of its legitimacy, played a key role in the social reorientation of Catholicism and the international legitimacy of the Third Republic.[53] By breaking its historical association with absolute monarchy, the Church sanctified neither democracy nor the Republic. The Catholic authorities who supported the Church's rallying saw conditions for rebirth in the unfolding of a political spirituality expressed through *social* action. To spiritualize politics meant investing not the state, but civil society.

With the Toast of Algiers in 1890, Cardinal Lavigerie declared the Church's support for the Republic. This raises a question: how should we understand that the Catholic Church proclaimed its rallying to the Republic in Algiers, within the colonial situation? The negotiations that led the pope to accept the Third Republic's secularization of schools seem to have given a central place to the colonial question. The pope's acceptance of laicization policies presupposed the maintenance of the Concordat and state financing of clergy in the colonies. The negotiations between the Republic and the pope show that the latter accepted the secularization of schools only on this condition.[54] Educational secularization thus took place under the imperial regime of the Concordat. For this reason, it assumed that the direct

---

52   Émile Poulat, *Notre laïcité publique*, Paris: Berg International, 2003. The word *catho-laïcité* is often used to describe this compromise.

53   Known in French as the *Ralliement*, the Roman Catholic Church acknowledged the political legitimacy of the newly established secular Republic after decades of defending the monarchy and accepted the Napoleonic model of empire as an interlocutor.

54   Baubérot, *Histoire de la laïcité*, p. 47.

diplomatic negotiations between the state and the pope had been possible only to the extent that France appeared on the international scene as a Catholic power. The creation of a properly colonial Church completely subjected to the secular state in Algeria facilitated negotiations, creating a provisory consensus that allowed the Republic and educational secularization to be imposed. But, in part, what led Leo XIII to back down before the Republicans was the maintenance of the Catholic missions in the colonies, and France's assurance of financial support through the Concordat. The institutions of the First Empire determined the possibilities for educational secularization, and secular schools were established under the Concordat. The promise of an expansion of Catholic universalism in Africa, under the protection of the secular arm of the Republican empire, led Leo XIII to agree to play by the rules of liberal democracy and the French Revolution. By doing this, he could continue to convert while also performing social works alongside the damned of the earth.

We should thus look to the diplomatic history of the Third Republic to understand the circuits that linked the unfolding of colonialism and the advent of social Christianity and liberal democracy. A *Diplomatic History of the Third Republic*, published in 1889, declared that the Republic, although secular, should continue to maintain diplomatic relations with the pope, for two reasons.[55] The first reason, in the domestic context, was state control of Church affairs in keeping with the provisions of the Concordat; the second concerned the politics France should develop concerning the Christians of the Orient.[56] The political emissaries of *Catholic* France in the Orient were direct legatees of the Egyptian Expedition. 'It is not to convert the Muslim populations that the Catholic missionary and the Protestant clergyman establish themselves in Syria or in Tunisia,' the author assured. 'If that had been the aim of this propaganda, then our role would to be disavow it and to stop those dangerous agents', since missionaries who wanted to convert the Muslims of Africa or of the Orient to Christianity 'could only arouse the fanaticism of the Oriental world against us'.[57]

---

55   Edmond Hippeau, *Histoire diplomatique de la Troisième République (1870–1889)*, Paris: E. Dentu, 1889. The author is a committed and enthusiastic Republican, while also Wagnerian.

56   Ibid., p. 291.

57   Ibid.

The goal of the missionaries' presence in the Orient was not to extend Christianity, but to consolidate France's ascendency over the Roman clergy by diplomatic means. Among other things, this strategy allowed the Republic to negotiate with the Catholic Church, and also the Church to negotiate with the Republic. From the other side of the pact, the Church's *Ralliement* was, first and above all, a strategy to regenerate Catholicism. It freed the Catholic Church from an age-old alliance with a monarchic order whose irreversible decline doomed it to weaken and eventually die. The *Ralliement* was therefore, from Lavigerie's point of view as well as Leo XIII's, a way of reasserting the Church's power and autonomy, inspired by the so-called ultramontanism that dominated the nineteenth century. It became common for both secular figures and Christians to define the West using the phrase 'Christian civilization'.[58] This reclaimed the Christian roots of France and of the modern world, and at the same time culturalized Christianity. By making Christianity the heritage of a modern Europe shared by the anticlerical and the religious, Catholics sought to reintroduce a spirituality that seemed to have been lost, or was at least menaced by the public life of liberal democracies. The concept of 'Christian civilization' allowed Catholic institutions to associate themselves with imperialism and with the Republic, without necessarily consenting to them spiritually. The Roman Church's relations to liberal modernity thus have a colonial aspect. In the double aim of inflecting democracy in a Christian and social way and re-establishing political spirituality, the Roman Church was indebted to its imperial and colonial history. The *Ralliement*, an international phenomenon that went beyond the frame of Franco-Algerian relations by implicating the Holy See itself, presupposed the French Empire's project of *secular* colonization as its condition of enunciation.

Lavigerie, as the founder of a new Catholic order, the White Fathers, attempted to restore the missionary project in Africa after it had been prohibited by the colonial authorities.[59] If the idea of massively converting Muslims to Christianity had been set aside since 1831, the Catholic missions attempted to break a new path to the heart of the secular frame that the colonial state's Concordat had imposed. In Algeria, Lavigerie

58   François Renault, *Le Cardinal Lavigerie*, Paris: Fayard, 1992, pp. 144, 246.
59   Oissila Saaïdia, *Algérie coloniale: musulmans et chrétiens: le contrôle de l'état (1830–1914)*, Paris: Éditions du CNRS, 2015, p. 89.

presented himself to the Muslims as a father, and addressed himself to them by *imposing* his love: 'I claim the privilege of loving you as my sons, even though you do not recognize me as your father. This privilege is conferred on me by my faith, which makes me see in you souls that have come from the hands of the same God, and are purchased with the same blood.'[60] With these words Lavigerie did not intend to *dehumanize* Muslims; on the contrary, he intended to *rehumanize* them by integrating them into Christian humanity. Sons of the White Father, they were created in the image of one and the same God, because it was the same blood – Christ's, sacrificed on the Cross – that redeemed all men, faithful or infidel, in one same act of redemption. Because the Muslims were *human*, according to Lavigerie, they had also been saved by Christ. The White Father speaking in the name of the Heavenly Father thus conferred to the Muslims the status of humans who are ignorant of the nature of their own humanity. He saved them as humans, but *not* as Muslims. He meant to convert them not just to Christianity but, indeed, to their own lost humanity, and so claimed to restore their trampled dignity.

The new missionary order founded in Algeria spread across Africa. The Christian missions employed the pastorate, a set of Christian practices by which pastors lead the flock of believers to their salvation. Lavigerie ordered the missionaries to 'draw close to the natives in all outward customs, in language first of all, in clothing, in food, following the example of the Apostle: "I have become all things to all men so that I may save them all."' His pastorate demanded that they adapt to African peoples by *translating* the message of Christ into their language and costume. Under no circumstance should the indigenous people be Francized, assimilated, or converted to European civilization. The heart or 'native interior' should be converted to Christianity, while the 'native exterior' was maintained intact.[61] Christianity, thus, had to translate

---

60   Cardinal Lavigerie, cited in Renault, *Le Cardinal Lavigerie*, p. 144. This address was Lavigerie's first open letter to the Muslims of Algeria.

61   Lavigerie, *La Mission universelle de l'Église*, Paris: Le Cerf, 1991, pp. 94–5. The 'Circular letter to the Missionaries of Africa regarding the theme of the first general chapter', written in Algiers and dated 11 November 1874, distinguishes between exterior conversion and interior conversion. Conversion of the interior was not intended to assimilate the indigenous to European cultural codes. 'We should be content, therefore,' Lavigerie wrote, 'to work on their hearts, their souls, their intelligence – in a word, their interior – to make them sincerely Christian, and on the contrary to conserve intact the indigenous exterior – clothing, the bedroom, food, and above all, language.'

itself into all languages and cross over the superficial barriers of the diversity of customs and mores. This missionary translation of Christianity outside Europe was theorized and tested on the Kabyles in Algeria, but it was in so-called sub-Saharan Africa that the model was fully deployed.

The Allocution d'Alger was pronounced at the departure of twenty missionaries to sub-Saharan Africa, on 29 June 1890. It defined the missionary pastorate and how converts should govern themselves. Since the conquest of Algiers, the construction of the colonial state had rejected the Church of Rome's missionary project. The risk of provoking a so-called Muslim fanaticism led to a prohibition of all missionary activity after 1852. But, for their part, the missionaries had never abandoned the project of conversion, which Lavigerie consequently inherited. The question of conversion was, therefore, at the heart of the conflict between two sets of actors in the colony: the secular administration and the missionaries. The conflict between their two missions led partisans of secular colonialism to support secular education, while missionaries such as Lavigerie moved into rural areas to deploy their project, in spite of the limits posed by a mistrustful colonial administration.

Lavigerie's pastorate focused on his apostles: they should 'suffer all things', while being careful to remain apolitical: 'Never take a side in any political cause, whatever it might be', Lavigerie exhorted. The only interests the apostle should defend were those of 'the Faith and of humanity'.[62] Respect for all established authority was the condition for the elevation of the religious, which would be persuasive only if it exceeded petty and profane interests. Separation between the missionary and the political was the condition of the apostolate. The White Fathers thus took up and spread the teachings of the colonial government in Algiers across Africa.

The pastor should not only preach but also practise universal love. Charity should be practised towards all, beyond the limits of any one community or confession, and exceed national differences through its translation. Like the secular colonist, the dignity of the missionary-colonist should be maintained at all costs. It should be proven 'by deeds still more than by words' that the missionaries' only thought was love for

---

62   Ibid.

all the nations of the earth.[63] Whether missionary or secular, the colonial power exhorted exemplary conduct and, accordingly, respect. This is what military and civil colonialism called the dignity of the Whites, the dignity of the colonists. The conversion of 'Berber' or Black Africans to liberation, whether Christ's liberation or the Revolution's, also required this dignity. Lavigerie thus invited the missionaries to be scrupulous about the signs and image they presented to the indigenous population. If the missionary pastorate was apolitical, this was because it was profoundly moral, affirming the pre-eminence of pastoral practice and its effects over merely verbal proselytism. The mission would convert the Blacks of Africa in the same way it converted the poor and orphans: by deeds and actions. One of Lavigerie's pastoral letters affirms this: in 'our pagan missions,' he wrote, 'we can do nothing until that day when – by our good deeds, by our suffering, by our death if need be – we have persuaded the poor populations surrounding us of our love for them, despite their degradation and errors!'[64] The *Charte des missions d'Afrique*, a secret memorandum he drafted in Algiers in 1878, develops this argument. If the Christian mission did indeed address the soul, it could penetrate it only through the pastor's exemplary conduct, since 'to change the heart, to inspire it to faith and virtue, one must oneself have preeminent faith and virtue.'[65]

Strict observance of Christian ritual practices and sacraments should not be demanded of the indigenous population. There could be no question of presenting them with every aspect of Christianity, Lavigerie declared. It would thus fall to the missionary superiors to decide whether to hide the worship of saints and images from them so as not to 'promote idolatry', 'in light of the superstitious tendencies of the Blacks'.[66] Nor, he added, could there be a question of immediate baptism. Only their *moralization*, an action expressed particularly in their abandoning matrimonial practices such as polygamy, could make them worthy of Christian baptism. Lavigerie thus declared that African souls should be gradually converted to the religion of Christ. Conversion implied, first of all, an *indigenization* of Christianity by maintaining local customs.

---

63 Ibid., p. 97.
64 Lavigerie, 'Lettre pastorale de Carthage', 1885, in ibid., p. 71.
65 Ibid., p. 109.
66 Ibid., p. 109.

Preparation for conversion to the Christian faith thus required the translation of Christianity into African languages and cultures.

In sum, the secularization of French institutions was directly connected to the Catholic mission in Africa. The drive to spiritualize liberal democracy by recalling its Christian dimension was the other side of what, for the missionaries, belonged to the indigenization of the missionary project. The alliance between the state and Christianity in the colonies was neither a betrayal of *laïcité* nor the revelation, at long last, of its Christian secret. It was precisely because colonial space was organized around conflicts and compromises between Church and state that the alliance was able to extend to the metropole and be internationalized through diplomatic means. The secularization of the state apparatus was determined by the Republic's negotiations with the Holy See, after the imperial Concordat had allowed Catholic missionary activity to shift its focus to Berber populations and the interior of sub-Saharan Africa. Christian colonialism was not the condition of possibility for a metropole falsely defined as secular; rather, the policing and colonial control of religious *cultes* set in place by the Napoleonic imperial state authorized the establishment of projects to secularize Christianity, as well as the expression of new Christian political spiritualities in the European metropoles in the context of liberal democracy.

French *laïcité*, thus, was not *imposed* as such in the colonies. It was not an article for export. That would imply that it had predated imperialism – that the Republic first became secular and then colonized. *Laïcité* was not an article for colonial export, simply because it did not exist before colonialism: *laïcité* was not invented and then imposed by the empire; its very construction resulted from imperial circulations between metropole and colony. In this sense, *laïcité* is only one, properly French, modality in the broader history of relations between secularization and empire. The secularization of France took place alongside and in tandem with the mutations of the empire's colonial strategies in Africa.

The colonial state in Algeria had tried to invent its own Islam by creating a 'Muslim *culte*'. The construction of an Islam with a central and representative authority was a consequence of the strategy of respecting religion and traditions, declared since the conquest of Algeria in 1830. Confessional pluralism, and its extension beyond Judaism and Christianity in 1830, should be seen as an effect of empire. Algerian

Islam became a religion surveilled and, at times, controlled by the French state. From the Muslim point of view, *laïcité* was thus tendentially reduced to what might seem like its opposite: the control of religion, the policing of rites and beliefs. This subjugation of practices and of believers identified as suspect certainly seems to contradict the generously liberal – but highly abstract – definitions of *laïcité* as state neutrality, the absence of religion in politics, or the simple separation of state and religion. But, in any case, the structural exclusion of colonial domination of Muslims was not in contradiction with the institutions of the First Empire. Today, these institutions continue to determine the practices of control and discrimination that, in public space, take the name of *laïcité*. The secularism of the imperial state and its colonial deployment in Africa were, therefore, not abolished by the regime of *laïcité* established after 1905. Laicization never meant the absence of state intervention within religious practice. Practices that exclude Muslims are faces of secularization in which its imperiality can be seen, not simple exceptions to the regime of *laïcité* established by the state. If the state no longer finances religions, it still regulates and surveils them through a set of practices still called today, in Title V of the Law of 1905, the 'policing of *cultes*'. The foundation of the First Empire was thus a crucial moment in the history of secularization and of French *laïcité*. The state's supposed secularism, like that of public education, was formulated under the imperial regime of the Concordat and the control of recognized religious traditions of practice. In any case, many of the Republicans who played a crucial role in educational secularization, such as Jules Ferry, had no intention of excluding the imperial regime from the control and financing of religions. A legal separation would only provoke opposition from those who were persuaded that the state would as a result lose all its power over a potentially seditious Catholic Church. The imperial state also deployed this suspicion of the Church outside the metropole, towards religions in the colonial space. The fact that the Law of 1905 was not fully applied in the French colonies does not indicate a betrayal of *laïcité*, but rather the maintenance of the Napoleonic system of *cultes* for reasons of public security and state defence. The 1905 law of separation did *not* abolish state regulation of religions. *Laïcité* does not consist in a separation of religion and politics, but in liberalizing the already secularized administration of religions as *cultes*. The privatization of religion and the Church did not mean they

would be treated as individuals, but that, henceforth, they would belong
to private rather than public law.[67] The state's colonial practices concerning religious matters belonged to a regime of controlling *cultes* that was
never completely abolished by the Law of 1905, not even in the so-called
metropole. The state still surveils and polices the *cultes*, even if it no
longer finances them.[68]

Of course, the idea of a pure and simple transfer of the policy of
recognized *cultes* to Algeria should be nuanced. The modes of organizing and controlling religious *cultes* were indeed transferred to
Algeria and other territories of the French Empire, but Islam was
never *officially recognized* as a *culte* by the French state. This
prevented Islam from being officially reorganized by state structures
in the metropole, unlike the Jewish and Christian *cultes*.[69] Islam thus
remained surveilled but not financed, kept under suspicion of radical incompatibility with the Republic and its so-called civilization.
The history of the colonization of Algeria coincides with the colonial
history of systematic non-recognition of Islam and the surveillance
of Muslims. We know, of course, that the secular idea and the colonial project went together in the minds of French Republicans in the
metropole. But this does not in any case mean, as we have seen, that
laïcité was imported on a massive scale or violently imposed on
indigenous peoples throughout the colonies. It means that the secularization of institutions in Europe and the deployment of missionaries in the colonies can be seen as two sides of a single process,
whose unity is imperial. It was through the many ramifications of

67   In Article 20, the Law of 1905 supressed the system of recognized *cultes* that
entailed the state's financial responsibility for them. Churches were no longer legally
public but, as constituted bodies, fell under private law.

68   Jacqueline Lalouette, *La Séparation des églises et de l'état, 1789–1905*, Paris:
Seuil, 2005, p. 15.

69   The official submission of Islam to the Napoleonic system of *cultes* was a project
of the Second Empire formulated by the Saint-Simonian counsellor Ismaÿl Urbain.
Urbain pressured the French state to recognize Islam as an official *culte* within the
empire. The 'Muslim *culte*', including its buildings and imams, should be recognized and
financed, he argued, and a 'Central Muslim Consistory' established on the model of the
Central Israelite Consistory of France. He argued this opinion in an intervention
published in *L'Époque* under the name Behaghel, on 26 July 1865. See Philippe Régnier,
'Le Discours colonial des saint-simoniens: une utopie post-révolutionnaire française
appliquée en terre d'islam (Égypte et Algérie)', in Pierre-Jean Luizard, ed., *Le Choc
colonial et l'islam*, Paris: La Découverte, 2006, pp. 69–70.

this project that the colonization of Algeria and Africa contributed to secularizing France, and Europe more generally.

It could be hypothesized that the exclusion of Islam outside of the social racial contract was what made such a contract possible: that France's action of ruling the Muslims it had transformed into colonial subjects, first in Algeria and then elsewhere, played a role in making the secular state into what it became. Might Islam, far from being a recent implantation in France and Europe, have been the 'excluded third' of historical *laïcité*? The non-application of *laïcité* in the colonies, rather than being an *exception* to the law separating state and Church, would precisely have contributed to making it possible in the metropole. The exception does not prove the rule, but constitutes the law itself. Thus, the condition sine qua non, for the secularization of state power, its violence, and its exclusions, seems to have been the deployment of Christian missions and control of the 'Muslim *culte*' in Africa. On the ideological level, European universalism was constructed by defining Islam as the alternative universal. This Islamic universalism was defined as both monolithic and religious. The Hegelian theme of a conflict of theologico-political universalisms thus haunted Republican universalism well after 1905, and still pervades contemporary philosophical gestures.[70]

The imperial relation between France and Islam constituted the very possibility of the Republic in the metropole. The task now is to develop this hypothesis by examining how the imperiality born in Egypt during the Napoleonic expedition was transposed in Algeria. My hypothesis is that the colonization of Algeria gave rise to a system of economic segregation, in which state racism systematically oppressed a subject defined as Muslim, opposing it to a secular citizen whose religious belonging could then be defined as 'indifferent'. This system of oppression was born from the vast project of transforming the Muslims of North Africa into colonial subjects. By making the colonial construction of Catholic institutions *appear* not as Catholic proselytism but, rather, as one recognized

---

70 Contemporary reflections on universalism continue to be haunted by this Hegelian gesture. Étienne Balibar, for example, reactivates the theme of the theologico-political conflict of universalisms in *Des Universels: essais et conférences*, Paris: Galilée, 2016, p. 73. Alain Badiou meanwhile approaches Christ and Christianity through the prism of his theory of the event: see *Saint Paul: The Foundations of Universalism*, trans. R. Brassier, Stanford, CA: Stanford University Press, 2003.

religion among others, the imperial power could guarantee not a princi-
pled secularism, but rather the stability of the colonial order. Through
Quinet, this colonial strategy of pacification declared that it was the secular and profane fulfilment of Christianity. It was deployed as a machine
to produce the appearance of religious neutrality, and project the signs of
this neutrality to the racialized Muslim subjects that colonialism needed
to convince of its sincere dedication to ending conversion. How did this
strategy of non-conversion contribute to the history of racism? How did
the theme of Muslims' inconvertibility lead to their racialization? How, in
a word, was the confrontation with Islam that suffused universalism
translated into the colonial institution of race?

3

Race and the Inconvertible: On Apartheid in North Africa

This chapter analyses the establishment of the *indigénat* in Algeria as a moment in the theologico-political history of race. The *indigénat* is an untranslatable word which refers to the legal status of indigenous peoples in the French Empire. Structured by inequality, the *indigénat* defined the indigenous populations of Algeria as French subjects but non-citizens. The *indigènes* or 'natives' belonged to the French *imperium* but could not be granted citizenship and thus equal rights. The indigenous population was legally defined via religion, as either Jewish or Muslim. By examining the ways in which Algerians were racialized by the colonial state, the chapter shows how the secularization of the empire led to a new form of state racism. The signifier of Islam became a racial name – literally a name for race – once Muslims were declared to be inconvertible but colonizable.

The *indigénat*, established first in Algeria and then extended to the French Empire in Asia and Africa, was a legacy of the Egyptian Expedition. The history opened by the aborted project of the expedition should be written beginning neither from Egypt nor from the so-called Middle East.[1] It was in the north of the African continent, in Algeria, that the imperial order of secularization was translated into a

---

1   As with many other scholars, I consider this category an imperial construct. See Michael Bonine, Abbas Amanat, and Michael Gasper, eds, *Is There a Middle East? The Evolution of a Geopolitical Concept*, Stanford, CA: Stanford University Press, 2012.

colonial order founded on state racism and the institutional segregation of Muslims. The mechanisms of the Concordat and the system of
cultes were applied in Algeria, and it was this colonial extension of
imperial secularization that short-circuited and blocked ecclesiastical
attempts to subjugate Algerian Muslims and Jews through colonization
based on Christian missions. The regulation and policing of religion
became imperial in the strong sense, articulating the secularity of the
bureaucratic metropolitan state with a colonial space that was rapidly
being integrated into the body of the empire itself. It was here that the
imperiality of secularization, born in Egypt while proclaiming itself
Muslim, introduced the colonial Manicheanism that put two worlds
face to face, in an opposition so radical that an infinite distance seemed
to separate them: the world of White Europeans, and the world of the
indigenous population, defined as Muslim. Race here was not defined
by skin colour: Whiteness did not define itself in contrast with
Blackness. Race referred to something other than the Blackness of
being that Frantz Fanon analysed. It referred to a systematic racialization of Islam that developed not from pure and simple repression but
from the codification of Muslim men's and women's religious and
matrimonial practices. After the Crémieux Decree granted Algerian
Jews French citizenship in 1870, the colonial administration legally
defined the colonized subject as a *French non-citizen Muslim*. This
establishment of a French nationality distinct from citizenship, formalized during the 1860s, was designated by the name *indigénat*. The colonial dissemination of the French imperial state's secular institutions
presided over the creation of the status of *indigène* in Algeria. The *indigénat* was the translation of imperial secularization into the register of
race. It designated a hierarchical structure that opposed White and
secular citizens, for whom religion was said to be 'indifferent', to
subjects juridically defined and racialized as Muslim.[2]

---

2   Empirical work by historians shows that this opposition was in part fictional,
and that it was never fully applied. At any rate, colonization never annihilated the
agency of the colonized. French nationality also became a way for Algerians to impose
themselves against the colonial state, while at the same time strategically claiming its
protection. The distinction of citizen and subject nonetheless describes the
administrative and ideological structure of colonial *racism* – a form of *apartheid* –
although it does not exhaust the complexity of colonial situations or the positions
occupied by the colonized, or even the institutional functioning of the state itself. See
Daho Djerbal, 'De la difficile écriture de l'histoire d'une société (dé)-colonisée', *NAQD*

It was as a function of their real or supposed belonging to what the West continuously called their *religion* that the indigenous population were racialized. Colonial secularization neither abolished religion nor neutralized it by diminishing its importance. On the contrary, it fixed and codified it; the empire interpreted Islam as a sign of race. To the extent that the imperiality of knowledge deciphered the rites of the colonized as so many symbols of a culture that it tried to understand in order to rule, its mission was distinct from the project of conversion to Christianity. It became a secular project, a *civilizing* mission. Far from separating religion and politics, secularization politicized religion and made it stand for race. The figure of the Arab typified how colonial racism saw Muslims: warlike but fanatical, courageous but violent, virile but religious. But these racial attributes went beyond Arabophobia for one crucial reason. It was as Muslims that the indigenous peoples – Arab, Berber, or Black – were racialized *by law*. Only the indissociably religious, racial, and legal category of Muslim allowed racism to function as *state* racism, as an *institutional* mechanism. It is possible that Islamophobia has inherited the contemporary fragmentation of this dynamic, this way of saying *religion*, the better to create racial effects.

Throughout this chapter, the word *race* refers to processes of racializing bodies by revealing their supposed religion. Race is an effect of violence exercised on subjects by colonial institutions such as the state or the police; it is neither a biological nor a cultural reality, nor a simple discursive or imaginary construction. Race is what authorizes imperial power to attribute violence to the bodies submitted to its yoke, such that its own violence appears with the artificial features of a pacifying counter-violence. Systemic racism thus authorizes colonialism to present aggression as legitimate defence. Racist discourses on fanaticism and terror attribute to Muslim bodies the form of violence that modern and liberal sensibilities are used to considering the most illegitimate and insupportable: theological-political violence, exercised in the name of God rather than of liberty or the nation. Because of this, the racialization of Islam and Muslims has a potential to intensify and

---

special series 3, 2014, pp. 213–31, and the entirety of this issue of *NAQD*, edited by Nourredine Amara, Candice Raymond, and Jihane Sfeir and titled 'Écritures historiennes du Maghreb et du Machrek'.

normalize violence whose significance is not always recognized. Irreducible to a simple discursive construction, race instead designates a real manifestation of state violence, whose reality is characterized by the constant possibility of putting to death.[3] Racial violence is an effect of this form of sovereignty, which was born in the West in the fifteenth century, in the wake of the Crusades: what I have called imperiality. Race proceeds from the imperiality of power; or, more exactly, from its becoming colonial.

Critical studies of race are characterized by the marginalization, if not the absence, of a nonetheless crucial question: How did the West's definition of religion produce particular effects of racialization? How did the real or supposed religion of a population come to function as race, and why do secularized societies, against all expectations, tend to intensify this type of exclusion? By ignoring these key questions, most studies of race show a methodological secularism that is often inherited from Fanon, and which may be the blind spot of his foundational work.[4] In this approach, the racialization of Islam is usually reduced to a particular case of a racism whose general definition pre-existed it. But it is impossible to grasp what the name *indigène* meant in the French Empire without understanding it in reference to a racial transposition of imperial secularization. The *indigénat* was a form of racism in which race could not be analysed independently of religion. Religion, here, referred to a reality that was constituted by the empire itself, and whose effects went beyond discourse. This reality was the appropriation by the state of ethico-juridical practices gathered under the name Sharia. It referred to a mutation of Islam produced through its internal secularization by colonialism, which made it into a set of laws in the modern sense of the term. The result was the translation of Islam by colonial law into 'personal status', which made it possible to establish the fact of being Muslim as a racial category.

---

3 On this Fanonian theme, see Achille Mbembe, *De la postcolonie*, Paris: La Découverte, 2020, pp. 19–22. This is from Mbembe's foreword to the second French edition.

4 See Mohammed Harbi, 'Postface' to Fanon, *Les Damnés de la terre*, Paris: La Découverte, 2002, pp. 304–9.

Inconvertible blood and Catholic Muslims

I will now sketch out the general lines of this argument, beginning from the margins of colonial space, to reveal something of the structure that governed the *indigénat* as a key institution of state racism. The marginal experience I discuss concerns the rare indigenous subjects who converted to Christianity, and the legal troubles they provoked. This trouble exposes the reality of race and its relationship to the inconvertible.

The rare colonized subjects who converted to Christianity, despite the colonial administration's efforts to limit missionary activity, were defined by the colonial administration after 1903 as 'Catholic Muslims'.[5] This well-known case signals, with a revealing strangeness, how *race* was spoken and deployed through the legal designation of the indigenous population as Muslim, troubling the supposedly self-evident borders of *religion*. Most theorists of racism treat religion as a given fact and race as a discursive construction. As we will see, race *and* religion are both colonial productions whose reality, although in no way a universal or even an anthropological fact, still cannot be reduced to simple discursive constructions. Separating race from religion renders institutions such as the *indigénat* incomprehensible because religion refers to a status and to a set of regulated practices which belong to the colonial apparatus of secularization. In the eyes of the law, religion was not something that indigenous subjects could choose. Contrary to what might be expected, the law's secularity seems precisely to have made religion into a category its members did not have the right to abandon. By their very marginality, the 'Catholic Muslims' demonstrated that conversion to Catholicism did not function as a vector of assimilation through which, by proximity to Whiteness, an indigenous subject could escape colonial status. Muslims would henceforth remain Muslims, so that they could be kept within the racialized status of colonial subjects. And it was

---

5   The Tribunal of Algiers published a ruling on 15 November 1903, according to which an indigenous subject who converted to Catholicism was still under the jurisdiction of repressive tribunals. *Muslim* therefore signified, beyond any belonging to the *umma* or profession of divine unity, a vulnerability to the arbitrariness of the state's racial violence. See Yerri Urban, 'Race et nationalité dans le droit colonial français, 1865–1955', PhD thesis, Dijon: Université de Bourgogne, June 2009, p. 131; André Bonnichon, 'La Conversion au christianisme de l'indigène musulman algérien et ses effets juridiques (un cas de conflit colonial)', PhD thesis, Paris: Librairie du Recueil Sirey, 1931.

secular law, liberated from the tutelage of God or the Church, that effected this legal fixation of religion by race and the consequences that flowed from it. Through the marginal examples of these indigenous Christians who continued to be defined as Muslims, racialization was materialized as an impassable limit. For religion to be racialized, it had to be fixed in the law of the empire as something other than an act of faith. The phrase 'Catholic Muslims' testifies to the presence of the racial at the heart of a 'religious fact' whose limits, and nature, were produced by colonial power. The state could deploy racism without ever naming *race* as such.[6] In this chapter, I argue that this racism historically precedes biological racism and is not reducible to it, while questioning the fact that the key question of how religious spaces are produced and racialized by power is generally absent in dominant analyses of race.

How is this analysis of race inscribed in the general economy of the imperial history of secularization? As a psycho-political reality rooted in violence, race is the manifestation of imperiality. The *racial* history of secularization is thus the history of its colonial mutations once colonialism opted not to destroy but to include Islam – and indigenous cultures more generally – in an attempt to transform it into a mechanism to subjugate the population. The codification of Islam as personal status, a typical effect of the secularization of law, was the foundation of race in the economy of the colonial state. This transformation of the very status of race is thus an outcome of imperial secularization, of which it is both a phenomenon and a clue or indication.

It was through the secularization of empire that the religion of indigenous people was racialized, to the point that their identity appeared to

---

6   Was the *indigénat* then a sort of racism without race, an ideal type of a cultural but not biological racism? The idea of a 'racism without race' was formulated by Étienne Balibar in a seminal essay, 'Is There a "Neo-Racism"?', in Étienne Balibar and Immanuel Wallerstein, *Race, Nation, Class: Ambiguous Identities*, London: Verso, 1991, pp. 17–28. According to Balibar, this new racism constitutes the generalization of a cultural racism in which 'bodily stigmata' are 'signs of a deep psychology . . . rather than a biological heredity'. Its model is antisemitism, where the essence of the Jew is 'that of a cultural tradition, a ferment of moral disintegration'. For this reason, Balibar diagnoses a 'generalized anti-Semitism', of which Arabophobia is a contemporary form. Balibar's analysis presupposes, without ever stating it explicitly, that at the root of this racism is a *culturalization of religion*, but he does not describe the process. The centrality of the racialization of religion and particularly of Islam in the creation of a 'racism without race' thus constitutes a blind spot in Balibar's analysis, and more generally in critical studies of race.

be irreversible and immutable (or inconvertible). Race thus appeared as the limit to all conversion, as the term 'Catholic Muslim' shows. The racialization of religion through the secularization of empire required not only that the borders of religion were imposed and delimited, but also that Muslims were defined as a community of inconvertible beings. What matters, in the following pages, is not whether this inconvertibility was presented as immutable or provisory, nor whether the violence of Islam was understood as a biological effect of Arab blood or a cultural formation, nor whether the idea was a simple pragmatic decision linked to the feasibility of colonization or a pseudo-scientific hypothesis inherited from Christian hatred of Jews and Muslims. For me, what matters here is to grasp how inconvertibility is the face of the racialized Muslim, the figuration of race beyond the diversity of its forms. Race is what, in the very body of the converted, presents an obstacle to conversion. Impure blood is first and above all what remains inconvertible and fundamentally suspect, even despite conversion to Christianity.[7] That race was created by an assumption of the other's inconvertibility is testified by the supposedly impure blood of the Jews and Muslims who converted to Christianity after the Reconquista. The laws of blood purity instituted by the Spanish empire, before the colonization of the Americas and the transatlantic slave trade, in effect constitute the matrix of race.[8] Race was born during the Reconquista, under the figure of inconvertibility of blood. It was generated from within the Christian logic of converting infidels, as reconfigured by the Spanish Empire. Its first victims were Jews and Muslims: the converted Moors of Muslim Andalusia, whose destruction was the womb of the Spanish Empire and the conquest of the Americas. The secularity of empire unfolded against the backdrop of this conception of race as inconvertible blood.

---

7   Race, as such, is not a nineteenth-century invention. To understand its matrix, it is necessary to go back to the laws of blood purity that the Spanish monarchy instituted against Jews and Muslims who had recently converted to Christianity after the Reconquista, and suspected of dissimulation. See Balibar, 'Is There a "Neo-Racism"?', and Gil Anidjar, *Blood: A Critique of Christianity*, New York: Columbia University Press, 2014, p. 76. In this chapter, I argue that the idea of an inconvertible blood puts Christianity in a state of crisis which is imperial. I also suggest that something new and irreducible happened when empires ceased to convert Jews and Muslims to Christianity.

8   I am intentionally taking up the formulation that Elsa Dorlin proposes, while questioning the 'genealogy' she proposes in *La Matrice de la race: généalogie sexuelle et coloniale de la nation française*, Paris: La Découverte, 2006.

Secularization took place once the inconvertibility of the Muslim *fanatic* gave way to a new and deliberate refusal of conversion to Christianity, thus engendering a politics of strategic and conscious non-conversion. Its most famous name is none other than the *civilizing mission*, the figure of secular conversion not to the Christian religion but to industrial modernity.

It will no doubt be objected that French Catholics and ethnologists opposed *Kabyles* to *Arabs*, considering the former to be more easily convertible to Christianity than other Muslims.[9] This discourse – which, it should be noted, was relatively marginal – wrongly understood the Kabyles as more convertible and thus less profoundly Muslim than the Arabs. This idea contributed to what is conventionally called the 'Kabyle myth', by which a certain French ethnology made the Kabyle into the colony's *convertible* subject. As an exception, and by its very marginality, this discourse signals that the operating rule of racism was the following: it was *as Muslims* that the indigenous population – Arab, Black, or Berber – were excluded as inconvertible. In addition, a crucial element of the myth by which the Kabyles were racialized was the idea that Islam was an Arab religion. The convertible colonial subject was thus the one whose Islam was defined as least authentic and least orthodox. French colonialism would also invent the connected myth of a 'Black Islam' (*islam noir*) supposedly distinct from an orthodox Arab and North African Islam, and generalize this distinction in the division of a White or Oriental Africa from a Black sub-Saharan Africa. In other words, inconvertibility was a racial property which colonialism attributed to natives *as Muslims*. The racial and ethnic distinction of natives as a

---

9 On the Kabyle myth, see Charles-Robert Ageron, 'La France a-t-elle eu une politique Kabyle?', in *De 'l'Algérie française' à l'Algérie algérienne*, Paris: Bouchène, 2005 (1960), pp. 13–17. For an analysis of the role of the distinction between Kabyles and Arabs within the Christian missions, see Karima Dirèche, *Chrétiens de Kabylie: une action missionnaire dans l'Algérie coloniale (1873–1954)*, Paris: Bouchène, 2004, and 'Convertir les Kabyles: quelle réalité?', in Dominique Borne and Benoît Falaize, eds, *Religions et colonisation: Afrique, Asie, Océanie, Amériques, XVIè–XXè siècles*, Paris: Éditions de l'Atelier, 2009, pp. 153–76. See also Carole Reynaud-Paligot, *La République raciale: paradigme racial et idéologie républicaine (1860–1930)*, Paris: PUF, 2006, p. 59; Patricia Lorcin, *Imperial Identities: Stereotyping, Prejudice and Race in Colonial Algeria*, London: I. B. Tauris, 1995, pp. 146–70. As we will see, this literature should be supplemented by considering a Saint-Simonian and Napoleonic *Arab myth* whose effects were much more important than the idea of Kabyle convertibility.

function of their degree of convertibility reveals a classification in terms of supposed degrees of faithfulness to Islam.

What happened when the colonial administration, in opposition to the Christian missionaries, deployed this racism to forbid converting Muslims to Christianity, so that they could be initiated into civilization and made into secular citizens? The strategy of non-conversion to Christianity that had structured the expedition was at the heart of the colonization of Algeria, and determined the structure of the colonial state that was implemented there. While the concept of secularization must inevitably be mobilized to explain the formation of ethnology in the nineteenth century, it needs to be defined in greater depth, and never reduced to a simple passing from the theological to the scientific, from religion to race. For this, we will need to understand how institutions themselves were secularized, going beyond the limits of a racism that they nonetheless constituted. The point of departure for this analysis is the deployment of French colonialism after 1830 under the sign of 'respect for religion'; at the same time, the prohibition of Christian missionary activity, which was suspected to provoke 'fanaticism' in the population, was made into one of the foundations of the legitimation of the colonial order and the production of indigenous consent to domination.

By developing a historical theory of the *indigénat*, this chapter tries to shed light on a contemporary phenomenon: the way in which the words *religion, fanaticism*, and *separatism*, applied to Islam, make it possible to deny the existence of race while putting racism to work. History is employed here in service of a critical aim: decrypting the mechanisms for racializing religion that are common to antisemitism and Islamophobia. Discourses on Judaism and Islam continuously racialize the cultural and the religious, without ever referring to race. The act of racialization that underpinned the *indigénat* was a process through which religion functioned *as* race, and race *as* religion. The indigenous Algerians were assigned to a racial formation whose existence necessarily troubles the arbitrary borders between the cultural, the biological, and the religious.[10] The reality of Islam continuously exceeds the borders

10   Ann Laura Stoler suggests that race is characterized by semantic polyvalence, and that the very power of racism consists in the ambivalence that makes race unstable and mobile. But Stoler doesn't analyse the making of religion as a central mechanism of this ambivalence, both in the metropole and the colonies. See Ann Laura Stoler, *Duress: Imperial Durabilities in Our Times*, Durham, NC: Duke University Press, 2016.

of what modern liberal societies recognize as religious. Colonial racism always recognized this in practice, while both explaining it in terms of the false idea of the Qur'an as a civil code and continuously searching to reduce Islam to the status of a mere religion. The secularity of the colonial state in Algeria was exercised through its power to define what was religious and to distinguish it from what was not. Imperial secularization thus refers to the way in which the state excluded indigenous lands from the private property regime, by defining the status of *indigène* through the racialization and codification of Islam.

This chapter demonstrates this by describing the institutional mechanisms of the *indigénat*. It thus analyses race indirectly, to the extent that it took the face of religion as the secularization of the empire progressed. The *juridical definition* of racial groups by their religious belonging was at the heart of a secular colonial law that continuously codified practices as connected to *personal status*. *Muslim* thus referred to the race of the indigenous subjects as much as to the codification of their modes of existence, or what colonial reason called their mores, through an Islamic law reconstructed by this reason itself as a sort of native family code. If it may appear to some readers as an analysis of religion more than of race, this is because its aim is precisely to uncover and dissolve the arbitrary but nevertheless powerful separation of race and religion. This separation betrays the tendency to marginalize, if not completely erase, Muslim experience in the West, which is marked by the inescapable reality of Islamophobia. I analyse fragments of the history of the colonization of Algeria by tracing the racial transpositions of imperial secularization, and the ways that the colonial state spoke of a tradition – Islam – that it continuously reconstructed by *codifying* it as race *and* religion. One of the stakes of this argument is to problematize a revealing lacuna in intersectionality, a sort of sign of its secularity. Intersectional discourses operate in light of the well-known trinity that articulates race, sex, and class. Religion is excluded, like a fourth party denied full rights and made invisible by the hegemony of this tripartite schema. Nonetheless, religion has a status analogous to the other categories, and is in constant interaction with them. Like race and gender, the supposed borders of the religious are produced by systems of power, which determine the very nature of what we call religions.

The assignation of the Muslim to theologico-racial inconvertibility serves as this chapter's guiding thread. In my view, this characterizes not *every* manifestation of race and racism but the way that race was deployed *juridically and institutionally* in the French Empire in the form of the *indigénat*. This will help us to understand what makes racism into *state* racism, and, at the same time, allow us to grasp the structure of the state structure from the perspective of race. The chapter's second aim is to show how the process of racializing Muslims was inscribed in the French establishment of a system of apartheid in North Africa. This policy, founded on state racism, was meant to establish the separate development of races that were born from the secularization of the empire. The idea of civilizing the indigenous population was materialized in a colonial state that tried dialectically to articulate two types of government: a *direct* form, based on the massive expropriation of indigenous lands and settler colonization in the urban areas; and an *indirect* form, based on strategic respect for customary chiefs and traditional institutions in the rural areas. Saint-Simonianism, a movement that was at once liberal and socialist, religious and industrial, played a key role in the articulation of this model of the colonial state, reprising the project of the Egyptian Expedition in Algeria. The Saint-Simonian programme of association contributed to founding this two-faced state, which assigned the indigenous subjects their place in a racial economy based on the productive utilization of their supposedly natural capacities. This colonial racism valorized each race's essential aptitudes, while, at the same time, it declared the dogma of their *perfectibility*. A critical analysis of its implementation by military force will help us to understand how the colonization of Algeria contributed to the colonization of the African continent.

This chapter's goal is not to reveal the origins of race, but to elucidate its functioning. There can be no question of *decolonizing* knowledge or power without an analysis of the imperial machine, of which race is never more than *a manifestation*. Race is the face that colonialism presents, and racism the experience through which the imperial machine orders death and threatens life. To dismantle this machine and stop its movement implies knowing how its mechanisms worked in the past, and how they still work today. Coming after the Crusades, the civilizing mission was meant to liberate people whom slavery had made unworthy of being truly human. No longer content to exclude them from humanity, it continuously prescribed how they would now be included. They were promised terrestrial redemption and renewed dignity by empires who spoke only in the name of liberty, after reducing millions of Black women and men to slavery. But the arrival of this redemption – subject to stringent conditions – was constantly and indefinitely deferred. The space of the colony unfolded in this time of infinite latency, suffocating the colonized, obliging them to breathe an unbreathable air and constraining them to live as humans already condemned to social death but constantly promised equality. Imaginary inclusion functioned as real exclusion. What would qualify a subject to become human, free, and a citizen also disqualified their existence. What made them unworthy to become citizens imprisoned them within a tradition that had been reduced to the arbitrary rule of ossified custom, and expropriated their lands as it did their dignity.[11] The double consciousness that haunted the colonized and still haunts their descendants – the impossible pressure to assimilate to White people if they ceased to claim their traditions, and of being pinned to a fixed identity if they claimed them – was the psychic effect of a doubling that was located at the heart of colonial institutions. What appears here is the double face of Leviathan, the imperiality of that biblical monster which, since Thomas Hobbes, we have identified with the state itself.

The double face of Leviathan

The policy of association formulated during the military colonization of Algeria, between 1830 and 1870, was in many respects an empire of custom. As the structure of a form of apartheid, it deployed a system of government comparable, though not identical, to what the British Empire would ultimately put in place in its African and Asian possessions, particularly in South Africa: spatial separation of populations based on race, together with indigenous tribes governed by control and support of their customary chiefs. But the crucial difference between apartheid in Algeria and North Africa and in South Africa was that, in the former, the race of the colonized race was the same as their religion, as it had been reconfigured and codified by the empire.

The decentralization of colonial power conducted in Algeria reconfigured the lives of communities throughout the African continent. By

---

11   Frantz Fanon, *The Wretched of the Earth*, New York: Grove, 1963, p. 9.

inventing the artificial categories of *ethnicity* and *tribe*, ethnographers arbitrarily defined these communities using monolithic and fixed identities, ignoring their implication in the precolonial transnational networks that took precedence over local communities.[12] Creating a two-faced state by deploying direct government in the urban areas and indirect government in the rural districts of the colony, the French army in Algeria initiated an embryonic version of the future colonization of the African continent. This double state corresponded to what Mahmood Mamdani has described as the structure that the majority of African states inherited from European colonialism.[13] According to Mamdani, the system of Apartheid in South Africa, far from being an exception, can be seen as a pattern for the racial segregation and indirect government of indigenous tribes and villages that Europe disseminated in different forms across the African continent. Consequently, a history of the deployment of European imperialism cannot take the colonization of equatorial Africa after the Berlin Conference in 1885 as its sole point of departure. A crucial part of this deployment was in play in Algeria from 1830, at work in the alliances and rivalries between French soldiers and Saint-Simonians. This history shows that imperial *traditionalism* was neither the rival nor the successor of civilizing *reformism*, as the classic historiography of the British colonization of India states. Beginning in the 1840s, French imperialism in Algeria made liberal reformism and the codification of indigenous customs coexist within the same governmental structure.

Indigenous uprisings and the spectre of fanaticism: at the heart of missionary conflicts

The colonial practices elaborated by the French Empire in Algeria were established to counter the numerous uprisings against the French army of Africa. These insurrections, organized from the 1830s on, through networks of solidarity that went beyond the tribal unit, did not use the language of nationhood to describe their developing unification. The

---

12   Jean-Loup Amselle and Elikia M'Bokolo, eds, *Au coeur de l'ethnie: ethnies, tribalismes et état en Afrique*, Paris: La Découverte, 1985, pp. v, 23.

13   Mahmood Mamdani, *Citizen and Subject: Contemporary Africa and the Legacy of Late Colonialism*, Princeton, NJ: Princeton University Press, 2018 [1993], pp. 16–34.

most famous of these was the insurrection led by Abd el-Kader ('Abd al-Qādir). Coming from a noble family in the west of the country, Abd el-Kader was a Sufi and disciple of Ibn Arabi.[14] Far from wanting to be a conqueror or to wield power, he was elected by a group of 'tribes' without having put himself forward, after his own father had refused leadership of the resistance movement against colonial occupation.[15] His abilities, rather than his ambition, were what destined him for the role, and tradition obliged him to consent to taking on the functions of emir (*amīr*).[16]

Abd el-Kader deployed a set of essentially guerrilla military tactics. His technique consisted in never remaining static, maintaining constant movement that short-circuited the enemy's targeting skills, and working in alliance with the environment. In a letter to General Bugeaud, he described the principle: 'We fight when we deem it appropriate; you know that we are not cowards.'[17] By choosing when to confront the enemy, and refusing to be hemmed in, Abd el-Kader saw the war neither as opposition to colonialism nor as a conflict between forces. 'For us to confront all the forces that march behind you would be folly, but we will exhaust them, we will pester them, we will destroy them selectively; the climate will do the rest,' wrote the emir. Working together with the climate and allowing it to work, this mode of struggle involved interaction with terrestrial forces. The emir described the anticolonial wave to Bugeaud in these terms: 'Do you see the wave that rises when a bird brushes with its wing? This is the image of your time in Africa.'[18] The emir's resistance was a permanent movement, always ready to deploy and redeploy in different territories according to its own insurrectional

14 Tom Woerner-Powell, *Another Road to Damascus: An Integrative Approach to 'Abd Al-Qadir Al-Jaza'iri (1808–1883)*, Berlin: De Gruyter, 2017, pp. 21–61; Raphaël Danziger, *Abd Al-Qadir and the Algerians*, New York: Holmes & Meier, 1977, pp. 51–88.

15 Woerner-Powell, *Another Road to Damascus*, pp. 25–6; Danziger, *Abd Al-Qadir*, p. 63.

16 Abd el-Kader reunited the tribes into an ethico-political community that covered two-thirds of Algerian territory between 1833 and 1848. It could be defined as a state only in a sense completely different from the territorial nation-state of the European type. For a description of it, and its organization, see Danziger, *Abd Al-Qadir*, pp. 180–209.

17 Cited in Jacques Frémeaux, ''Abd el-Kader, chef de guerre (1832–1847)', *Revue Historique des Armées* 250, 2008, p. 4.

18 Ibid.

needs. After its defeat, which notably involved the French side's failure to respect the treaties it had signed, Abd el-Kader's resistance was succeeded by a multitude of other attempts, such as the ones led by the Mahdi Bu Zian or El-Mokrani.[19]

The policies of segregating Muslims and surveilling their activities was established to counter these uprisings. They were a permanent menace, which the colonizers referred to systematically with the racialized term *fanaticism*. The use of this word had been generalized by Volney and the Lumières, and it let the military reduce an eminently complex discourse to a vague idea of *religion*. The colonial government's opposition to Christian missionaries largely derived from the terror aroused among the settlers by the supposed fanaticism of Muslims. The prohibition of Christian missions during the first twenty years of the conquest was not a result of a direct transfer of the imperial state to the colony, or of a linear process of secularization that began in Europe before it spread to Africa. If colonialism was secularized, this developed through the modes of violence exercised against anticolonial uprisings, and then the stabilization of counter-insurrectional war by an institutional mechanism that operated through law.

By arousing the settlers' terror, ideas of fanaticism and the supposed inconvertibility of Muslims worked as so many operators of this secularization. Insurrections like Abd el-Kader's fed the profound uneasiness inhabiting the colonizers' minds and bodies as to the necessarily fragile maintenance of an illegitimate order. They led the colonial state not only to establish itself as a space of secularity, but also to disseminate a racism which, while also deployed against the Jewish populations of Algeria, reduced the category *Muslim* to the status of colonized indigenous subjects. Islam appeared to Europeans as the principal *cause* of the uprisings. The historiography inherited from colonialism has consistently and wrongly reduced these movements' many dimensions to a principle of religious causality, or a static and abstract idea of tradition. From the beginning of colonization, the members of the French army of

---

19   On the theme of Mahdism during the 1849 insurrection in Algeria led by Bu Zian, see Julia Clancy-Smith, *Rebel and Saint*, Berkeley: University of California Press, 1994, pp. 92–124. It is generally considered that after the repression of the insurrection led by the Kabyle chief El-Mokrani (Al-Moqrani) in 1871 the Algerian resistance entered a period of latency, which cleared the way for its 'nationalist' phase in the following century.

Africa and their allies put this historiography's conceptual presupposi-
tions into practice by defining *jihād* not as a concept embodied through
ethical practices, but as the religious foundation of a violence supposedly intrinsic to Islam. Racist discourse could then ascribe fanaticism to
the supposed manifestation of the Arabs' naturally violent character,
inherent to their race.

Once the colonizers came to see the traditional and political organization of Muslim practices as the source of revolt, maintaining the docil-
ity of the colonized called for extinguishing their supposed fanaticism.
By affirming the inconvertibility of Muslims in the present, colonial
administrators declared that the principal goal of the colonization of
North Africa could no longer be to convert the indigenous to Christianity.
This declaration had an impact on colonizing practices, starting with
the suspension of the Roman Church's missionary project and the
construction of a colonial state founded on Napoleonic institutions. A
civilizing mission was then explicitly formulated by Saint-Simonians
such as Barthélemy-Prosper Enfantin and Ismaÿl Urbain, leading to the
idea of converting the indigenous population to civilization. The colonial state thus invented new procedures to interfere in the sphere it
defined as religious, while at the same time promising to respect the
principle of religious liberty and embrace tolerance. Indirectly penetrating indigenous society through the secularity of colonial education, and
more specifically the instruction of women, who were seen as a strategic
point of entry to the secret space of the so-called 'Muslim family', was
typical of this type of colonialism. These approaches operated as a
machine for producing signs, born of the will to master appearances.
Not only did colonial education have to present a religiously neutral face
to Muslims, but secular education also had to appear to Christians as
Christianity realized through profane actions. To understand how the
colonization of Algeria was a gesture of secularizing empire requires an
examination of the conflicts between secular power and Christian institutions, as well as the spaces in which they took place.

The history of conflict between secular and Christian missions begins
with a failure: that of the Roman Church in Algeria. Despite its constant
efforts, it was not able to transform the colonization of Algeria into a
large-scale conversion of indigenous people to Christianity – in a word,
to make colonialism into evangelism. From 1831 on, the Church of
Rome attempted to found a missionary order in Algeria led by an

autonomous vicarate, and so to regain the influence it had lost in the metropole after the Revolution. Conflict broke out between France and Rome, which hoped to exempt the colony from the Concordat and the imperial state's control. The Concordat dictated that clergy were subject to the political authorities, which Rome refused. The French state wanted to preserve its say in appointing bishops and its control over the clergy, which went against the interests of the Catholic Church. These conflicts of sovereignty, which took place between 1831 and 1833, led the imperial state to impose institutions of religious control in Algeria. It would control the Catholic Church and Christian missions, to the detriment of the pope, and refuse the missionary orientation that Rome wanted.[20] The result was a de facto prevention of indigenous conversion to Christianity – a prohibition that characterized the colonization of Algeria. The secularization of the empire was manifested in the way the state controlled and dominated religions in the absence of conversion, or even by virtue of its impossibility.[21]

In 1850, the governor general of Algeria commissioned a report on the practices of conversion that were taking place in the territory despite the prohibition.[22] The report submitted to the minister of war on 5 January 1851 reiterated what would come to constitute a sort of doctrine: missionary activity was harmful to the colonial order, and an obstacle to 'pacification'. It proposed an interpretation of resistance to the conquest according to which Muslims had defended their *religion*, rather than a nationality or a government. They would thus accept colonial domination only by virtue of the promise, more moral than truly juridical, that the first governor general had formulated: respect for their religion.[23] The report's conclusion stated the principle that justified the prohibition of missionary activity until 1852, and its limited and monitored authorization afterwards: any policy of massive conversion or conversion officially supported by the government could not avoid awakening the

---

20 Oissila Saaïdia, *Algérie coloniale: musulmans et chrétiens: le contrôle de l'état (1830–1914)*, Paris: Éditions du CNRS, 2015, p. 111.

21 Ibid.

22 Ibid., pp. 184–5. On the prohibition of missionary activity, see Pierre Vermeren's remarks in *La France en terre d'islam*, Paris: Belin, 2016, p. 57.

23 This expression appears in the 'Extrait de la convention entre la général en chef de l'Armée d'Afrique et le dey d'Alger', cited in *Rapports sur la prise de la ville d'Alger*, Paris: Gautier, 1830, p. 19.

Algerians' resistance and increasing the mobilizational power of Muslim organizations, which colonialism disqualified as fanatical. The primacy of conversion to civilization over conversion to Christianity thus structured the colonial administration. It was not that the colonial state was hostile to missionary activity on principle: in the last instance, reasons of *security* and maintaining order were what justified the strategy of non-conversion to Christianity.[24] They contributed to the development of the theme of the indigenous population's irreducible inconvertibility 'as Muslims', despite their accessibility 'as Arabs'.[25]

This racial theme of inconvertibility had been developed from the end of the eighteenth century with the publication of new biographies of Muhammad that presented him as Arab legislator. 'One is excessively fatigued', wrote the Orientalist Konrad Engelbert Oelsner, translator of Sieyès and an actor in the French Revolution, 'in reading our Christian authors, to see Mohammed treated as an instrument of the Devil and an impostor in every phrase he pronounced or that was addressed to him.'[26] The Orientalist declared, with a disconcerting certainty still shared by some of our contemporaries today, that Muhammad 'did not believe in the visits of the angel, that important piece in his game'.[27] This change of paradigm led to defining Islam as a colonizing civilization, founded on a religious civil code whose practical genius was opposed to the spirituality and love that the Gospel offered.[28]

The racialization of the Muslim as fanatical conqueror flowed from this secular critique of Christian Orientalism. 'Granting nothing to the

24 Saaïdia, *Algérie coloniale*, p. 89.

25 Ibid., p. 86. See also Maurice Landrieux, *Les Trompe-l'oeil de l'islam: la France puissance musulmane*, Paris: P. L. Lhaine, 1913: 'The native, as Arab, would be accessible; as Muslim, he is inveterate.'

26 K. E. Oelsner, *Des Effets de la religion de Mohammed*, Paris: F. Schoell, 1810, p. 15, note 1. The Orientalist thesis of imposture can be found in a classic text by Humphrey Prideaux (1648–1724), an Orientalist and man of the Church of England. Humphrey published his work on Muhammad in 1653 under the title *The True Nature of Imposture Fully Displayed in the Life of Mahomet with a Discourse Annexed, for the Vindicating of Christianity from this Charge; Offered to the Consideration of the Deists of the Present Age*. It was translated into French by Daniel de Larroque in 1699: Humphrey Prideaux, *La Vie de l'imposteur Mahomet*, Paris: chez Jean Musiern, 1699. The text continued to circulate and be read until the end of the eighteenth century. See the key role it still played in Baron d'Holbach, *The Spirit of Judaism*, London, 1770, foreword, p. ii.

27 Oelsner, *Des Effets de la réligion*, p. 15

28 Ibid., p. 32.

senses, but much to the imagination', Islam 'makes the Muslim genius dark and fanatical'. Muslims' character, or their race, appeared as an effect of the religion of Muhammad. 'The moral austerity, ardor to propagate the faith, and warlike enthusiasm that move them were its consequences; more universal even than the religion of Mohammed, a frame more vast even than that of political forms, which assimilated the conquered to the conquerors and joined them in a community of sentiments, opinions, and customs', Oelsner continued. It was thus 'military spirit, much more than art' that 'gave them their conquests', and 'led to the establishment of colonies, whose agricultural spirit was protected by the anti-feudal legislation of the Qur'an'.[29] By expressing this thesis in a volume edited by the Orientalist Sylvestre de Sacy, Oelsner established the warlike and fanatical violence of Islam as a theme in the then-nascent social sciences.[30]

This theme, along with the transformation of Muhammad from Antichrist to legislator, had already been formulated during the Enlightenment, under the pens of Rousseau and Condorcet.[31] By the end of the eighteenth century, it was at the heart of the emerging secularity of European reason. Before it had emboldened Napoleon, inspired by his readings, to imagine himself as the great legislator of the Orient, it established a series of comparisons, which Hegel inherited, between Islam and Robespierre's Terror.[32] These comparisons went to the heart of the revolutionary event itself, and led Robespierre's enemies to compare him to a Muslim fanatic.[33] 'In his *politico-religious* code, Mahomet severely prohibited the *freedom of opinions* such that only his own would prevail', wrote one of Robespierre's enemies.[34] 'Robespierre also scrupulously included in his lists of prohibition anyone who had dared to

---

29   Ibid., p. viii.

30   Oelsner's book demonstrates the growing interest in Islam during the Revolution and through the empire. This interest followed the Egyptian Expedition and the development of academic Orientalism under the aegis of Sylvestre de Sacy. The book's academic recognition helps us understand its considerable success. Its influence can be traced as far as Hegel's lectures on the philosophy of history, Saint-Simon, and Auguste Comte. See Marcelle Adler-Bresse, 'Le Manuscrit Lichtstrahlen d'Oelsner, document inconnu de la révolution française', *Annales Historiques de la Révolution Française* 186, 1966, pp. 556–60.

31   See Oelsner, *Des Effets de la religion*, ch. 1, notes 38 and 39.

32   Ibid., ch. 2.

33   Louis La Vicomterie de Saint Samson, *Les Crimes des empereurs turcs, depuis Osman I jusqu'à Selim IV*, Paris: Bureau des révolutions de Paris, 1794, p. ix.

34   Ibid., p. x. Emphasis added.

publish doubts about the goodness of his character or the infallibility of his principles.'[35] Under the Restoration, this theme was applied to the entire French Revolution, as counter-revolutionary thought accused all the revolutionaries of being fanatical Muslims.[36]

In the wake of these comparisons, Muslims became the incarnation of savage violence, and of the most radical illegitimacy. Hegel formalized this racial representation at the same time that he condemned the Black African to bestial nature and the ahistorical world of childhood.[37] As the Revolution of the Orient, Islam deployed the One as the single goal of all existence. While it thereby liberated the Orient from the caste system, according to Hegel it lost all connection to the world and to the particular. This led Islam to develop a conquering fury that was as ephemeral as it was fanatical. From here, the Muslim became the very type of the warrior whose elevated virtue coexists with a propensity to violence. Hegel's Muslim is the man of destruction engendered by abstract freedom.[38] He incarnates the supposed violence of pure monotheism that the celebrated Orientalist Ernest Renan would attribute to Semites.[39] In the colonial situation, this racial theme gave rise to the idea of North Africans' congenital aggression, which a host of discourses tried to derive from cerebral structure or blood.[40] At the heart of these different racial representations was the idea according to which Islam

---

35   Ibid., pp. xi–xii.

36   Walter Scott, *Vie de Napoléon Buonaparte*, vol. 4, Paris: Imprimerie de Cosson, 1827, pp. 151–2.

37   G. W. H. Hegel, *Philosophy of Mind*, Oxford: Oxford University Press, 1971, p. 44.

38   Hegel, *Philosophie der Weltgeschichte*, Hamburg: Meiner, 1996, pp. 458–9; *Vorlesungen über die Philosophie der Weltgeschichte*, Frankfurt: Suhrkamp, 1986, pp. 428–9.

39   Gil Anidjar, *Semites: Race, Religion, Literature*, Stanford, CA: Stanford University Press, 2006, pp. 28–33. See the commentary on Hegel's texts as the racial invention of the 'Muslim' in Anidjar, *The, Jew, the Arab: A History of the Enemy*, Stanford, CA: Stanford University Press, 2003, pp. 3–39, 128–33. Islam, represented as law, is devoid of all substance and all properly *theological* interest, in comparison to Judaism and Christianity. As we have seen, this Orientalist idea has derived from relations between legislation and prophecy since Rousseau and Oelsner. The idea of Islam's practical genius led to racializing it as a law that confounds the religious and the political. The theme of the Law is biblical and Pauline, even if it was reinvested in a particular manner in the nineteenth century by institutional Orientalism.

40   See Fanon's text, 'From the North African's Criminal Impulsiveness to the War of National Liberation', in *The Wretched of the Earth*, pp. 219–33.

racially constitutes the Muslim's 'dark and fanatical' character. The racialization that took place through the theme of fanaticism implied that Muslims are fundamentally impermeable to all ideas other than Islam.

How did the racial theme of fanaticism lead to the idea of Muslim inconvertibility? On 5 January 1851, General Charon delivered the previously mentioned report to the minister of war. From within what I have been calling a conflict of mission between the colonial administration and Christian missionaries, Charon declared that the Muslims had defended their religion, not a nationality or any government. He noted that they had accepted colonial domination only because the first governor general of Algeria had promised to respect their religion.[41] Charon thus rejected missionary activity as detrimental to the colonial order, to the extent that any large-scale or official policy of conversion could not avoid awakening the Muslims' supposed fanaticism, and so would lead to anticolonial insurrection. The weak success experienced by attempts at conversion could be explained by the too-great theological resemblance between Islam and Christianity. The report deployed a key argument: because the Qur'an had borrowed its practical prescriptions from the Bible, and because it lacked an evangelical spirituality, Muslims could not help but remain unmoved by Christianity. Only a supposed 'improvement' of their intelligence by education could make them sensitive to it; hence the primacy of education over conversion.[42]

The report mobilized the concept of fanaticism to explain the French inability to convert by Muslims' incapacity to be converted. It is not so much that Oelsner's ideas were directly translated into the field, but rather that the field itself and its vicissitudes made them necessary. The terror inspired by the permanent menace of insurrection fed an uneasiness that gave these racial discourses their force of conviction. They established the supposed fanaticism and inconvertibility of Muslims as the constitutive threshold of colonial power. The theme of the inconvertible was one way in which colonial actors represented to themselves the limits of the imperial order, and the force against which they established colonialism as permanent counter-insurgency. It was not only the transfer of French institutions to Algeria that led colonialism to become

---

41   Saaïdia, *Algérie coloniale*, pp. 184–5.
42   Ibid., p. 185.

secularized. It was the refusal of colonization, of which Abd el-Kader's insurrection was only one episode, that forced the government to invent new colonial practices. It was because Muslims imposed themselves on the colonizers as *impossible to convert* that secular education had to be given the task of taking over from conversion to Christianity, once Christian propaganda appeared to be a menace to public order.[43] The indeterminacy of the slogan 'respect for religion', pronounced from the moment that Husayn Dey capitulated in 1830, exceeded the frame of law. By its extra-juridical nature, colonialism after 1830 retrospectively invested this promise in an indissociably strategic and moral way. The reasoning was simple: because colonial authority rested on the moral ascendency engendered by civilizational superiority, it required a strict respect of commitments in order to gain consent. As long as everything had been done to respect Islam, to support missionary activity after first having prohibited it, according to the report, would be a denial of the undertakings of the first twenty years of colonization.[44] Because the preceding governors had not supported the Christian missions, the government would be betraying its word if it supported them now. This inconsistency would destroy the colonizers' credibility in the eyes of Muslims. The colonial government could not become Christian again, since it had won the war as secular. Its secularity was a point of no return. Seeking to authorize missionary activity while, at the same time, limiting it to prevent the potentially disastrous effects of Christian proselytism, the report laid out an alternative strategy that it presented to Christians as a technique of *preparing for conversion*.

This technique consisted first and above all in extinguishing 'fanaticism', so as to end all desire for resistance and create in the colonized subjects not only consent but an interest in colonization. The government exhorted the settlers to publicly display signs of virility, morality, and dignity for the indigenous population to see. This was a calculated strategy of *moral effects* on the Muslim spirit. The primacy of the morality of effects was connected to the primacy of secular education over Christian missions. This education consisted in 'teaching' Muslims to separate politics from religion, which had to occur before any spiritual conquest could be envisioned. 'The priority' was 'to rally' and 'prepare

---

43   Ibid.
44   Ibid., p. 185.

minds and win hearts, before attacking beliefs'. It would be necessary, the government declared, to wait for 'the time when the European population would display more moral mores, drawing the natives closer to the French and making them more accessible to new ideas'; but, also, to wait 'until the light shines within their minds through instruction, so that the natives will understand that the political is independent from the religious'. The state's production of a separation between the political and the religious was posed as the condition sine qua non of the colonial order and of any possible conversion to Christianity, which accordingly had to be temporally deferred. Without a separation of the state from missionary activity, the Muslims could only continue to see 'the missionaries as agents of the authorities'. Without it, the missionaries' 'words' would be seen as 'orders', and 'apostolic approaches would be received as moral violence'.[45]

In the eyes of the empire itself, what the secularization of colonialism implied was nothing other than a will to govern Muslims as colonized subjects, no longer exterminating them as enemies of Christ, in the logic of the Crusades, or converting them to Christianity. In order to justify this strategy of non-conversion, rather than relying directly on the word of God, the government compared religions with one another. It declared that 'the Muslim religion is too close to Christianity for the Muslims to be able to grasp its full superiority'. Because 'the Law of Mahomet took from the Gospel the greatest part of its human prescriptions, it differs only in the spiritual dimension, in the divine faith that perfects the human soul'. And so, 'to appreciate the superiority of Christianity, their intelligence must be developed', something 'that is possible only with time'. Faced with the supposed inconvertibility of the Muslim, the separation of the political and the religious by secular education became a condition sine qua non for any possible conversion to Christianity, which would have to be conjugated in the future tense. The secularization of colonialism appeared as the only possible means to access the interior of indigenous minds and hearts, the only way to break the hostility of the colonized by extinguishing what it deciphered as the religious motivations of their hatred.

The idea of a secularization of Christianity through empire presupposed a definition of Islam as a religion of law that owed its power to the

---

45   Ibid.

Bible, which Muhammad had plundered to write the Qur'an. This act of comparison made it possible to deduce Christianity's superiority: Christianity was a religion of spirit and love, fundamentally distinguished from an essentially practical Islam founded on constraint and legalism, nothing more than a simplified and bastardized Christianity.

The educational mission was thus reaffirmed: only the transformation of their intelligence by secular instruction could prepare Muslim minds to grasp the moral and religious superiority of Christianity. Only such a separation would allow the Christian mission to appear as 'purely religious', and no longer as an instrument of colonial power. The colonial administration's position was clear: the colony must remain a space of secularity, within which a publicly declared principle of separation between the Catholic missions and the state coexisted with rigorously limited missionary activity, controlled and surveilled by the government. The missions must receive no official support, since missionary activity could not be associated with any government participation. Any such association would necessarily make the missions appear to Muslims as a military technique, and French colonialism as Christian colonialism.[46] Colonization thus demanded that the government break with the logic of the Crusades, or at least stage this rupture for the Muslims to see.

At the same time, while missions were strictly prohibited in the rural areas governed by the army, they were permitted in the cities, which were dominated by European settlers. The Christian missions would have to accept the lines that spatially divided the colonized territory into civilian and military zones if they wanted to take their place in a colonial space governed by a secular state. Concerning the 'interior populations', the governor declared that 'the only possible mission is to make them love France, even if this means protecting the Muslim *culte* in order "to put hate and fanaticism to rest" '.[47] The colonial project of 'pacification' implied extinguishing the hatred of the invaders that was constantly expressed through revolts; and Christian missions were reputed to be less and less capable of this, compared with secular education. What remained for the clergy were 'all the good deeds' by which it could stand out and attract orphans and other lost souls. By encouraging these works, the government hoped to tame Muslim subjects through the

---

46   Ibid., pp. 185–6.
47   Ibid., p. 186.

intermediary of missionaries who would content themselves with preparing for a currently impossible conversion.[48] The strategic aim of the acts of charity, authorized and encouraged by the colonial power, was the extinguishing of resistance. This led to the subordination of all missions, secular or religious, to a single task that was presented as absolutely central: education. The moral transformation of Muslims required that the activities of secular schools would be accompanied only by charitable works. In a word, the clergy had to *socialize* its actions. Thus, the colonial government's position was neither purely Christian nor strictly secular, and still less was it anticlerical: it was a compromise position whose role was to make a consensus between the government and the clergy possible within the colonial space.

In the majority, Catholics accommodated the governor general's circumscription of their missions' space of activity. Charitable works, whether scholarly or medical, were provisory instruments of penetration, since they were carried out in anticipation of direct preaching. The period of latency that separated the present from future conversion was the colonial mission's real space of activity. In principle, the secular school prepared for conversion to Christianity; but, in reality, it deferred it to an indeterminate horizon.[49] The missionaries thus had to cease preaching – and turn themselves towards the most vulnerable. Their charitable activities were organized around those two great institutions of control: the school and the hospital. A new model of missionary conversion opposed the efficacy of action to vain dissertations and sermons, and declared that only practices of social charity could go to the root of Muslim resistance and 'fanaticism'.[50] The *realization* of Christian duty in the world should take place not only through preaching or monastic life, but through social and profane activity. The project of secularization shared by the Christian mission and the civilizing mission was imposed as the one and only possible way to convert souls, the one viable technique to produce the consent of subjects defined as *indigènes*.

The imperial order of secularization was the matrix of the opposition between two great strategies of rule, whose conflict was at the heart of the French colonial empire: assimilation and association. The first

---

48 Ibid.
49 Ibid.
50 Quinet, *Le Christianisme et la Révolution*, p. 149.

referred schematically to direct government that tended to destroy indigenous institutions and apply a law identical to that of the metropole. The second could be compared with a form of indirect government that consisted of maintaining the customs of colonized society, relying on traditional chiefs to gain its submission. These two great policies were formulated against each other in the confrontations between the colonial state and indigenous uprisings in Algeria from 1830 to 1870. While, in truth, the two were constantly entangled and overlapping, they corresponded respectively to two camps: the settlers themselves, who supported civil direct administration, and the army, which supported a more indirect government of what would come to be called *tribes*. If settler colonialism triumphed massively after the fall of the Second Empire, the history of the imperial policy of association cannot simply be described as failure. In effect, the military and governmental strategies put to work during the phase of territorial conquest in Algeria did not disappear; they were disseminated in other spaces of the French Empire in Africa. We thus need to determine how the concept of association was constructed, by examining the central role played in the process by an industrial and socialist movement: Saint-Simonianism. This investigation aims to analyse how the project of the terrestrial fulfilment of Christianity and Islam by industry was transposed into a structure of colonial government comparable to apartheid. It was first and foremost in the metropole that the idea of association was formulated in opposition to the established churches, as a 'new religion' that went beyond past religions in order to emancipate man, before it metamorphosed into the project of ruling colonized populations.

The Saint-Simonians, or the industrial reprise of the Egyptian Expedition in Algeria

Once God no longer represented supreme truth, romantics and liberals spoke of what they called religion with a strange certainty.[51] The more they sought to liberate themselves from the spectres of a transcendent God whom they understood as jealous, Oriental, and inhuman – because

---

51 On the spread of an atheological and supra-confessional concept of religion after 1848, see Maurice Agulhon's remarks in *1848 ou L'Apprentissage de la République, 1848–1852*, Paris: Seuil, 1992, p. 23.

incapable of love – the stronger and more imperceptible became their certitude that man creates religion. From then on, religion would signify not the theological rigour of doctrine, but the communitarian bond and mystical impulse proceeding from a universal essence expressed in each tradition. Religion was grasped as the essence of community, and Christianity could then become the announcement of a social and humane community to come. Seeing itself fulfilled in opposition to Christian institutions, the new religion pushed beyond Christianity itself, to embrace all confessions in a higher, post-Christian unity.

The imperial policy of association, invented by Saint-Simonianism between 1830 and 1840, was a product of this mutation in the concept of religion. Saint-Simonian industrialism carried this mutation to its furthest consequences, by making secularization the founding dogma of a new religion. The understanding of religion as having been created by humanity did not lead the Saint-Simonians to reject it. Once the concepts of humanity and religion became interwoven, only a new religion could bring the advent of a new man. And, once religion appeared as an invention of man, it was possible to search for ways to invent new religions.

The dyad of man and religion allowed the Saint-Simonian philosophy of history to articulate a key theme of socialism: the exploitation of man by man, and its coming abolition by the universal association of men. Here, Saint-Simonianism was merely pursuing the definition of universalism articulated by Hegel as the fulfilment of the divine on Earth. Through this, Saint-Simonianism hoped to reunite all the outcasts of society under the direction of engineer-emancipators who would lead the world to liberation brought by industrial progress. In preaching the improvement of the condition of the most hardworking classes, and of women, Saint-Simonians aimed to reconcile humanity's races and religions in a unity that, far from assimilating them, would embrace them all without confounding them. This union by association would take place through a mystical body realized by industry, a new church that would associate the damned of the earth with grand industrial projects conducted by master engineers. As a result, although the doctrine seduced quite a few women and Parisian workers at the start of the 1830s, it spread mainly among young engineers from the École Polytechnique and the École des Mines, making Saint-Simonianism an effective ideological force for French and European industrialism.

The Saint-Simonians saw Enfantin as their messiah. It was during his imprisonment, at the height of the movement's failure and political impotence in Europe, that the most devoted of them decided to leave for what they called the Orient. There they hoped to find the one they called 'the Lady', and to unite her with their messiah, Father Enfantin. After being turned out of Turkey, they went to Egypt to propagate their religion of industry, not by amassing converts but by constructing modern infrastructure. Industrializing projects were acts not only of piety but also of virility. In their view, the West as industrial actor incarnated the masculine principle *par excellence*. The most emblematic of their projects was piercing the Suez isthmus by constructing a canal. They proposed a programme of technical and scientific cooperation to Mehmet Ali, who had succeeded Bonaparte as governor of Egypt.

The sixth session of the *Doctrine* of Saint-Simon narrated the universal history of humanity and proclaimed what was to follow: 'Man has, until today, exploited man. Masters and slaves; patrician and plebeian; lords and serfs; landowners and farmers; idle and worker; here is the progressive history of humanity to our day.'[52] With this dogma, the *Doctrine* cut history literally in two, dividing it at a present marked by revolutionary crisis. The history of the past had been dominated by slavery; the history to come would liberate humanity as a whole. It was thus necessary to prophesy the beginning of a new era, breaking the chain of time that had enslaved men. 'Universal association, that is our future' was the Saint-Simonian rallying cry. The end of the exploitation of man by man had a name: association. Its liberal principle, inherited from the revolutionary period, proclaimed the legitimacy of merit over birth: 'To each according to his ability, to each ability according to its works, here is the new law that replaces that of conquest and birth.' In the empire of this new law, 'man will no longer exploit man', but rather 'man, associated with man, will exploit the world which is given over to his powers'. The end of the exploitation of man by man therefore coincided with the beginning of the exploitation of the *globe* by *industry*. The liberation of the slaves who peopled the earth presupposed the exploitation of the planet by industrial activity.

---

52   Émile Barrault, Armand Bazar, and Prosper Enfantin, *Doctrine de Saint Simon: exposition, première année, 1828–1829*, 3rd edn, Paris: Au Bureau de l'Organisateur, 1831, p. 38.

Nonetheless, the Saint-Simonian conception of industry cannot be reduced to the extraction of fossil riches through mining, although it also has this meaning. Industry was first of all the moral accomplishment of a duty to work that was imposed on the free subject. Industry affirmed that 'idleness is contrary to nature, impious, harmful to all and to your own self', and ordered: 'You will work.' It called on the human race to form 'a peaceful army', and forbade it from saying 'this is impossible'.[53] By doing this, it reduced the enemies of this army, the partisans of blood and heredity, to the status of anthropophages, eaters of men. The reactionaries were 'savages', 'primitives'. This philosophy of liberation was expressed as a history of religions: a progressive science of man whose steps were moments in a continuous religious evolution. The 'general tableau of the development of the human species' that imperial philosophy drew through the history of religions allowed it to stage the discovery of the great law of human progress. This was composed in three stages, symbolized by three cities. The three stages of human religious development were fetishism, polytheism, and mono-theism. The 'three great inaugurating cities of the human race' were Jerusalem, the imperial Rome of the Caesars, and the Rome of the medieval Christian Church. But the people born respectively of Moses or the Old Testament, Numa or the Roman Empire, and Jesus or the New Testament were declared to be dying. The *Doctrine* then presented the questions that would constitute the great problem of the future: Who will be 'the father of the future race'? Where will the new Jerusalem, centre of a fourth historical epoch, be found?

These questions were answered by a philosophy of the history of religions. Because Islam and Christianity were defined as two universal religions in constant conflict, they appeared as anticipated forms of the empire of association. From here, industrialization and the expansion of banking networks to a global scale could be seen as actors of secularization, which took the place and function of the religions of the past. Industry was thus religion because it followed and surpassed the great religions of the past by realizing, here in *this world*, the salvation that they had promised in the other, thereby revealing their secret. A religion whose catechism was secularization through industry, Saint-Simonianism declared that the networking of the world by means of

---

53   Ibid., p. 39.

communication would materially and concretely realize the communion of all men in this world. As a result, we cannot simply understand Saint-Simonianism as a religion of progress whose object was no longer God. The Saint-Simonians intended to found a civilization that would dissolve the old religions, to liberate themselves from the crushing transcendence of a supposedly secret God by affirming the existence of the divine, because they were convinced that it was present in the industrial activities that transformed the globe. While setting up industrial techniques as genuinely religious practices, the Saint-Simonians declared a determined dogma that can be understood as the beating heart of theologies of industrialism: the transformation of the earth by man, the industrial exploitation of the globe, was the extension of divine creation. Through this transformation, the oppressed of all the earth would one day come into association to realize collectively an immense and global social project. Their association would result in a unity that would be nourished by differences of sex, race, and class, rather than suppressing or abolishing them. This socialism that Marx and Engels disqualified as utopian differed from communism only in terms of how the universal association would be brought about. It opposed to the revolution of European workers a universal proletariat governed by an army of engineers, who would supervise humanity's development thanks to their mastery of natural forces.

Saint-Simonianism was thus one of the first organized non-state movements that tried to generalize a theology of liberation that included not only European workers, but also women and the non-European world. It is the epitome of a properly imperial inclusion of difference as such. Outside Europe, the Saint-Simonians wanted to realize global association through a double project: the industrialization of North Africa and the revalorization of the feminine, which they identified with the senses and the Orient. The first country in North Africa where they attempted to realize this project was Egypt. The result was the building of the Suez Canal, intended to materialize the nuptials of an Orient defined as sensual, material, and feminine, and a West understood as rational, spiritual, and virile. The project of secularizing heaven through industry thus led, via the scaffolding of Saint-Simonianism, to the invention of a key theme of racial Orientalism in which Europe is identified with virility and the rest of the world with femininity. This racial sexualization of continents did not counteract paranoiac representations of the super-virility of Black, Arab, or Muslim men. On the contrary: the super-virility of the other became the psychoanalytic manifestation of the instability of colonial domination, the experience of the possibility of a reversal of assigned roles and the capture of White women by non-White men.[54]

By declaring that the new world would be born from the union of the two poles of the globe and the two sexes, Saint-Simonian industrialism expressed the order that European colonialism *wanted to* impose. The Suez Canal played a crucial role in this symbolic economy. It was to be the material sign of a greater union, on a cosmic scale: the union of feminine and masculine, as well as of the earth and man himself. The nuptials of man and the globe through the industrial transformation of the earth were prophesied by industrialism as secularization in action. Colonial Orientalism was thus only one aspect of a general cosmology that declared that the earth should be progressively united with man, alongside and in pace with the progress of industry. The theme of the 'resurrection of the Orient by the West', formulated by Volney's Orientalism, can be read as a formula that anticipated the industrial projects to which French engineers and Egyptian elites would devote themselves in the nineteenth century.[55]

It was in Egypt, over the course of 1833, that the Saint-Simonians first attempted to convert the legacy of the expedition into a policy of indus-trialization. From this point on, imperialism would be based on the idea of systematic exploitation of underground riches on a global scale, rather than on war of conquest. Michel Chevalier's writings from 1830 on, and Enfantin's writings in Algeria, only extended this thinking. By becoming industrial, imperialism identified the reality of secularization (whose order it professed) with techniques of mineral extraction and other modes of dominating nature. It was by subjugating nature that

54 Frantz Fanon, *White Skin, Black Masks*, New York: Grove, 2007, pp. 137, 144; Ann Laura Stoler, *Carnal Knowledge and Imperial Power: Race and the Intimate in Colonial Rule*, Berkeley: University of California Press, 2002, pp. 44, 58–60). Stoler emphasizes the limits of the distinction between the feminine Orient and the masculine West as analysed by Edward Said. My argument on this subject is that this distinction was specific to Saint-Simonianism and was articulated as the extension of a particular philosophy, even if Said reasonably made it a sort of *emblem* of Orientalism.

55 Ghislaine Alleaume, 'L'École polytechnique du Caire et ses élèves: la formation d'une élite technique dans l'Égypte du XIXè siècle', PhD thesis, Lyon: Université de Lyon II, 1993.

industrialism would now try to fulfil religion on Earth. The word 'religion', which the Saint-Simonians themselves used to describe their doctrine, should not fool us, because, in reality, what they professed was nothing but an exit from religion: the imperial secularization that would take place through the world's unification by proliferating steam engines and railways. The Saint-Simonians described the material realization of this order through the alliance of technique and science as 'religion', and identified it with the practice of industry itself. Rather than grasping industrialization as one religion among others, we should understand how industry made religious practice into a singular phenomenon. By wanting to conduct ritual practice through industrial activity rather than in the church, by making industry a church in itself, industrialism gave rise to policies of restructuring Africa and Asia whose consequences went far beyond what we define as religious. Industrialism as theorized by the Saint-Simonians was not a secularization of theology. It was a theology of secularization, a doctrine that chose colonization as the site for the terrestrial accomplishment of salvation, and that understood the divine only as a desire to liberate man from the old religions and illusions of transcendence.

The policy of association was situated at the intersection of the colonial, industrial, and theological. It was thus a modality of the imperial order of secularization. Through its industrial turn in Egypt, Saint-Simonianism became one of the most coherent philosophies of nineteenth-century industry and imperialism. It was not only a systematic theory, but also a decisive actor in the colonial exploitation of the earth and its subsoils through industrial and racial imperialism.[56] But it was in Algeria that Saint-Simonianism participated in creating an effective colonial institution. We thus need to understand how imperialism was constructed through the attempt to associate Islam and Muslims with industry, and how, beyond its apparent failure, it contributed to the colonization of North Africa and the Middle East. A key architect of the becoming-colonial of association in Algeria was Ismaÿl Urbain. While remaining a Saint-Simonian and never abandoning Catholicism, Urbain

---

56 Reynaud-Paligot, *La République raciale*, p. 27. Certain Saint-Simonians, such as Gustave D'Eichthal and Urbain, who was for a time the former's secretary, were members of the Ethnological Society of Paris. Jules Michelet and Victor Schoelcher, who would abolish slavery in the French colonies, were also members.

strategically converted to Islam, crossing the threshold at which Napoleon and his army had faltered during the Egyptian Expedition. Becoming Muslim, for Urbain, meant uniting himself with the colonized and gaining respect through the practice of prayer. His act of conversion was to be a living symbol, the incarnation of the union of Christianity and Islam in a higher unity. Beyond his real motivations or the question of his sincerity, this act was characteristic of the type of imperiality deployed beginning with the Egyptian Expedition. We will follow its trajectories to the heart of the Second Empire's policies in Algeria.

Imperial dignity or the terrestrial redemption of the indigenous

The speech Napoleon III delivered in Algiers in September 1860 drew directly on the Saint-Simonians' colonial project. 'In our hands,' the Emperor declared, 'conquest can be only redemption, and our primary duty is to occupy ourselves with the wellbeing of the three million Arabs the conquest has placed under our domination.' Providence had called the empire 'to expand the benefits of civilization on this earth'. This meant, the emperor continued, 'raising the Arabs to the dignity of free men', and 'extending instruction to them, while also respecting their religion', and thereby improving their existence. 'This is our mission,' the emperor declared, and maintained with all the confident certitude of the colonizer that the Europeans would not fail in Algeria.[57] The secular arm of the imperium would realize the redemption of the indigenous population on this earth, not in heaven. This was because the empire itself was an act of secularization: the terrestrial realization of the salvation of all, in this world, through prosperity. The Second Empire claimed by this to restore the lost dignity of the Arabs, presenting indigenous dignity as a gift from the empire to the colonized subjects it racialized. This imperial concept of dignity cannot be reduced to the abstract principle of undifferentiated humanity. On the contrary, the dignity the empire promised to the Arabs corresponded to the recognition of a particular and irreducible status, and so distanced itself from the abstract

---

57   Cited in Charles-Robert Ageron, 'Peut-on parler d'une politique des "royaumes arabes" de Napoléon III', in M. Morsy, ed., *Les Saint-Simoniens et l'Orient: vers la modernité*, Aix-en-Provence: Édisud, 1990, p. 92.

universalism that would claim to whiten Arabs by making them into Frenchmen.

This model of imperial liberation developed from White abolitionism.[58] From 1830 on, the abolition of slavery and 'Barbary piracy' was a humanitarian motif in the conquest of Algiers.[59] This project was imposed on colonial and racist forces as a demand to break with the old practices of the slave traders. 'Become worthy of being free': this was what the colonial mission now wanted to impose on the indigenous Algerians. Thanks to wage labour, this project promised material improvements to the colonized, the only thing that gave real legitimacy to colonial actions. The task was thus imposed on empire as a duty, the only way to confer a *real* and not illusory dignity to the indigenous subject. Redemption would no longer take place in another world whose invocation had justified slavery on Earth, but terrestrially, through liberation in the here and now. This was, therefore, an act of secularization working through a social rather than a pious charity: Christianity finally fulfilled by the profane actions of the empire.[60]

---

58   Marcel Dorigny, 'Anti esclavagisme, abolitionnisme et abolitions de la fin du XVIIIè aux années 1840', in Pascal Blanchard, Sandrine Lemaire, and Nicolas Bancel, eds, *Culture colonial en France: de la Révolution française à nos jours*, Paris: Éditions du CNRS, 2008, pp. 67–90. Dorigny shows that the Enlightenment abolitionists envisioned a gradual exit from slavery. All the abolitionist societies were gradualist. Considering the liberation of contemporary slaves to be impossible, abolitionists aimed to improve their living and working conditions and help them gradually attain freedom. Abolitionism was thus not anticolonial; on the contrary, it aimed to save existing colonies from disaster and to create new ones. For Enlightenment abolitionists, the goal was to found African colonies in a continent no longer depopulated by the slave trade.

59   Jennifer Sessions, *By Sword and Plow: France and the Conquest of Algeria*, Ithaca, NY: Cornell University Press, 2011, pp. 29–38.

60   Did colonialism secularize the old imperial dignity of the king? In the Middle Ages, according to Kantorowicz, the dignity of the royal function was distinct from the person of the king. It thus referred to a reality that exceeded its representative. See Ernst Kantorowicz, *The King's Two Bodies*, Princeton, NJ: Princeton University Press, 1997, p. 440. Colonial dignity referred neither to divine transcendence, nor even to the dignity of the royal function as such. Nonetheless, dignity served the function of maintaining the moral prestige needed to justify the hierarchy on which the colonial and racial order rested. On the maintenance of dignity as a concern for the colonizer in his relations with the indigenous population, see Emmanuelle Saada, 'The Empire of Law: Dignity, Prestige, and Domination in the "Colonial Situation" ', *French Politics, Culture and Society* 20, no. 2, 2002, pp. 98–120. As Saada shows, the example of the *métis* demonstrates the loss of prestige and dignity that follow from a lack of respect for racial divisions.

It was through respect for their traditions that the 'Arabs' would be transformed into subjects who were autonomous but associated with the empire, which claimed to speak in their name and used their suffering to articulate the idea of redemption on Earth. This was why, in the eyes of the emperor and his Saint-Simonian counsellors, Algeria could not be an 'ordinary' colony or a 'colony properly speaking'.[61] It was to be the 'trial site' for a colonial organization whose productive efficiency was based on the institution of racial segregation.[62] This new imperial order involved a project of secular conversion presented in opposition to conversion to Christianity. One of its inventions was the idea of reforming Islam.

The reform of Islam and conversion to civilization

A theme constantly recirculates in Western public spheres: the need to reform Islam so that it will at last be compatible with the demands of the modern world. It was in Algeria, during the colonial occupation, that this question of the compatibility of Islam and modernity presented itself. None of the actors of French colonization of Algeria considered Islam fundamentally incompatible with French citizenship; but they made acquisition of citizenship subject to the condition of reforming the religion of the indigenous population. Through this, the Second Empire became the architect of what would after 1865 become the *indigénat*.

The discourse around the compatibility of Islam with modernity was constructed in debates between partisans of assimilation and association, between the settlers and the imperial administration. What this debate owes to colonialism cannot be reduced to the choice of one solution or the other. The idea of a modernizing reform of Islam and of Muslims was only one of the empire's faces. What colonialism imposed was this interrogation of Islam's compatibility with modernity, a question whose terms were imposed at the same time as the construction of the racial status of the *indigène* as French non-citizen. Race was positioned as the border of

61   Letter from Emperor Napoleon III to Maréchal Pélissier, 6 February 1863, cited in Ageron, *De 'l'Algérie française' à l'Algérie algérienne*, pp. 135–6.
62   Prosper Enfantin, *Le Colonisation de l'Algérie*, Paris: Bertrand, 1843, pp. 116, 488–95.

citizenship, and racialization was expressed through the language of cultural and religious difference. As the historian Judith Surkis has shown, this was intrinsically linked to the management of polygamy and matrimonial practices that the colonial administration had resolved not to abolish but to regulate by codifying Muslim law.[63] The status of the *indigénat* – the establishment of institutional racism – was the result. If the settlers themselves formulated the idea of an innate incompatibility between Islam and modernity, the thesis of their compatibility was defended by an imperial and liberal faction that claimed to know the path that, in some distant future, would integrate Muslims into imperial citizenship: 'There is nothing irreconcilable between the Muslim natives of Algeria and Frenchmen.'[64]

By articulating the idea of 'converting Muslims to civilization', Urbain became the principal theoretician of the process of secularizing 'native' modes of life in the French Empire. His supposed 'conversion' to Islam could not be separated from this reforming function, which let the empire claim 'Islamic' authority over indigenous Muslims, as Bonaparte did in Egypt and Faidherbe did in Senegal. This act of conversion was meant to facilitate penetration into indigenous society. But it would also contribute to the establishment of the *indigénat*, while making the secularization of Islam into the condition for future emancipation in the form of obtaining French citizenship. By deferring indigenous access to citizenship in the name of a dignity always to come, the Second Empire reduced Islam to a 'native' tradition, and made complete secularization the one condition for access to citizenship. The colonial reconfigurations of Islamic traditional ethics into a sacred family code that belonged to private and customary law were the interior mechanisms of the *indigénat*, which was then transferred to the empire's other colonies. Thus, the dignity of the indigenous subject and his conversion to citizen would result from the abandonment of any political readings of his religion. Urbain explicitly stated the principle of this new secular conversion:

---

63   Judith Surkis, 'Propriété, polygamie et statut personnel en Algérie coloniale, 1830–1873', *Revue d'Histoire du XIXè Siècle* 41, vol. 2, 2010, pp. 27–48. For a comparative and synoptic perspective on the *indigénat* and its relations to French colonial law, see Emmanuelle Saada, 'La Loi, le droit et l'indigène', *Droits* 43, no. 1, 2006, pp. 165–90.

64   Thomas Ismaÿl Urbain, *L'Algérie pour les algériens*, Paris: Michel Lévy Frères, 1861, p. 8.

We are not concerned with the religious question. It would have importance in a Catholic and absolutist state, but under an empire defined by a political constitution that consecrates freedom of conscience, we are concerned for the citizen rather than the believer. It is not a question of knowing whether Muslims will one day become Christian; from a political point of view, this is an idle question that we do not even have the right to raise. We want only to establish that it is not impossible to make them French.[65]

The conversion of the Muslims of Algeria to civilization rather than to Catholicism is presented here as the keystone of the imperial system. An empire of association must break with all practices of evangelization. Becoming a citizen could no longer require conversion to the Catholic religion, because in the metropole Jews and Protestants were recognized as citizens of the imperial state. As Catholicism was no longer the state religion, Muslims had to be able to become legally free and equal French citizens, on the condition that they secularize themselves and reform their reading of the Qur'an. 'Conversion to civilization' was thus nothing other than the reform of a religion imprisoned by its confusion with political and profane life. 'As long as the natives have not made a radical separation between the spiritual and the temporal, as long as their worship and their religious dogmas are in contradiction with our Codes, they cannot be granted the title of French citizens.'[66] From here on, a reform of the reading of the Qur'an would be expressed as the condition for any future equality between Frenchmen and the indigenous population.

The *indigénat* was articulated in Algeria with the expression of a secularization of the reading of the Qu'ran as the horizon for future emancipation: 'The Qur'an must become a purely religious book, without effect on civil legislation.' 'This progress is not impossible', wrote Urbain, since other 'peoples have left theocratic organization and arrayed themselves under a secular government without abdicating their beliefs'.[67] The secularization of Islam would need to coincide with

---

65   Ibid., p. 8. The constitution Urbain is thinking of is the 1830 Charter, which abolished the status of Catholicism as state religion that the Restoration had re-established.

66   Thomas Ismaÿl Urbain, *L'Algérie française: indigènes et immigrants*, Paris: Challamel, 1862, p. 6.

67   Ibid.

the formation of a Franco-Muslim union, brought about through a purely religious reinterpretation of the Qur'an that would be the condition both of promised equality and present inequality. As long as Muslims did not reform themselves in conformity with the empire's demands, Urbain suggested, they excluded themselves from equal citizenship. The empire's constitution of Islam as an indigenous family code was thus the other side of this call to reform. It founded colonial law, creating the *indigène* while prescribing the conditions for its coming abolition, which made it a provisional status. That this personal status could be described as a sort of family code, as I propose, means that the *indigénat* was established at the intersection of two processes: the codification of the Sharia and the tendency to identify its field of application with 'private' familial domesticity.[68]

For the Qur'an to become a purely religious text, and for Muslims to come to dissociate the political and the religious in Islam, Urbain had to assume the existence of a differential progress, which he opposed to abstract universalism. He declared that there was a particular path proper to the indigenous subject, in the image of the imperial dignity Napoleon III had promised the Arabs. The attribution of legal equality thus implied that the empire would search the Muslims' hearts, and that by consultation or surveillance it could come to know their religious interpretations of the Qur'an. The empire distinguished acceptable practices and beliefs from unacceptable ones, following a model of separation of the political and the religious that had never existed anywhere outside of a handful of minds, and which was constantly made obsolete in practice. The theme of the law of God, the idea according to which Islam had confounded the temporal and the religious, was presented as the source of the indigenous religion's theocratic impurity. By transgressing the norm of separation with its supposed theocratic impurity, Islam seemed to have excluded itself from the city, legitimating the racial domination of colonized subjects in the eyes of the empire and its settlers. The Qur'an would have to become a purely religious text if the colonized were to aspire to citizenship and equality with the French. This injunction was *laïque avant la lettre*, if only because it was a

---

68   See Talal Asad, *Formations of the Secular: Christianity, Islam, Modernity*, Stanford, CA: Stanford University Press, 2003, pp. 230–1; Samira Haj, *Reconfiguring Islamic Tradition*, Stanford, CA: Stanford University Press, 2004, pp. 153–87.

command to secularize expressed as a will to reform Islam. Through Urbain, Saint-Simonian socialist and the emperor's principal counsellor on Algerian affairs, the project of reforming Islam was identified with the possible emancipation of indigenous subjects. The imperial party, in opposition to the settlers, thus decreed what Islam had to become if Muslims were to be 'worthy of citizenship'. In this way, the principle of separation between spiritual and temporal, of which the West was supposedly the herald, became a religious norm prescribed by reformist discourse. The *indigène* was the one who remained incapable of converting his religion to civilization. In this figure, race appeared as a legal fabrication embodying the supposed inconvertibility of Muslims.

The primary opponents of indigenous access to equality and citizenship were the European settlers themselves. The imperial state needed to maintain the horizon of a possible emancipation of indigenous subjects, provided that they reform their religion. The injunction to reform Islam, and the practices of policing inconvertible Muslims, spoke to how the French Empire, from the metropole and in opposition to the brutality of the settlers, saw indigenous emancipation as a step towards enfranchisement and citizenship by self-determination. It was thus imperial counsellors, and not the European population in the colonies, who first invented the *indigénat* and indefinitely deferred equality in the name of a reform of Islam that remained always to come. In Algeria, the empire first tried to create its own Islam by setting the cultural conditions for access to political citizenship. The institution of democratic citizenship is structured by this imperial contradiction, which constitutes its interior limits and exclusionary potentials. The definition and then the progressive imposition of a reading of the Qur'an as a 'purely religious' text was in a sense a sign of the singularity of the civilizing mission. In effect, telling Muslims how to read the Qur'an determined the way in which colonized indigenous Muslims were permitted to nourish a hope of being humanized, recognized in their dignity as full members of humanity. Muslims were invited to reconsider the foundations of their own tradition by reducing them to what the imperials called a 'religious text'.[69] It was through the lens of this purely religious reading of the

---

69 That the Qur'an is a religious text is not self-evident. This is not because it is a political or politico-religious text, as colonialism claimed. The Qur'an is, first of all, a recitation. *Iqra*, from which *Qur'an* is derived, means both to recite and to read. The Qur'an may exist as a codex (*mus'haf*), but this mode of existence does not exhaust its

Qur'an that the empire distinguished who was emancipated and thus worthy of becoming a citizen, by measuring how much indigenous subjects' opinions and actions conformed to this norm. Colonial racism was fed by this legal establishment of the religious borders of the secular citizenship that founded its legitimacy. It was only an effect of the governing of tradition as family code, and its reduction to a set of customs. This reconfiguration of tradition was the matrix of colonial racism, which preceded and determined the institution of the *indigénat*. The secularization of power produced by this colonization was based on a struggle with the supposedly inconvertible Muslim. It was thus the spectre of 'Islamic terror', to use Hegel's words, that the colonial establishment of the civilizing mission and the *indigène* was trying to conjure away. The menace represented by the Muslim fanatic was the institutional foundation of race and racism in colonized Algeria.

This colonial domination is incomprehensible if reduced to simple repressive negation. It worked by reinterpreting Islam and tradition. Colonialism did not suppress the juridical aspects of Islam in their entirety. Instead, it led to a reconstruction of Muslim ethico-juridical institutions in the terms of Napoleonic private law, confining them to the space of the family, the sacred, and personal status.[70] Rules of life became 'native customs', reduced to the status of simple articles in a family code. This colonial creation made Algeria a crucial testing zone for what 'Islamic law' would become when subjected to European imperialism. The politics of reform underpinning the legal definition of the *indigénat* were neither a Republican assimilatory policy nor a liberal reformism; they were an imperialism of association that governed Muslim subjects by reconstructing their tradition and ritual practice. The colonial state that reconstructed a legitimist 'Muslim *culte*' was also an empire of custom. The colonial policing of religions was part of French indirect rule. The empire that wanted to construct its own Islam by subjugating Muslim authorities was the same one that governed them through the intermediary of tribal chiefs. Through one single

---

reality as vocal writing. The reduction of the Qur'an to a religious text was thus absurd, and it derived from a decision that was also an ontological impoverishment. In this sense, colonial reason did indeed deploy situated and local ontologies, as functions of its power of naming.

70   Saba Mahmood, *Religious Difference in a Secular Age: A Minority Report*, Princeton, NJ: Princeton University Press, 2015, pp. 119–20.

gesture, it secularized religion, tribalized its power, and racialized the population.

Urbain's trajectory shows that the formation of colonialism in Africa presupposed the articulation of a project of reforming Islam, whose principal actor was the imperial state that had emerged from the French Revolution and the Egyptian Expedition. Converting indigenous people to civilization implied not only converting civilization to their religion, but also translating it into their language and adapting it to their customs. Thus, while Urbain's defence of Muslims' potential access to citizenship set the conditions for that access, he also helped to turn Islam into a family code whose juridical recognition would contribute to creating the status of *indigénat* under the Second Empire. We should now examine the structure of this colonial institution of race, which was based on a delimitation of the religious by a secular state. How was secular citizenship established as a practice of racial exclusion, while constructing the Muslim subject as its religious frontier?

The distribution of equality, or how 'Muslim' became a name for race

Republican history declares that by establishing the *indigénat* the colonial empire betrayed the principles of equality and liberty conveyed by the French Revolution. In this view, the *indigénat* was a juridical monstrosity, the product of a regime of exception.[71] But as the following analysis will show, it was by articulating liberty and equality with the principle of recognizing cultural difference that the *indigénat* was, so to speak, deduced from the principles of 1789. In fact, the imperial state intended to apply the principle of respect for equality and liberty through a legal order adapted for the governing of colonial populations.

'The Muslim is native, the native is Muslim': this was the constitutive equation of the *indigénat*, which was born in Algeria and then transferred to the empire's other colonies. Being 'Muslim' referred to a *legal* status. Someone was said to be *indigène* if they possessed French nationality without enjoying citizenship. After the Crémieux Decree in

---

71   Olivier Le Cour Grandmaison, *De L'indigénat: anatomie d'un 'monstre' juridique, le droit colonial en Algérie et dans l'empire français*, Paris: La Découverte/Zones, 2010.

1870, the indigenous Algerian was a French Muslim but not a citizen. But the juridical invention of the status of *indigène* that the Muslim would finally incarnate after 1870 was a creation of the Second Empire. Jews, implicitly *indigènes* on the same grounds as Muslims up until the Second Empire, were only officially defined as French non-citizens between 1865, the date of the *sénatus-consulte* that established the *indigénat*, and 1870, when Jews were granted citizenship by the Crémieux Decree. As Algeria was part of France, the *indigène* was of French nationality but not a French citizen. Among other texts, the principle was expressed in a ruling delivered on 24 February 1862 by the Imperial Court of Algiers. It began with a principle of integration into the imperial body of the nation: the population of an annexed territory possesses the nationality of the empire that annexes them.[72] But exceptions to the legal status that would normally follow from French nationality were possible when the different populations were not 'homogeneous'. It was the legal production of difference between traditions that determined the *indigénat* as legal mechanism, not the production of racial difference as such: the 'two populations differ profoundly in their religion, mores, the constitution of marriage, and the organization of the family'.[73]

What imperial law recognized and instituted as colonial difference was not only the plurality of religious beliefs. The object of the empire's juridical reason was the set of rules that governed the behaviour and everyday life of the Muslims and Jews of Algeria. Respect for these rules was translated into respect for customs, which contributed to legitimating the *indigénat* in law, in the name of liberal principles. Muslim law was thus reduced to no more than a sort of family law, which made it possible to manage the indigenous population through specific customary law. From here, Algerians' practices and ways of life became readable, signs of a specific personal status protected and regulated by the empire's tolerance, and for this very reason incompatible with citizenship. This procedure gave colonial law the status of exception, and established the inequality of indigenous subjects and French citizens as a legal reality. But what led to this establishment was the liberal empire's apparatus of secularization, not a rejection of the principles of liberty

---

72   Cited in Urbain, *L'Algérie française*, p. 4, note 1.
73   Ibid.

and equality. Such an institution cannot be analysed as a betrayal of these principles, which official Republicanism considers to be the legacy of the Revolution. It was by virtue of the principle of legal equality issued from the Revolution that what would ultimately be formalized under the name *indigénat* was developed. The recognition of Islamic and Israelite 'personal status' was presented by the 1862 ruling as de facto inequality between Europeans and Algerians: a given, that had pre-existed its legal establishment and imposed itself like a fact of nature on a colonial administration that had agreed to respect it.

From here, the empire could present granting citizenship to the *indigène* as a contravention of the principle of legal equality. De facto inequality implied de jure inequality, by virtue of the very principle of equality.

> Considering that by stipulating, for the various fractions of the native population, the maintenance of their religion, their property, their commerce, and their industry, the contracting parties above have by this very fact understood that, while becoming French, the different members of this population are not admitted to the enjoyment of those rights conferred by the quality of French citizenship, and that indeed a great number of the rights conferred by the personal status of Muslim or of native Israelite cannot be reconciled with the duties imposed on French citizens, whose yoke cannot be shaken off except by contravening the principles of public order and even of the penal laws under whose double protection the French nation lives.[74]

In this way, the institution of the *indigénat* was imposed as a colonial contact between French and indigenous parties.

Respect for freedom of religion was also at the heart of the construction of the *indigénat*. It was precisely because the empire claimed to tolerate the religion of its indigenous subjects that it excluded them from citizenship. The colonial reconstruction of the ethico-juridical tradition of Islam as religious and customary law was the institutional matrix of race and of the *indigénat*. This process of racialization by codification followed from imperial secularization: being Muslim no longer

---

74 Decree cited in Urbain, *Algérie française*, p. 5.

referred to a status opposed to the French state's Catholic identity, which thus had to be abrogated by conversion or extermination. On the contrary, Muslims would need to remain culturally and racially 'Muslim' in order to be maintained in the status of the *indigénat*. The reduction of Islamic tradition to custom thus made the racialization of Islam and Muslims possible. Through it, the French Empire created the juridical matrix that initiated the *indigénat*, in the name of equality and freedom, but also of the *dignity of the indigenous*, understood not as individuals but as members of a collectivity.

Mores and customs related to the family and the regulation of marital unions were crucially important in the colonial formation of race. The traditional practices accompanying these mores and customs constituted racial difference. Colonial law's focus on the family and questions of matrimony can be explained by the fact that the secularization of the empire took place at the intersection of sex, race, and religion. As a process of transforming the Sharia into family law, the secularization deployed by the state constituted a new colonial domesticity, within which it tended to confine the indigenous people it racialized. The violent domestication of racialized bodies instituted by the *indigénat* was only a means of governing a Muslim sexuality defined by colonial discourses as polygamous, religious, and oppressive.[75]

Indigenous sexuality and religion were entwined fields, from the point of view of a colonial administration that constantly described sex in terms of Islam and Islam in terms of sex. Islam meant much more than a simple religion in the eyes of imperial rationality. It triggered the colonial affects that racist discourse constantly if reluctantly betrays.[76] Islam was not racialized as a system of belief but, as we have seen, as a set of matrimonial practices, at the centre of which was polygamy. White French men who conquered and then administered Algeria felt polygamy to be a sexual privilege, which inspired a series of contradictory affects in them. It engendered a profound sexual rivalry which led them, between fantasies of the harem and the reality of rape, to desire symbolic

---

75   After the 1880s, the *indigénat* gave rise to a specific penal regime inaccurately called the *Code de l'indigénat*.

76   On the relations between sex and race in the colonies, see Stoler's pioneering work *Carnal Knowledge and Imperial Power*. On secularism and sexuality, see Joan Scott, *Sex and Secularism*, Princeton, NJ: Princeton University Press, 2018.

or real possession of the bodies of indigenous women.[77] But such extreme practices were marginal. The authorities attempted, on the contrary, to maintain order by respecting racial separation. Immediately after the conquest, the 1830 text of the capitulation of Algiers thus promised to respect the religion of the indigenous population as well as *their women*. This double mention inaugurated the articulation between governing of sex and governing of religion, the node around which the *indigénat* would be legally constituted more than thirty years later.[78]

How the secularization of Islamic law contributed to the expropriation of indigenous lands

The legal establishment of the *indigénat* took place under a regime opposed by the settlers themselves, and whose policy of restricting settler colonization would be defeated after the fall of the regime in 1870. The colonial project, whose first step was racial segregation and respect for indigenous property and customs, failed under pressure from the settlers and their institutional supporters. But it determined the legal establishment of what would remain at the centre of colonial order until the anticolonial war of liberation: the personal status of the so-called Muslim *indigène*. In a word, despite its defeat, the military policy of association continued to structure the policy of assimilation constructed in opposition to it from top to bottom. Indirect government made direct colonial government possible, and without it the latter would not have been able to express race as the constitutive limit of assimilation to France and Europe.

If direct colonialism was the dominant policy applied to Islam, the constitution of a council of jurisprudence in 1858, which substantiated the idea of transforming Islam from inside, belonged to a French

---

77   Judith Surkis, *Sex, Law, and Sovereignty in French Algeria, 1830–1930*, Ithaca, NY: Cornell University Press, 2019, pp. 1–11.

78   The *sénatus-consulte* of 1865 is generally cited as the text that definitively inaugurated the *indigénat* in colonial Algeria, despite a series of preparatory texts, particularly in 1862 and 1863. See Surkis, *Sex, Law, and Sovereignty*, p. 95. The 1865 text attempted to fill a gap and clarify an ambiguity concerning the status of Muslims and Jews that had been present since 1830. According to Surkis, after French citizenship was granted to the colonists in 1848, the year Algeria was divided into *départements* and integrated into French territory, the question of the indigenous population's nationality had remained suspended.

tradition of indirect government. Maréchal Vaillant was one of the cata-
lysts of this politics of adapting Islamic *institutions* to 'French ends', as
opposed to destroying them pure and simple.[79] The settlers and their
supporters, for their part, called for the end of all Muslim law, which led
to the dissolution of the council in 1875, two years after the Warnier
Law marked the victory of settler colonialism through the quasi-total
expropriation of the indigenous population. Despite this dissolution,
and the European settlers' call to destroy all remnants of Islamic law, no
destruction of personal status took place, and thus no complete assimilation. While the official rationale was tolerance, in reality assimilation
would have meant legal equality, and it thus menaced the colonial order.
This situation, which exemplified the French impasse in Algeria, was an
effect of association at the very heart of assimilation, the active trace of
the policies of indirect government at the heart of the civil administration. The result of this entanglement was an apartheid effect, the sovereignty of the double-headed Leviathan.

What secularization produced in colonial space can be seen in the drive
to construct a Muslim *culte* along with the transformation of the Muslim
legal system into a confessional law exclusively applied to Muslims.
Through this, the fact of being Muslim became the foundation of a *personal
status* that determined and named race. What a culturalist approach would
define as Islam or religion should thus be understood instead as a set of
social formations deriving from the manifestation of processes of secularization in the transformation of religious and traditional institutions. The
colonial state's institutional racism was one face of this imperiality of secularization. Racial designations derived from its construction of the
supposed limits of what the colonial state named and defined as *religion*.
The state surveilled, suspected, and deciphered the bodies it governed as so
many *signs* of an essence it named *race*. Processes of racialization such as
Islamophobia or antisemitism, which function by assigning individuals to
their supposed religion, are decisive manifestations of the theologico-
political, and thus properly imperial, dimension of racism.

The state's construction of the borders of the religious and non-
religious determined the policies of expropriation put to work in Algeria.
These left the indigenous population with only usufruct rights and

79   Allan Christelow, *Muslim Law Courts and the French Colonial State in Algeria*,
Princeton, NJ: Princeton University Press, 1985, pp. 110, 130–7.

legally created *tribal* and collective property, in a sort of state socialism that had been developed through the Saint-Simonian concept of association since 1847. Thus, the juridical reconstruction of Islam as indigenous religion and personal status determined the institutional mechanisms that led to the institution of apartheid. It was the matrix not so much of race as such, but rather of its deployment by the state, and its other face: the simultaneous invention and government of the *tribe*. Imperial secularization led not only to state racism but also to a policy of segregation based on the creation of tribalism and ethnic divisions that had not existed before colonialism. The imperial reconfiguration of Islamic tradition was the corollary of the birth of apartheid in North Africa.

Apartheid in North Africa

Up to at least 1870, French colonialism in Algeria oscillated between two concurrent strategies: the massive expropriation of land through the generalization of private property, and the legal recognition of indigenous collective property by imperial law. That is to say, it oscillated between two modes of subjugating the Muslims of Algeria by destroying their networks of solidarity and capacity to organize insurrections. The second approach, formulated by the Saint-Simonians, was the matrix for the French Empire's colonial policy of association. As opposed to assimilation, association can be provisionally defined as a form of indirect rule. It was constructed during the armed repression of native uprisings, and formulated by Urbain and Napoleon III in the 1860s. Despite its apparent failure, its legacy would persist in the *indigénat*, as well as in Algeria's Saharan regions. This is why the colonization of Algeria by military power cannot be reduced to the history of its supposed assimilation by France. Not only was this assimilation never total, it was itself a founding myth of French colonialism, which any critical analysis should put in question. The process of military colonization in Algeria contributed to the invention of techniques of rule that did not disappear when the policy of massive expropriation was adopted and the military regime was replaced by a civilian regime. We should thus see the policies of the 'Arab Kingdom' (Royaume Arabe) as the expression of a project of racial segregation.[80] This was no Franco-Muslim entente, a tolerant liberalism that unfortunately failed due to the European settlers' lack of refinement; rather, the Royaume Arabe was fragmented and disseminated after the fall of the Second Empire across the rest of North Africa, where it took the form of the protectorate. By beginning from this margin of colonial history, this utopia defeated by settler colonialism, we can describe the anatomy of the colonial state, the nature of its sovereignty and of its racism. The heart of this imperial organism, the *indigénat*, was not a project fomented by the expropriating settlers and their allies. Its genesis can be found in a series of misses, non-events, and failures by the Saint-Simonian movement and the policy of the Royaume Arabe.[81] The doctrine of *association* as it was invented in Algeria followed a singular trajectory, interrupted in 1870 and then reactivated and disseminated by so-called late colonialism in Africa. My contribution to the debate on the origins of the *indigénat* derives from the reconceptualization of the imperial misses in the settler colony. In my view, the *indigénat* was the trace left by colonial Saint-Simonianism, despite or perhaps by virtue of its failure, at the heart of a colonial system dominated by the expropriation and settler colonialism the Saint-Simonians had sought to limit. Understanding the history of the state that supported this settler colonialism on its margins by examining the actors who tried to develop a different type of colonialism will allow us to understand fully the birth and structure of the *indigénat*. The centre of the empire can be illuminated from the margins that its development would ultimately doom to failure. One of these margins, with one such 'negative history', was the theory of the perfectibility of the *indigène*.[82]

---

80 The Royaume Arabe is an ambiguous notion referring to the model that Napoleon III wanted to implement in Algeria. Sometimes interpreted as the will on the part of Algeria's enemies to designate Abd el-Kader sovereign of Algeria, it in fact referred to a system of *apartheid*, where the customs of the native tribes would be *protected* (separated) and the settlers thereby contained.

81 On this kind of historicity, see Ann Laura Stoler, *Along the Archival Grain: Epistemic Anxieties and Colonial Common Sense* (Princeton, NJ: Princeton University Press, 2009), pp. 2–4, 105–10. Saint-Simonianism can be seen as a set of archives with their own historicity, irreducible to the history of French colonialism or to the colonial archive.

82 Ibid., pp. 106–8.

The theory of racial development, or how imperial racism defined the indigène as a perfectible being

> Can the Muslim be perfected? A singular question! If progress is the
> law of humanity, could we claim that any race, people, or agglomera-
> tion of living beings, would by their beliefs be placed outside of the
> conditions of the general law? Evidently, the beautiful theories of
> modern philosophy are not applicable only to Frenchmen, Europeans,
> and Christians. Arabs, Orientals, and Muslims must be subject to the
> same law; like us, they are perfectible and they progress.[83]

In this text, Urbain employed a theme common to colonial racisms: the
perfectibility of the indigenous subject. It has been deployed in various
places, each time in order to contest the assimilationist project that aims
to make non-White indigenous persons into false Europeans. In the
Dutch colonies in South Africa, this discourse on indigenous perfectibility was articulated with a critique of abstract universalism and of an
emancipation of colonized races that would lead to an impossible repli-
cation of the European model in the colonies.[84] The discreet but insist-
ent centrality of indigenous perfectibility shows that opposition between
assimilationist racism, founded on a valorization of so-called métissage,
and a racism of pure exclusion, founded on blood purity, is simplistic.
The persistence of this discourse attests, to the contrary, that colonial
racism never functioned as an abstract and Eurocentric universalism,
but instead deployed a concept of race understood as a disposition to
evolve in a particular, and irreducible, way. A reading of Urbain's text
will help us to develop this hypothesis.

In formulating the theme of indigenous perfectibility, Urbain offered
a theory of the evolution of human races to respond to the claim that
Arabs could not evolve, and that Islam could not be reformed or cease
to be a theocratic religion. Nature and history, in concert, showed that

---

83 Urbain, L'Algérie pour les algériens, p. 9.

84 'We do not want to create imitation Europeans, we just need perfected natives';
AR, KV 28 March 1874, no, 47M, archive cited in Stoler, Along the Archival Grain, p. 105.
The phrase refers to what the colonial administrators in the Dutch Empire called
Inlandsche kinderen, 'native children' born from unions between European men and
indigenous women. It recalls a later but much more famous discourse: that of General
Jan Smuts, one of the founders of the Apartheid system in South Africa.

the differential progress of the races was the great law of humanity. The association of European and indigenous that he aimed for did not postulate that the White race was essentially superior to the Black or Arab race, but, rather, that each community ought to work and evolve in conformity to its race, and should not be betrayed or impoverished by violent assimilation. Urbain's racism was not biological. He defined race as the social and cultural production of an essence that was transformable and perfectible. Races could progress, and their essences could transform. Colonial racism, therefore, was not an abstract universalism, and its theoretician – himself originally from a French colony – declared, against any abstract application of the principle of progress, that Arabs and Muslims evolved in a way that was irreducibly specific. 'The Muslim is perfectible' because he is human; 'but for him perfection will not be pursued by the same paths as for us'.[85] In expressing this theory of perfectibility as the differential development of human races, this imperial counsellor did not dehumanize Muslims; he proscribed how they should evolve and convert to civilization, without needing to be assimilated to Whites or Christians. His strategy consisted in tracing multiple pathways of progress, diverse ways in which the aptitudes of each communitarian group could become productive.

The secularization of Islam was thus the programme of evolution specific to the 'Oriental races', Arab or Berber, and appeared as the condition for the becoming-citizen of the Muslim subject that it humanized. This double project of the secularization of Islamic tradition and the association of the races was the beating heart of the Second Empire's policies in Algeria. In colonial Algeria, the secularization of Islam was expressed as the other side of a project of segregation in Africa. According to Urbain and the emperor, there was indeed a solution to the imperial integration of Muslims into France; but the racialization of Islam, its codification by colonial law, and the constitution of the tribe as administrative entity were the necessary first steps. The call to reform Islam in order to convert the indigenous population to 'civilization' was a crucial aspect of the model of racial segregation. It constituted the formula of 'perfectibility', which was nothing but an apartheid project whose supposed aim was to create an improved Muslim subject. Far from any abstract universalism or assimilation, this call sketched out a

---

85   Urbain, *L'Algérie pour les algériens*, p. 13.

gesture of exclusion by inclusion, the inclusion of indigenous subjects into the body of the empire. It wove the threads that dialectically connected assimilation and association as two faces of the empire and of its racism.[86] Its strategy organized the mobilization of the other through a colonial mechanism of totalizing rule.

In articulating his theory of the perfectibility of Algerian Muslims, Urbain did not use a discourse founded on the supremacy of the White race. As witnessed by his writings and correspondence, he himself did not identify as White.[87] During his voyage to Egypt, he declared in Suez on 18 February 1834:

> O you, all you *martyrs of labour, black, slaves, proletarians of all nations*, of all colours, you who are the *reprobates of this world*, do you know that among men there is an apostle who works for your glory and happiness? You do not know me, you do not know where I come from, or what I want . . . I am from the torrid Americas, I have black blood in my veins.[88]

This extraordinary declaration racialized the idea of the liberation of the proletariat and transported it outside of Europe, and beyond class. Expressed in the name of the wretched of the earth, it declared that the goal of industry was the redemption of slaves and the excluded. Urbain thus set himself up as living proof of the perfectibility of the indigenous subject, and described the trajectory of a being who, although he participated in the colonial project, never renounced his Black heritage. He posited the necessity of the development of races subjected to colonialism as an emancipation that could never be reduced to becoming European. The colonial model that flowed from this was the spatial

---

86   It is worth noting that Raymond Betts, in his classic study of French colonial theory, mentions no Saint-Simonians. See Raymond F. Betts, *Assimilation and Association in French Colonial Theory, 1890–1914*, New York: Columbia University Press, 1960.

87   In a poem composed in Egypt in January 1834 titled 'Au Miroir du père' (In the Father's Mirror), Urbain identified himself as 'of black and enslaved race'. See Anne Levallois, *Les Écrits autobiographiques d'Ismaÿl Urbain: homme de couleur, saint-simonien et musulman (1812–1884)*, Paris: Maisonneuve et Larose, 2004, p. 28; Gustave D'Eichthal and Ismaÿl Urbain, *Lettres sur la race noire et la race blanche*, Paris, 1839, p. 30.

88   Poems, Bibliothèque de l'Arsenal, Fonds Eichthal, Ms 13735, p. 58.

separation of the races that Fanon would describe at the beginning of
The Wretched of the Earth.[89] Its history goes back to the beginnings of
the colonization of Algeria.

The manufacture of race, or the spatial segregation of Muslims

The principle of 'decentralized despotism', which the model of association developed and put at the heart of a doubled colonial sovereignty,
was not the exclusive property of the Saint-Simonians. It was articulated
beginning in the 1830s by the French administrators of Algiers, who
declared the imperative of governing tribal populations in the country's
interior through the intermediary of their chiefs.[90] If the system of
protectorate as formulated by a certain Cerfberr was deemed impossible, it sketched the outlines of a politics of strategic fragmentation of
colonial government, in order to govern the interior tribes.[91] A letter
from Guizot to Bugeaud, the general charged with combatting the insurrection led by Abd el-Kader, formalized this solution in 1841. The July
Monarchy's minister of foreign affairs offered as the only possible organization for the future colony of North Africa a 'clear, rigorous delimitation between two territories: one directly occupied by France and given
to European settlers, the other ruled indirectly in the name of France
and left to the Arabs'.[92] In this letter, the broad strokes of what would
become a policy of segregation were presented by the French state. This
doctrine of spatial distribution and the separation of racialized populations did not remain merely on paper. Far from being a simple and
tacitly guarded suggestion, it was effectively put into action by Bugeaud
and the military authorities, before being taken up and theorized by
Saint-Simonianism under the name of association.[93]

---

89   Fanon, *The Wretched of the Earth*, p. 15. Fanon notes that 'apartheid [is] but one
method of compartmentalizing the colonial world'.

90   Léon Blondel, *Aperçu sur la situation politique, commerciale et industrielle
des possessions françaises dans le Nord de l'Afrique au commencement de 1836*, Paris:
Imprimerie Royale, May 1836, p. 42; Léon Blondel, *Nouvel aperçu sur l'Algérie:
trois nécessités en Afrique: conserver, pacifier, coloniser*, Paris: Delaunay, 1838, pp. vii,
143–58.

91   Auguste-Édouard Cerfberr, *Du Gouvernement d'Alger*, Paris: Dumont, 1834, p. 5.

92   Pierre-François Guizot, *Mémoires pour servir à l'histoire de mon temps*, vol. VI,
Paris: Michel Lévy Frères, 1864, p. 388.

93   Enfantin, *Colonisation de l'Algérie*, p. 480.

Enfantin intended this policy to be extended not only to the country-side but to the cities as well. Systematizing the policy of spatial segregation used by military colonization, he declared that the indigenous Muslims should be placed 'beside us but not mixed with us', 'close to us but not under us, as they are in the cities, where we physically and morally crush them, and they harm and bother us'.[94] Thus, he continued, 'the Moorish population should be the population base of native villages that we will establish beside our civil colonies; that is to say on the outer line of the enclosing trench'.[95] Here this Saint-Simonian formulated not only the principle of the indigenous ghetto, but also a strategy of indirect government that ran counter to the faction of French administrators who, in his opinion, had been seduced by 'the idea of governing the Muslims, of administrating them directly, under their eyes'. Enfantin saw this policy of direct government as related to interventionism in the religious sphere. In effect, it would lead to 'becoming their interior police', and 'even meddling in their mosques and religious festivals'. 'This would be fine if we were aiming to make ourselves Muslims, but it is not the way to make the Muslims good friends of the French.'[96] Here, again, it was the need to deploy a colonialism founded on moral respect and freedom of religion that demanded indirect government, and made association the only technique adequate for ruling Muslim subjects. Again, this policy did not remain mere words. It contributed to *spatially* organizing the colonial state's rule over Algerian land, and to articulating a programme of governing the so-called tribes, formalized under the name of association.

How the colonial domestication of Islam led to a decentralized government of tribes

The model of segregation and government that the Saint-Simonians called *association* was one effect of the supposed inconvertibility of the colonial subject. The model of governing 'Arab tribes' by controlling their chiefs was first formulated as a way to construct a mechanism of rule that would make armed violence superfluous by operating through

94   Ibid., p. 481.
95   Ibid., p. 482.
96   Ibid., p. 480.

subtler and more pacifying institutional means. The matrix of this solution was a counter-insurrectional strategy born during the war against
Abd el-Kader and systematized after his surrender. The colonial policy
of association as conceived by Urbain developed from a double refusal.
The maintenance of tribal leaders' authority was set back to back with
their pure and simple destruction.[97] The future colonial state ought to
generalize neither indirect nor direct government, but to deploy both as
the two faces of Leviathan, two aspects of the doubling of the state's
institutional mechanisms. This model of colonial government functioned by fragmenting the networks of solidarity and unity that ethnographers would call tribes. The function of the policy of association was
thus to destroy any means of power to unify these groups, to unite
communities through insurrectional action.

Urbain interpreted this unification as an effect of Islam, understood
as a causal factor but also an archaic and still-religious form of patriot-
ism and national sentiment. These 'peoples, having no nationality, take
up the name of *Allah* as the only possible rallying cry whenever danger
is shared and imminent', he wrote. Islam appeared as a religious unity
substituting for the still-embryonic nation. 'Faith and homeland share
the same banner' only because 'religion is the sole bond that can unite
the tribes'.[98] Abd el-Kader's *jihād*, incorrectly translated as 'holy war',
appeared to the colonizers as an effect of the confusion of the political
and religious that, according to Urbain, characterized Islam. The
colonial state should therefore act in a secularizing and counter-
insurrectional way, inserting itself between the tribes in order to divide
them. It would literally take religion's place by fulfilling its supposed
function. This would subject the tribes to a single and unique power
without encouraging them to unite, and submit them to the central
power of the colonial state the better to fragment them: in sum, it would
make them dependent on a single and sovereign power that functioned
to create disunity between tribes. This strategy of pacification operated
through an always provisory and limited decentralization of colonial

---

97   Ismaÿl Urbain, *Algérie. Du gouvernement des tribus. Chrétiens et Musulmans,
Français et Algériens*, Paris: Just Rouvier, 1848, p. 27: 'It does not follow from this that we
ought to destroy the Arab military or religious aristocracy; it is a question only of
causing order and justice to triumph, and taking a place above the aristocracy in the
hierarchy of power.'

98   Ibid., p. 23.

power, which was meant to rule the tribes through the intermediary of their chiefs.

To dissolve the matrix of insurrection would require the empire to secularize by distancing itself from all religious causes or missions, and in the same movement to decentralize. From 1848 on, Urbain maintained that the 'native' populations should be convinced at all costs that France pursued no religious interests.[99] Strict policing should be exercised against those whom Urbain considered fanatics, and they must, at all costs, be dissuaded from taking up arms. Recruiting faithful indigenous agents who could act as links in the colonial chain was part of this politics of counter-insurrection and secularization. The *marabouts* would be put under surveillance, 'enriching them with favours and presents, while pushing them towards the exclusively religious life from which Abd el-Kader tried to bring them out to mingle in the world of politics'. Indigenous life would be secularized through tribal government, and indigenous subjects maintained in purely religious life. A politics of secularization that announced its tolerance towards religion was thus at the heart of the racial segregation that the colonial state established under the name of the *indigénat*.

The 'tribe', Urbain declared in the 1840s, was the most important 'social element' in the Algerian society France was to colonize. To found a colonial order in Algeria not by war but by the supposedly peaceful mechanism of stable institutions implied 'administratively constituting the tribe', 'connecting it to a common centre', and 'engaging its interests' to 'make it contribute to maintaining order'.[100] For this reason, according to Urbain and the Saint-Simonians in Algeria, governing indigenous society required creating new institutions, rather than importing the ones already in place in the metropole. The colonial institution should impose a legal system through which tribes would be administratively recognized and governed. Linking the tribes to a common centre implied that government would be able to act throughout the colony by means of collaboration in colonization. Urbain criticized models based on pure and simple expropriation and the reform of indigenous customs, because these implied a permanent colonial war that, in the colonizers' own opinion, would destabilize colonization and make its rule

---

99   Ibid., p. 24.
100   Ibid., p. 12.

precarious: 'Upending the natives' customs and usages, removing them from their territory, pushing them into the southern regions where all social improvement will be more difficult; all this is to prepare major obstacles for the future, and in some sense to perpetuate the precarious character of our rule.'[101] This strategy of colonization was a criticism of the policy of massive European immigration. Urbain aimed to make Algeria something other than a settler colony. He hoped to assimilate not only the Kabyle tribes to the colonial regime; in his opinion, it was the 'Arab population' that should be admitted 'as one element of our projects of colonization.'[102] But neither was his colonial model reducible to a simple generalization of indirect rule. If he maintained that most indigenous people would obey only their own chiefs, he also said the colonial army had 'an unfortunate eagerness to delegate' authority 'to native chiefs, under the pretext of giving their full attention to developing colonization.'[103] By declaring that more was needed than simple reliance on the chiefs of the Arab tribes, he questioned the practice of the first military leaders in Algeria. It was necessary to 'administer ourselves', he wrote, and so to guarantee 'the settlers' security'.[104] But his criticism of indirect government as applied by the army did not lead him to support a model of direct government. It rather led him to invent a mixed model, one that could not be clearly separated into direct and indirect aspects.

Urbain brought a decisive metamorphosis to the concept of association, and participated in its translation to the colonial situation. The policy of the empire of association was presented as a productive employment of races according to their own particular capacities, in the interests of a colony that supposedly belonged to all of them. The Arabs should be associated with agricultural work, not exterminated, or pushed towards the desert. 'There remain noble families, for whom the time has come for their despotic preponderance to be reduced, and for them to be made into administrators within the hierarchy.' For this reason, Urbain declared, indirect government should be established in the majority Muslim regions. In these areas, the colony's political

---

101 Ibid., pp. 6–7.
102 Ibid., p. 7.
103 Ibid., p. 9.
104 Ibid.

interests 'did not demand the exercise of direct authority'; and it 'would be wiser to delegate a portion of power to the natives'.[105]

The colonial state in Africa had a double face, a power that racialized the indigenous in spaces dominated by European civil society, and tribalized them in the rural regions. Its theory and still experimental and fragmentary practice were debuted in Algeria during the period of military government between 1830 and 1870. It may be objected that during this period direct and indirect government were merely debated as two possible but distinct modalities of colonial power. Still, as early as the 1840s, Urbain had conceived colonial association as a synthesis of these two modes of government. What was needed was neither indirect nor direct government, he wrote, but an association of the two within a single colonial power. As colonization was the association of direct and indirect powers, the rationality that governed it should make mutual and differentiated use of the two. 'A tribe that can be assimilated, whether to a commune or canton, should be commanded by natives; but any authority charged with centralization and the surveillance of several *kaïds* should be French.'[106] According to this policy, colonial organs of centralization would be governed by Frenchmen, while those that performed a decentralization of power would administratively recognize the tribes and leave the task of governing to indigenous chiefs. If the tribes were ruled by the authority of their associated chiefs, French agents would need only to 'look after the interests of our rule and direct the administration of the tribes'. According to Urbain, the creation of the *Bureaux Arabes* had 'begun to realize this improvement' – that is, the relative decentralization of colonial power between the many tribes with the support of *kaïds*, *marabouts*, and chiefs.[107]

The coloniality of power consisted in pacification through the use of mixed government, and preparing the tribes for a future contribution to the general progress and prosperity of the empire. By first recognizing tribes as administrative entities, Urbain declared, the colonial state would one day be able to convert these groupings into towns or villages.[108] Indigenous governance thus would pass through different steps

---

105   Ibid., p. 19.
106   Ibid., p. 27.
107   Ibid., p. 22.
108   Ibid., pp. 25–6.

towards a progressive 'harmonization' of the races. In Urbain's eyes, the 'Muslim', the 'Oriental', and the 'Arab' were races produced by social institutions. For this reason, the races were said to be perfectible and subject to the law of historical progress. They could be transformed only by respecting their particular, irreducible, and specific laws of development. Such was the racial foundation of the imperial order of association, which took the form of a doubling of the colonial state, the beating heart of the stated policy of the Royaume Arabe.

The industry of race in agricultural colonization

If the settler colonization that unfolded in Algeria on a massive scale after the fall of the Second Empire was founded on the expropriation of indigenous lands, in reality the policies supported by the Saint-Simonians that codified forms of indigenous property had been crucial preparation for this process.[109] From 1851, the state was nakedly established as proprietor of *aarch* lands – indigenous collective lands, which the indigenous population would from then on enjoy only with usufruct rights. The dynamic of expropriation that triumphed definitively with the Warnier Law in 1873 was already at work, by virtue of the necessity, in order to establish colonial agrarian capitalism, of creating a proletariat by dispossessing Algerians.[110]

It is in no way surprising that the conflict between the European settlers and the empire was structured around the question of private property and expropriation, a key element that underpinned the activities of colonial law and relativized the ideological opposition between *assimilation* and *association*. But any analysis that simply reduces the violence of law to that of capitalism or its initial accumulation will leave

109   It is often claimed that the *sénatus-consulte* of 1865, by wanting to preserve and protect native lands, actually contributed to facilitating their expropriation. The opposition between indigenophiles and settlers was thus above all discursive, even if it was reflected in the legal field and determined the process of writing colonial law.

110   Mahfoud Bennoune, 'The Origin of the Algerian Proletariat', *Dialectical Anthropology* 1, no. 3, 1976, pp. 201–44. Note that from 1851 on the French state distinguished collective indigenous property, *aarch* lands, from land designated as *melk*, which it defined as individually owned. Auguste Warnier, it should be noted, was himself a former Saint-Simonian. The conflict between settlers and imperialists was also overdetermined by the religious, sectarian, and secular movement of Saint-Simonianism, and its fragmentation in Algeria.

aside the question of imperial secularization: the construction of borders between religion and politics that opposed a *religious* Islam to a *political* Islam. An anonymous response to Urbain by a group of settlers reformulated the idea of the necessary separation of the political and the religious, which Urbain himself had posed as a condition for Muslims becoming citizens. It was necessary 'only to cling to the separation of spiritual and temporal in the Qur'an', the settlers insisted; 'property must be subject to the Napoleonic Code', and they assured that 'no Arab would refuse this'.[111] Rather than referring the separation of temporal and spiritual to the future, giving the indigenous population time to appropriate the principle for themselves, the separation should be immediately applied. Since the colonial state in Algeria was to be merely an extension of the French state – since Algeria was France – the same right of property should be applied. The argument was clear: because the Qur'an could not be recognized by a secular state as a text with authority over the temporal, it could not regulate property, which belongs precisely to what is not and cannot be religious. French property law should thus apply to Algeria, generalizing private property by the expropriation of indigenous lands. This additional project of secularization served to legitimize expropriation and settler colonialism. Secularizing the law meant expropriating the indigenous population. But the settlers' legitimation of expropriation relied on the reduction of Muslim law to personal status. Imperial secularization thus determined the massive dispossession of the indigenous population by force of law. It made it possible to institute private ownership of Algerian land, and gave legal grounds for it to be appropriated by the settlers. This subjection of property to the Napoleonic civil code was actualized by the Warnier Law – introduced by a former Saint-Simonian – which, from 1873 on, made Algeria definitively and irreversibly a settler colony subject to settler interests.

It is through the invention of the debate over Islam's compatibility with modernity that I propose to analyse the ideological matrix of the expropriation of land in Algeria, and thus of apartheid. The two sides, the emperor's party and that of the European settlers, clashed over a key question: the reform of Islam, understood as a condition for the civilization of colonized subjects who were no longer to be converted to

---

111   Anonymous, *Algérie: immigrants et indigènes*, Paris: Challamel, 1863, p. 22.

Christianity. As we will see, this question was connected to the problem of *property* as it was deployed in the colonial situation. The imperial party, Saint-Simonian in tendency, declared that indigenous collective property should be maintained and codified, and its owners maintained as agricultural actors in the colony. The settlers' party, for its part, defended a policy of expropriation and the generalization of settler colonization based on the application of French private property law. The crucial conflict that played out in the debate over the compatibility of Islam and modernity set in opposition an agricultural colonialism based on the massive expropriation of indigenous lands to the profit of European agriculturalists, and a colonialism that associated European industry with agricultural work performed primarily by indigenous subjects: that is, imperial union versus settler colonization. The two economic models corresponded *schematically*, as we have seen, to two models of colonization in Africa: direct government and indirect government.

The failure of the colonial model the Second Empire had tried to establish in Algeria was sealed by the massive expropriation of indigenous land after 1870, to the benefit of the settlers and more generally of European private property. But the victory of settler colonialism in Algeria did not prevent military imperialism from inventing and putting to work techniques that, in other colonial spaces, would contribute to the maintenance and regulation of indigenous customary property. The policy, advocated by the Saint-Simonians, of conserving indigenous agricultural lands by respecting a principle of collective ownership can thus be compared with what European empires would later apply in order to govern so-called *tribal* African communities. In this model, settlers are not farmers: they should be engineers and capitalists, circulating the colony's agricultural products on the markets while exploiting its subsoils. Following this model, the colonial conservation of indigenous lands contributed to the deployment of a system of agriculture based on private property and bank credit. *Preparing* the inconvertible Muslim to perceive the moral superiority of Christian Europe thus meant, very concretely, that the colonized peasant should be morally converted to integration in the capitalist economic circuit. The idea of colonial agricultural credit was formulated as early as 1830, in Michel Chevalier's *Système de la Méditerranée*. There, the subjugation of agriculture to bank credit was presented as an instrument of general pacification. But it was Abd el-Kader's surrender that opened the debate over the agricultural colonization of Algeria. Seeking to define a method for the most durable colonization of the country, army leaders and Saint-Simonians asked which economic model should be applied. Colonial 'pacification' techniques thus played a role in determining the economic structure of the colony. It was the military that first developed a model of colonization based on a military-agricultural complex, an association of soldiers and farmers. They theorized the deployment of military-backed agriculture as a condition for the colony's economic development. The colonial state would submit agricultural lands to credit, under military protection. The accumulating of agricultural capital would thus progress through the intervention of the military government and the imperial state.

This model of military-agricultural colonization was not unanimously supported by the French settlers. Urbain challenged it, declaring that it would lead necessarily to a dangerous expropriation of indigenous lands, as well as excessive state intervention in the colonial economic sector, which could only be to the detriment of the accumulation and circulation of capital. His liberal position, which he expressed in the 1860s under the Second Empire, was contrary to the recommendations of certain members of the Bureaux Arabes before Urbain's rise to prominence. One of them, Paul-Dieudonné Fabar, had proposed to 'found a society in Algeria that both knows how to defend and how to fertilize the soil'.[112] His response to the question of counter-insurgency was a long-term stabilization of the colonial order through the 'pacification' of the indigenous population, and a future settler colony founded on the expropriation and privatization of land: this 'society will be born in the midst of those same populations it will have stripped of their territory'. These were superior in number, 'hostile by instinct, by fanaticism, and perhaps the most restless, bellicose, and best organized for revolt of any in the entire world'. 'The first colonial centres' could therefore only be established 'by possessing all the conditions of force that have assured our pre-eminence over the vanquished race'. Because an unrestricted colonization would be too weak to confront the Algerians' insurrection, the author recommended setting up a colonial economy

---

112 Paul-Dieudonné Fabar, *Camps agricoles de l'Algérie*, Paris: J. Correard, 1847, p. 2. Fabar was a military captain close to the French military leader Eugène Daumas.

founded on state violence. 'This great role of pioneer belongs only to the state', since only it has the power to invest 'without fear of amortization', and so to 'sink the first colonial markers into conquered soil'.[113] The only way to found a stable colony in which the races would be pacified, Fabar declared, was to subject land to the secular law of the imperial state.

This model of settler colonialism was defined as a way to resolve the question of governing the tribes. In it, the organization of agriculture was an act of war. By the proliferation and settling of colonized lands, the tribes would be encircled. Thus 'the native tribes, closed in on all sides by our population centres, will be reduced to powerlessness', Fabar predicted, and the subsequent reduction in the budget of the army of Africa would serve to develop industry and commerce. The unpopularity of the colonization of Algeria in the metropole would also be addressed, the captain wrote, because imperialism is popular only when it fertilizes land, submitting it to the banks and yielding profitable returns. The riches produced by the European settlers in Algeria for the profit of France and the French would make African colonization popular in the metropole. Then, and only then, could the military colonies become economic centres, sites of capitalist investment, by being 'conferred to the most clear-thinking private interests, more ingenious than the administrators'. The colonies would need to 'call on large capital, because only this can obtain from African soil the productive capacity that constitutes its superiority'.[114]

According to these officers, who from the start had opposed the liberal model the Saint-Simonians promoted, the colonial state would clear the way for capital by developing a model of agricultural entrepreneurship founded on direct collaboration between the banks and the army. 'These reflections' on colonial agricultural development 'lead us to desire that good agronomists with a knowledge of Algeria' be 'placed at the head of vast enterprises'.[115] If colonization were to endure, the settlers would need to become rich.[116] The agricultural projects would need to be protected by the army to ensure their security.[117] This military plan for economic development was not marginal. It enjoyed the

113   Ibid., p. 3.
114   Ibid., p. 4.
115   Ibid.
116   Ibid., pp. 11–12.
117   Ibid., p. 13.

support of the French government and had a partial triumph after the fall of the Second Empire, in the context of civil government in Algeria. The law of 24 February 1847, which Fabar cited, institutionalized military-agricultural colonization and so participated in the accumulation of colonial capital colony through state violence.[118] The granting of agricultural encampments to soldiers was legalized; soldiers' time spent in Algeria was counted into their retirement pensions, and they were granted credit towards the creation of agricultural encampments in Algeria.[119]

It was thus that, around 1840 in Algeria, a crucial economic support of French agrarian capitalism was born, which would only be fully established in the metropole after 1880 and in the century that followed: agricultural credit. The unilateral application of a model of strictly agricultural colonization was precisely what the strategy of imperial association had meant to avoid. As we have seen, in his defence of association, Urbain stated that Muslims should be responsible for agricultural work, while industrial works should remain in the hands of European settlers. This organization would uphold a mode of agriculture based on indigenous social organization, making agricultural colonization into an anachronism: 'The native peasant is preferable to the European farmer, who is not in a good condition to produce cheaply and to live with dignity and health while working.'[120] At least at first, the Europeans had 'more to learn from the natives than to teach them'. But the administrative constitution of collective tribal ownership as a productive agricultural entity, as Urbain proposed, presupposed that agriculture would be subordinate to mining capital – the 'solid and fertile terrain of the immigrants', through which the European presence would prove its superiority. In this model of industrial colonization, the settlers were 'knowledgeable and the natives ignorant'; in Urbain's words, the settlers 'were capable, while a lack of special education and of capital made the natives incapable'. Racial division was a division of labour: 'We bring intelligence and capital . . . the native supplies labour and primary materials.'[121]

---

118   Ibid., p. 14.
119   Ibid., p. 94.
120   Urbain, L'Algérie française, p. 63.
121   Ibid., p. 64.

It was the underground riches of Algeria that would feed the development of the colony and the racial division of labour. Urbain prophesied that 'the seven or eight hundred million pieces of money buried and hidden in Algeria, so to speak, will come up from the earth and come to the aid of European capital'. Agriculture 'will no longer remain outside of the industrial movement, which will embrace large and profitable farms, new model sheepfolds, stud farms, the transformation of natural products, means of transport, and lastly precise instruments and the application of steam and the chemical arts'.[122] Agriculture would be subject to industry. What Urbain theorized was the circulation of the colony's agricultural products on the market. While production would remain 'native', it would fall to the settlers to transform the products of indigenous labour into merchandise, and to reap the benefits.

The European settlers would be neither proletarians nor peasants, but engineers who would convert agriculture into an industrial system based on the combustion of coal and the use of banking credit. This racial division of labour was the condition under which the colony could be pacified, and the only way to make the indigenous subjects participate in colonization was to make them beneficiaries of a 'genuine public prosperity, whose effect', Urbain assured, 'would be felt as far as France'.[123] The principle was simple: 'for immigrants, industrial colonization', and 'for natives, agriculture colonization'; 'industry to the immigrants, cultivation to the natives'.[124] That a certain number of European settlers in the coastal regions might remain peasants would not, Urbain believed, challenge the founding principle of this 'great division of labour'. The submission of agriculture to capital would 'advance the exploitation of the earth'.[125]

This racial division of agricultural labour implied the continuation of indigenous social organizations, namely the tribe and its chiefs. By 'abolishing the nobility, who are accustomed to commanding, and the scholars, who possess influence, we tear from the masses their most

---

122   Ibid.
123   Ibid., p. 65.
124   Ibid., pp. 65–6.
125   Ibid., p. 66. Apart from 'the creation of markets, means of communication, dams and irrigation canals', civilization should teach 'the value of agricultural shows, competitions, and expositions'. These competitions would modernize and advance agriculture.

cherished traditions', Urbain declared.[126] By rejecting purely agricultural colonization, Urbain was rejecting 'the system that made' the state
into an 'entrepreneur of colonization'. He intended to 'transfer to industrial establishments the encouragement given to artificial cultivation'.
This was not a question of doing for industry what the state had done
for agricultural colonization, which was currently foundering in its
'exaggerated protection and interference'. 'The state should make things
happen,' he wrote, 'it should not do them itself'.[127] This was a model of
the colony as mixed economy: the state was not itself an agricultural
entrepreneur, but simply one cog in an agricultural industrialization
that would begin in Algeria and then radiate to France. Leaving industrial initiative to the European settlers, associating the indigenous
population without assimilating them, and making their majority into
agricultural workers and a minority into a supporting military force;
this was Urbain's colonial programme.

The modernization of agriculture he proposed was linked to a
policy of reforming Islam, but also to the *racial*, *religious*, and *ethnic*
division between Arabs and Kabyles. Urbain's book, which served as
an inspiration for the legal foundation of the *indigénat* under the
Second Empire, closed with a refutation of the 'favourite argument of
the extreme colonizers'. This was the argument regarding an innate
incompatibility between Islam and European civilization.[128] But
Urbain's response was not only to affirm that Islam as reformed by the
empire would be compatible with 'civilization': from the outset, it set
itself on racial terrain, maintaining that the capacity of the Arabs to
be regenerated by the French Empire was undeniable. History attested
to their past grandeur, and it would thus be 'to give the lie to history
to deny the Arab's abilities'.[129] The history of their medieval conquests
in Spain and Europe showed, 'according to magnificent testimonies',
what 'this vigorous nationality' could 'do in the path of progress if
nothing blocked its intellectual and moral development'.[130] Islam's
tolerance towards Christians in Spain, and its love of study and poetry,
became so many signs of the Arabs' intelligence and greatness. The

126   Ibid.
127   Ibid., p. 65.
128   Ibid., p. 70.
129   Ibid.
130   Ibid.

transmission of the sciences to medieval Christians was presented as support for a sort of Arab myth. Urbain's praise of the conquering Arab nationality was doubled by his criticism of the tyrannical conquests of the Turks, who had merely plundered and degraded the Arabs. Because the Arabs had resisted the world's greatest military power, Urbain declared, they had not fully degenerated; the Turkish yoke had not made them lose their capacity for civilization. In this schema, 'Kabyles' and 'Berbers' appeared as races less noble than the Arabs. France could not restore the lost greatness of the 'Berber races', but it could make them experience 'a transformation analogous to what Islamism was able to perform during the seventh century of our era'.[131] Through this, according to Urbain, they were destined to become a source of industrial labour.

The Saint-Simonians' ethnology even included a political project that consisted of making strategic use of 'Arab nomadism'. Because, in Urbain's eyes, it seemed easier to 'civilize' sedentary populations than nomads, he believed the tribes should be pushed to become sedentary, as the military had been doing. But, the Saint-Simonian added, the nomads could also be mobilized for a specific task: helping French colonialism to penetrate the Saharan region. His defence of a decentralized despotism founded on collective ownership by 'native tribes', rather than total expropriation, was part of a broader idea: that of conquering the Sahara. Here, Urbain was in the direct lineage of the colonial project Enfantin had formulated, which not only made a link between the Arabs' pastoral mode of life and collective property, but also sought to make them instruments for the penetration of 'sub-Saharan' Africa.[132] In this way, as a crucial aspect of the policy of association, the project of French colonization of the Sahara and the invention of a properly racial division between White and Black Africa began to unfold in concert.[133]

---

131   Ibid., p. 72.

132   Enfantin, *Colonisation de l'Algérie*, pp. 70–1.

133   On Faidherbe's role in this division of two Africas, see Amselle and M'Bokolo, eds, *Au coeur de l'ethnie*. Saint-Simonian networks played a key role in the first exploratory journeys in the Sahara, as the case of Henri Duveyrier shows. Duveyrier's voyage was published under the title *Exploration du Sahara: les Touaregs du nord*, Paris: Challamel, 1864. Duveyrier was the son of Charles Duveyrier, a member of the Saint-Simonian sect. These voyages were the basis for Charles de Foucauld's explorations, and his call for France to govern the Sahara as a region separate from Algeria. On these

Racial divisions of Africa

The Saint-Simonian strategy of association testifies to the inseparability, from the empire's point of view, of the colonization of Algeria and the colonization of all of Africa. The colonization of Algeria was globally envisioned as a door that opened onto the interior of the African continent, passing through the Sahara. This project had existed since the Egyptian Expedition, which already envisioned the conquest of Algeria as a step towards ruling Africa. 'Algiers must be an appendage of French territory', wrote the minister, poet, and geostrategist Lamartine; and 'a root that we will cause to grow into Africa, beneath the sea'.[134] Not only should France

> protect the coastline, which will give us an immense influence in the Mediterranean, that spot in the world towards which all the political destinies of Europe and Asia seem to push forward to be decided; my thinking goes further: we ought to occupy the interior itself, under the command of an illustrious marshal who will govern it, select its important locations, and establish our influence there forever.

The Orientalization of Africa

As we have seen, the idea of European settlement in Algeria, understood as the doorway to French colonization of Africa, was born during the Egyptian Expedition. It is well known that, during this aborted attempt at colonization, Egypt became the object of a new scientific reasoning. But the *Description de l'Égypte*, the multi-volume work the Expedition produced, was not only a discourse on the Orient. It was also a geographical text that treated Egypt as a part of Africa. Its definition of Egypt did not include the word *Orient*, because the term does not refer to any rigorous geographical entity.[135] The word *Africa* was used to define

questions, see Dominique Casajus, 'Henri Duveyrier et le désert des saint-simoniens', *Ethnologies Comparées, Centre d'Études et de Recherches Comparatives en Ethnologie* 7, 2004, pp. 1–14.

134 Alphonse de Lamartine, *La Question d'Orient: articles et discours*, Brussels: André Versaille, 2011, p. 130.

135 Napoleon Bonaparte, *Campagnes d'Égypte et de Syrie*, Paris: Éditions de

Egypt, presented as a strategic point from which it would be possible to undermine British commerce and its rule in India. Egypt's geographic importance was seen as a determining factor, because of its location at the crossroads of three continents – Europe, Africa, and Asia – and of their commercial exchanges.[136] Its conquest would clear the way for imperial policy to restore the civilization and prosperity of Egypt – a sort of French conquest of India – but also for the emergence of a powerful Egyptian nation whose first task would be to 'civilize Africa' by associating it with the empire. This is the conclusion of the *Description de l'Égypte*. What the expedition initiated, and what gave birth to Orientalism in Egypt, was a process of Orientalizing northern Africa, rather than the Orient itself, as Edward Said claimed. The northern part of the African continent was represented as the Orient in relation to the West, and then quickly distinguished from an Africa defined as Black and sub-Saharan.

The 'semitic hypothesis' – the racial construction of the Arab and the Jew as two figures of *pure monotheism* – played a role in the construction of the racial division between sub-Saharan Africa and North Africa.[137] This can be seen in Henri Duveyrier's writings on the Touareg: because the Arabs were 'semites', they were considered to be closer to Jews than to the Berber Touaregs.[138] The grand Hegelian construction of Africa as the Black continent situated outside of history unfolded within the vaster economy of colonial knowledge. It would contribute to the imposition of racial divisions onto African populations, notably through the mediation of French colonial ethnography, as it was constructed from 1830 on, between North and West Africa.

What was at work in the establishment of Saint-Simonian networks was a crucial act of Orientalization. What was first Orientalized by imperialism was *not* the Orient but *its West*: the Maghreb and North Africa. This Orientalization materialized among the Saint-Simonians and Ferdinand de Lesseps himself, during the construction of the Suez Canal. As French colonialism unfolded, a process took place of *racially*

l'Imprimerie Nationale, 1998, p. 49: 'Egypt is part of Africa. Situated at the centre of the continent of antiquity, between the Mediterranean and the Indian Ocean, it is the natural storehouse of the Indian trade.'

136   Ibid., p. 89.
137   On the 'semitic hypothesis', see Anidjar, *Semites*, pp. 6–9, 13–38.
138   Henri Duveyrier, cited in Casajus, 'Henri Duveyrier et le désert', pp. 8–9.

identifying Africa as the Black continent, and *Orientalizing* North Africa. The racial geography of Africa that Hegel deployed was one of the receptacles where the imperiality of knowledge would be written. But what authorized Hegel to exclude Africa from world history – by reducing the Black to the status of child and animal, of human in formation – was the construction of religion. The first sign of the supposed inferiority of the Black race was the religion attributed to them: fetishism.[139] The matrix of race in Africa, as in Europe, was thus a construction of religion that separated and hierarchized 'Orientals' and 'Africans', 'fanatics' and 'fetishists', 'semites' and 'savages'. The colonial invention of the inconvertibility of the Arab Muslim goes hand in hand with the invention of so-called 'African fetishism'.

From imperial association to steam power

Despite its failure in Algeria, can a critical study of the policy of association lead us towards a comparative analysis of European colonialisms as they were configured from the nineteenth century on? The first element of an answer is that the opposition that Hannah Arendt makes in her *Imperialism*, of a French imperialism based on assimilation and a British imperialism of indirect government, does not stand up to historical analysis. The opposition itself was an *ideological production of competing colonial empires*. It allowed and still allows French imperialism to avoid seeing Algeria as the birthplace of a form of apartheid irreducible to the project of assimilation, and allows British imperialism to see indirect government and the Commonwealth as forms of government more respectful of indigenous traditions. The history of Algeria, subjected to a total colonialism in which the state deployed forms of both 'direct' and 'indirect' government as two faces of the same rule, shows the limits of this conventional distinction.

Another element of an answer can be found in the energetic dimensions of the concept of imperial association. Our first clue is a passage by Ismaÿl Urbain: 'The application of *steam power* to industry, the substitution of machines for human labour, gas for lighting and heating, railroads, and electricity, have encountered the most lively opposition, and more than a few years were needed before these inventions

---

139   Hegel, *Philosophy of Mind*, pp. 42–3.

were popularized.'[140] Although the policy of association was still encountering resistance, Urbain promised that the progress it was sure to create would triumph, just as technical progress had won out over the obstacles and reactionary formations that had blocked its path. There is more at stake here than a simple analogy between steam power and the model of apartheid supported by Urbain. The very foundations of the empire of association were industrial: the use of steam power as energy to drive machines and production, of gas and electricity. The policy of association that legally structured apartheid in Algeria was the shared work of secularization and industrialization, inseparable from the emergence of an economy based on the combustion of coal along with agrarian capitalism. This fossil economy was propelled in France by the Second Empire, in the attempt to catch up with British capitalism. Saint-Simonian networks were among its decisive mechanisms.[141]

How, then, to understand the coincidence between the new forms of exercise of colonial violence that were born from the imperial order of secularization, and the unfolding of an economy based not only on agrarian capitalism but also on the combustion of fossil fuels? For nineteenth-century observers, the religious promise of the kingdom of God seemed to have been realized and then to be dissolving into this world, as steamboats and railways were meanwhile beginning to cut across the planet. We should, therefore, analyse the power of empire – which claimed to convert the world to civilization rather than to re-enact the Crusades, submitting men to 'free labour' rather than slavery – by grasping its energetic foundations, and show how the birth of secular and liberal empires coincided with the formation of a capitalist economy based on the exploration and appropriation of underground resources. How did the imperial order of secularization participate in the coal-fired processes that would lead to the emission of massive amounts of carbon dioxide into the atmosphere? Did the

---

140   Urbain, *L'Algérie pour les algériens*, pp. 139–40. My emphasis. The model of agricultural development he advocated for France in Algeria was the one used by the English and certain German states.

141   David Pinkney, *Decisive Years in France, 1840–1847*, Princeton, NJ: Princeton University Press, 2014, p. 24; Colin Mooers, *The Making of Bourgeois Europe*, London: Verso, 1991, pp. 83–9; Roger Magraw, *France, 1815–1914: The Bourgeois Century*, Oxford: Oxford University Press, 1983, p. 159.

Saint-Simonians, by ordering the fulfilment of Christianity on Earth via its exploitation and the birth of a new form of empire, herald what we now call fossil capital? For these questions to be answered, we will need to broaden our scope beyond the single case of the French Empire. Only a comparative perspective will allow us to deploy a more planetary perspective to this global problem.

4

Anatomy of the Fossil State: Geopolitics of Climate in Europe and Beyond

How did the secularization of empires transform capitalism into a fossil machine? By what mechanisms did it make the combustion of coal – and then of oil – necessary, contributing to the emission of carbon dioxide into the atmosphere? In answering these questions, this chapter tries to understand how the policies of secularization pursued by European empires led to underground exploration in search of fossil fuels. Its goal is neither to determine the major culprit responsible for global warming by uncovering a primary cause hidden beneath the figure of humanity or capital, nor to lay out a definitive explanation. Instead, it tries to describe the extra-economic dimensions of climate transformation by showing how the mutations of imperiality participated in the birth of a capitalist economy founded on fossil fuel combustion. It describes how imperial secularization played a driving role in the advent of the climate catastrophe. This hypothesis requires us to describe how the violence of most modern imperial states – its counter-insurrectional practices and techniques of colonial war – are at the heart of what is called the Anthropocene. The word *secularization* does not describe a process that progressively gave birth to capitalism through a sort of teleological necessity; it refers, rather, to a set of powers that have determined the fossilization of capitalism. Understood as an effect of the metamorphoses of imperiality, secularization appears as the keystone of the initial accumulation of *fossil* capital.

I begin by showing how, from the sixteenth century on, the secularization of Church goods facilitated the extraction of coal. I then describe how

European empires were secularized by overturning the economy of conversion on which they had been based since the Crusades, permitting the launch of a capitalist economy founded on the extraction and large-scale combustion of fossil fuels that extended to the whole of the planet. From their desire to fulfil the Gospel on Earth, while liberating a man still enslaved to a God whose transcendence seemed merely a product of the 'Oriental' imagination, these empires threw the planet into irreversible upheaval.

What, then, are the threads that connect imperial secularization to global warming? How did imperiality graft itself onto the flesh of European states, determining the mechanisms of their industrialization? Why did these states need to be, or become, empires in order to develop a fossil economy? To what extent was the imperial secularization of the state a condition for both the emergence and the introduction of fossil capitalism in Europe? These are the questions that will occupy us in the following pages.

On the fossil state and its relations with capital

If the concept of the Anthropocene plays a role in obliterating the specific role that Europe and capitalism – and England and the United States – played in the advent of global warming, the concept of the Capitalocene, created by eco-Marxists, tends to marginalize the role played by the *secularization* of the state and of *colonialism*.[1] A critique of fossil capitalism without a critique of the imperialist states that made capital accumulation possible will remain blind to the role of violence in history. By situating imperiality and secularization at the heart of state violence, my approach tries to grasp the properly *theologico*-political dimensions of these empires as contributors to the advent of the Anthropocene. The concept of the fossil state is thus a critique of the tendency to underestimate the role of the state in the emergence of the fossil economy, an underestimation that characterizes both the narratives of the Anthropocene, which make undifferentiated humanity the major culprit in climate mutation, and Marxist analyses centred on the critique of capitalism. A description of the

---

1   For an analysis of the limitations of Marxist histories of climate change in terms of capital, see Dipesh Chakrabarty, 'The Climate of History: Four Theses', *Critical Inquiry* 35, no. 2, Winter 2009, p. 212.

anatomy of European fossil states will also show how inter-imperial competition presided over the generalization of practices of fossil fuel extraction and combustion that spread across the planet as a whole. Analysis of the imperiality of the fossil state, rather than the concepts of modernity or capitalism, will allow us to analyse the interactions between capital and the colonies, as well as the ways in which state reforms in the nineteenth century prompted a forced and vertical conversion of societies to fossilization.

From the 1820s onwards, the industrial revolution led to the formation of a new economy based on the extraction and combustion of coal, no longer for domestic reasons but as a source of energy for textile production and steam ships.[2] By substituting coal for water as productive power, the mutation of British capitalism unleashed around 1830 became a decisive factor in the warming of the planet, by emitting massive amounts of carbon dioxide into the atmosphere. Steam-powered machines and railways were the technical materializations of this fossil economy in the nineteenth century, when it was dominated by coal. It was only in the following century that oil would be significantly introduced into the mechanisms of fossilizing capitalism.

How did coal become a key actor in British industry? By what means did British industrial capitalism, around 1830, come to make the combustion of coal the primary source of energy for textile production? The use of coal, born within textile production by the substitution of the steam engine for the water wheel, cannot be explained by a simple logic of profit. If we follow Andreas Malm's account, water power remained globally more profitable than steam.[3] It was because the steam engine allowed the textile economy to mobilize and govern workers more efficiently that capitalists began to generalize its use. The mobility of coal let production centres be relocated to towns and cities, where they could employ the urban labour force. For the same reason, steam liberated the production of surplus value from the meteorological constraints that nature had put on it. Production was no longer constrained by climate and geography, as it had been when it depended on waterways; it was now free to relocate to

2   Andreas Malm, 'The Origins of Fossil Capital', *Historical Materialism* 21, no. 1, January 2013, pp. 15–68.

3   Andreas Malm, 'Who Lit This Fire? Approaching the History of the Fossil Economy', *Critical Historical Studies* 3, no. 2, 2016, pp. 224–6.

the cities. Up to this point, Malm's account is articulated around the agency of three factors: the mobility of coal; the availability of workers in urban centres; and meteorological factors. It was not in isolation that steam came to be established in textile production, but only to the extent that the mobility of coal made it possible to employ the urban labour force without needing to relocate workers near waterways, despite the overall lower cost of using water as a productive force. Here, Malm introduces a properly ideological factor: the idea of absolute mastery, the total control offered by steam in comparison to water and the natural elements, played a role in the capitalist economy's passage into the fossil era. The logic on which this conversion depended was based not only on calculation, but on mastery of the mobility and speed of production as well as the most lucrative possible exploitation of labour.

The unfolding of this rationality was entangled with the way that capital was abstracted from nature and its spatiotemporal limitations. It does not seem to me that the mobility of coal and the other factors Malm mentions are able, by themselves, to account for the emergence of the fossil economy. If we want to understand how factors like the mobility of coal and exploitation of urban labour power were able to work effectively on English capitalists, another series of factors needs to be invoked. As Malm himself shows, the mobility of coal was initially not sufficient to convince textile producers reticent to use the steam engine. It was only later, when the state forced them to, that they abandoned the water wheel in large numbers. The state's legislation, in turn, had itself been forced by the workers.

In response to a series of workers' uprisings, and despite pressure from the owners of the spinning mills, the British Empire instituted the first law limiting workers' hours, the Factory Act of 1833. Shortly after, beginning in 1847, this was followed by other legislative measures. The workers were protesting against the arbitrary extension of working hours that resulted from the meteorological constraints affecting textile production organized around hydraulic power. The possibility of freedom from meteorological constraints thus only helped to bring about the age of coal, because the use of steam allowed capitalists to respect the law limiting working hours. While the shift from water to coal as productive power in cotton spinning mills did, indeed, in principle, make it possible to employ labourers in the urban centres, what actually led the majority of British textile producers to abandon the water wheel for the steam engine had nothing to do with a simple calculation of gains. After numerous attempts to work around the law, the steam engine was imposed as the only way to produce surplus value while respecting the limitation on working hours dictated by the state. And, so, the fossilization of capital came to be imposed as inevitable: productive intensity had to be augmented by the use of the engine, so that greater surplus value could be wrung out of a reduced duration of labour. The birth of fossil capital was thus entwined with the passage from what Marx called absolute surplus value, based on the extension of working hours, to relative surplus value, based on the intensification of production by the use of machinery. Capital only deployed relative surplus value because the state was forced, by the insurrectional activities of the workers themselves, to issue laws limiting working hours.[4]

If we admit that no logic intrinsic to capitalism, no teleological separation from nature based on the dynamic of abstraction, suffices to explain the process by which steam power was generalized, then we must try to grasp the fundamental importance in this process of social and political violence. This violence is, however, irreducible to class struggle, to a simple conflict between worker and capitalist, to the extent that it engages what we are calling imperiality. The set of factors related to capitalism could not have led to the generalization of the fossil economy except as components of a process: the process by which the imperial state regulated social violence. The British imperial state, not the intrinsic logic of capitalism, was the real vector of abstraction that led fossil capital to become more adequate for the demands of productivity and mobility, as well as legal constraints. It was not only conflict between workers and capital but also, and perhaps above all, the regulation of this conflict by the liberal state and its neutralization by the force of modern law that played the main role in tipping British textile production into the fossil economy.[5]

---

4 Karl Marx, *Capital, A Critique of Political Economy: Volume 1*, New York: Penguin, 1992, pp. 533–4.

5 On Barak, *Powering Empire: How Coal Made the Middle East and Sparked Global Carbonization*, Berkeley: University of California Press, 2020, p. 116. The workers, Barak notes, 'forced the state to intervene between them and employers in managing the safety of their persons both inside and outside of the mine in terms of nutrition, subsistence, insurance, schedule, and wages. They fought . . . in order to secure these "labor" rights.' From this point of view, 'steam engines' were 'absorbed into this statist game'. My argument aims to develop this suggestion, which Barak formulates but does not analyse systematically.

The later appearance of practices of oil extraction confirm this, as if by anticipation: the fossilization of capitalism was an effect of counter-insurgency. It was in trying to neutralize the protests of British workers and miners, whose power was based on the material organization of coal extraction and combustion, that the British state was led to make oil the principal energy source for the Royal Navy, bowing to the wishes of the petrol companies. The relations between the emergence of liberal democracy and carbon dioxide emissions have to do not only with the series of conflicts between workers and capital, but also with the way in which *the state* fossilized capital while seeking to dismantle other powers that opposed it.[6] Understood in terms of a state sovereignty, the democratization of politics that emerged from the workers' organizing made possible by the establishment of the coal economy constitutes one moment in a larger process of secularizing empires. As we will see at the end of this chapter, the upheavals in geopolitical equilibrium that followed the weakening of the Ottoman Empire after the end of the eighteenth century allow us to understand the relations between secularization, empire, and global warming.

I argue that the role played by the imperial state in the explosion of the oil economy displays a structure that might help us understand the birth of fossil capital itself. This structure connected military imperialism, in the form of the Royal Navy, to the state's domination of workers in the metropole. It attests to the indissociable character of these two processes, two faces of the imperiality that are the lungs of the state. It allows us to grasp the way in which the state used steam ships as a weapon of colonial war, before textile production had definitively converted to the coal economy. This should be stressed: the birth of the fossil economy cannot be reduced to class interest; it was an effect of the interaction between military imperialism and industrial capitalism that was made possible only by the liberalization of the state apparatus in its secular form.

---

6   Timothy Mitchell, *Carbon Democracy: Political Power in the Age of Oil*, London: Verso, 2011, p. 63. I follow Mitchell in grasping the properly and irreducibly political dimensions of the mechanisms leading to global warming. While Mitchell puts the emergence of political democracy at the heart of the climate question, I insist on the central role of the state in regulating power relations which have led to formal 'liberal democracy' only in some parts of the West and not in the non-Western most polluting economies.

Imperial expropriation of Church lands and subsoils

The Marxian analysis of the dynamic of the primitive accumulation of capital argues that a crucial part of this process took place in England and determined the emergence of agrarian capitalism by the overthrowing of feudal relations. The nobility or landlords, who, until then, had used lands only for limited production, gave way to capitalist proprietors who received competitive rent by exploiting lands with the use of salaried agricultural labour. Land would be cultivated only by capitalist farmers, whose principle was productivity. The unfolding of this process was integrated into a general dynamic of land expropriation made possible by the monarchic state. Its keystone was the birth of modern property law, which after 1640 allowed capitalist landlords to expel peasants who failed to pay rent due to low yields.[7] This system, as it manifested in the process of enclosures,[8] gave birth to the first urban proletariat through a massive and unprecedented exodus of expropriated peasants to the cities.

The birth of capitalism in the British Empire was not only agrarian. From the sixteenth century on, it was linked to the proliferation of exploratory and extractive mining with a view towards large-scale production, due to the scarcity of coal and charcoal. This coal was required not to turn the steam engine, which would be invented by James Watt only in 1784, but to meet domestic heating needs, particularly for expropriated peasants who had become urban workers. Even if it was not inevitable that it would lead to a fossil economy organized around the steam engine, this coal-based capitalism retrospectively appears as a key moment in the primitive accumulation of fossil capital.[9] This analysis not only shows the central role of state violence in the

---

7   Karl Marx, *Capital, A Critique of Political Economy*, vol. 1, New York: Penguin, 1992, pp. 877–85.

8   Ibid. Enclosures were lands appropriated by British capitalists after the policy of massive expropriation of peasants that Marx places at the heart of the primitive accumulation of capital.

9   This is the moment that Malm says coincides with what he calls the *Elizabethan Leap*. Andreas Malm, *Fossil Capital: The Rise of Steam Power and the Roots of Global Warming*, New York: Verso, 2016, p. 320: 'The primitive accumulation of fossil capital is the process by which capital is invested in the production of fossil fuels while at the same time dissolving the bond between the direct producers and the earth, fencing off nature as private property, dispossessing farmers, hunters, herders, fishermen . . . contributing to the creation and expansion of capitalist property relations.'

expropriation of peasants through enclosures. It also attests to the existence of another, properly theologico-political dimension of the appropriation of lands and subsoils, which involved relations between the
empire and the Church.

A series of confiscations of Church lands by the British state played a
central role in the primary accumulation of fossil capital, and contributed to transforming underground coal reserves into private property.
With an edict in 1566, the monarchy renounced ownership of mineral
resources apart from gold and silver. Before the edict, however, the
obstacle to coal mining had not been the state, but, rather, the Church.
On the lands where the great mines of north-east England would proliferate were monasteries, and their mineral resources therefore belonged
to the Church.[10] While the monks tolerated the extraction, sale, and
domestic burning of coal from monastic lands, they had no appetite for
the kind of growth that could lead to the development of an industry.
According to the historian John Nef, their discipline made them little
disposed to invest substantial sums of money into mining or to encour-
age their tenants to make such investments. For example, when the
archbishop of Durham leased out mines, the contract was expensive and
relatively short, and accompanied by restrictions that prevented the
development of any intensive or lucrative mining activity.[11] Because
monks and archbishops were not economically dependent on the exploitation of their subsoils, no expansion of productivity or reinvestment of
surplus was part of their horizon.

With the edict of 1566, the monarchy intended to support the expansion of the mining industry by authorizing private ownership of mineral
resources, particularly coal. But the state's edict of privatization presupposed the series of expropriations of Church goods by the Tudor
monarchy, first under Henry VIII and then under Queen Elizabeth. By
dissolving the monasteries and appropriating their properties and
lands, the state had taken ownership of the majority of the kingdom's
mineral riches, which it could then privatize by transferring them to
the market. This secularization of Church goods contributed to facilitating capitalist investment into mining by removing ecclesiastical

---

10 Ibid., p. 322; John Nef, *The Rise of the British Coal Industry*, vol. 1, London:
Routledge, 1966, pp. 136–7, 144–56.
11 Ibid.

restrictions. The appropriation of ecclesiastical lands by merchants made possible by the state expropriation of Church goods gave rise between 1570 and 1580 to a dynamic of primitive accumulation of fossil capital. The coal mines located under Church lands were captured by the state and reinvested on the market in a process of privatization. The transfer of properties that led to the expansion of the mining industry before the emergence of the fossil economy was thus indissociable from an act of secularization: the expropriation of the Church. The prerequisite for the appropriation of underground riches to enable intensive coal production and the expropriation of peasants was an act of secularization carried out by state violence, which was at the heart of the dynamic of capital accumulation.

This act of secularization, on which the birth of capitalism depended, was an imperial act. It was part of the dissemination of imperiality, not only because of its indissociability from the colonization of the Americas, slavery, and the imperial rivalry between Britain and Spain, but also, and above all, because it followed from the attribution of the status of empire to the British Kingdom, in opposition to the Church of Rome. 'The Kingdom of England is an Empire': with these words, from the start of the sixteenth century, the monarchy declared its imperiality.[12] This formula testifies to the overlap between the imperial and the secular that was at the heart of the state and at the foundations of underground resource extraction. It attests that the monarchy's control over the Church and appropriation of its land, initiated by the royal establishment of Anglicanism after the Reformation, was intrinsically linked to the *imperial* nature of the sovereignty that the state claimed over its territory.

Underground dragons

This dynamic of secularization cannot simply be reduced to the state expropriation of ecclesiastical lands. It also had an ideological dimension, which involved a new way of understanding the subterranean. This

---

12   David Armitage, *The Ideological Origins of the British Empire*, Cambridge: Cambridge University Press, 2000, pp. 34–5. The phrase 'this realm of England is an Empire' is first found in a letter to Henry VIII from his counsellor Tunstall, dated 1517, before being reprised in 1533 in the preamble to the Act of Appeals.

meant ridding it of the non-human beings that had inhabited it in the medieval imagination. Most domestic coal consumers had discovered in its sulphurous smell a clue to the existence of a subterranean world peopled with demonic spirits. Into the first years of industrialization, the descent into the entrails of the earth aroused miners' fears.

As industrial and fossil capitalism developed, representations of a subterranean world peopled with a multitude of extra-human forces were discredited and treated as the superstitious beliefs of the lower classes. But still, even the most respectable scientists were not absolutely certain these subterranean beings did not exist. In 1665, Robert Boyle, one of the founders of modern chemistry and of the Royal Society, encouraged his colleagues to conduct scientific research in order to determine whether frightened miners had truly encountered such demons in the underground.[13]

This history would be repeated in other stages of the accumulation of fossil capital, outside the West. The French Empire in Indochina encountered similar beliefs. A mandarin declared to the *chargé d'affaires* of the governor of Cochinchina that a dragon lived beneath the earth. Imperiality immediately reduced the declaration to an easily identifiable theme: the 'superstition of dragons'.[14] What the governor's *chargé d'affaires* described as a superstition was presented as a major obstacle to the exploration and extraction of coal: 'We can be sure that on occasions it will be impossible to exploit some seam whose concession we demand, as some additional dragon will be imagined whose inviolable retreat it is.' Seeking a sign of the subterranean dragon, colonial reason immediately translated the mandarin's reply into the language of supposed charlatanism and sacred prerogatives. The dragon 'is not visible to ordinary

---

13   Thomas Princen, Jack Manno, and Pamela Martin, eds, *Ending the Fossil Fuel Era*, Cambridge, MA: MIT Press, 2015, pp. 55–6. On the relations between the demonic and subterranean, see the pioneering work by June Nash, *We Eat the Mines and the Mines Eat Us: Dependency and Exploitation in Bolivian Mines*, New York: Columbia University Press, 1979. See also Michael Taussig, *The Devil and Commodity Fetishism in South America*, Chapel Hill: University of North Carolina Press, 2010 (1980), ch. 8, pp. 143–54. The title of this chapter is 'The Devil in the Mines'.

14   Letter from the *chargé d'affaires* to the governor of Cochinchina, 10 February 1882, ANOM, GGI fonds, n. 12712. The drafting of this letter coincided with the installation of the Freycinet cabinet. The author declared that the superstition of the dragon 'was not imagined exclusively against us'. 'It exists in reality, but is more common and strongly held among the literate than the common people.'

people' because 'only certain soothsayers have the gift of determining these sacred locations', according to the rendition by the *chargé d'affaires* of the mandarin's speech. The latter tried 'roughly' to describe 'the shape of the dragon in the mountains', which seemed 'unintelligible' to the French *chargé d'affaires*. Nonetheless, the mandarin assured him that the dragon did not reject cartography, that it was even 'possible to draw a map of the dragon'. The governor insisted on knowing how to be on guard 'against false dragons'. He rejected the idea of a map. It 'would serve us little, since it could always be corrected after the fact, on the pretext of an oversight or a revelation'.

The governor continued to reconstruct the subterranean tradition that seemed to him to have been imagined to oppose his power: 'It seems that by digging into the ground, we run the risk of piercing a vein of the Sacred animal, and from this accident terrible misfortunes would result; that is, I believe, the fall of the reigning dynasty'. The governor offered the example of European mines: 'I said to the Minister that in Europe we had dug into the soil in all directions without encountering even the smallest dragon, and without these excavations causing any cataclysm'. The mandarin 'objected that the Chinese shared the same superstition, and that it was for this reason that they had suppressed the construction of railroads on their territory'. The *chargé d'affaires* concluded with these words: 'I imagine that for his part he thinks that it is for lack of dragons that Westerners are Barbarians, or vice versa'. The fossil economy implied a profane readability of the underground world, liberated from all 'superstition'. Dragons had to cease to exist so that underground empires could unfold. In the form of geological and mineral exploration, secularization was also a condition for the *ideal* appropriation of the earth and its subsoils by industry.

Ownership of the subsoil and the state's underground sovereignty

As we have seen, it is impossible to analyse the emergence of the fossil economy in nineteenth-century England without examining the mutations of imperiality that took place within relations between Church and state. The birth of this economy required the transformation of state institutions by the Reform Bill of 1832. These reforms, by contributing to the construction of a liberal and administrative state, were, in some sense, a translation of the industrial revolution into the language of political institutions.[15] The United Kingdom was attempting to catch up, in political and reformist terms, with Revolutionary France, just as France with its Revolution was attempting to catch up economically. It was not by chance that its detractors attacked the Reform Bill as French, atheist, and revolutionary, all marks of the imperial order of secularization.[16] The issue was that the reform of the state apparatus was directly connected to the granting of the right to exercise parliamentary functions to the Jews and Catholics of the kingdom.[17] The state recognized religious diversity, and rejected the idea of a confessional uniformity of public life in the empire. Religious reforms thus accompanied constitutional reforms. After 1812, the penalties for rejecting the doctrine of the Trinity were abrogated. The years between 1828 and 1833, the emergence of the age of coal, thus coincided with a moment of transformation in relations between the British imperial state and the Anglican Church. Evangelicalism played a major role in this dynamic of secularization, which commenced in 1828 with the abrogation of the Test and Corporation Acts, according to which no one who was not a member of the Anglican Church could hold official function, unless he subscribed to thirty-nine of the Church's articles of doctrine.[18] The following year, in 1829, the Roman Catholic Relief Act allowed Catholics to sit in Parliament. In 1832, the right to vote was finally granted to those who were publicly hostile to the established Church. From then on, dissidents were permitted to vote, and Parliament ceased to be of Anglican confession.

This religious liberalization of institutions had nothing to do with moral tolerance: it was the reverse side of the imperial state's reinforcement of its power over the official Church and its control over dissident churches. The official Church now found itself subordinated to the state. The state-Church was reinforced by the abolition of the Church-state, making control of the official religion a one-sided relation. Because it

---

15   Harold Underwood Faulkner, *Chartism and the Churches: A Study in Democracy*, New York: Columbia University Press, 1916, p. 9.

16   UK Parliament, *The Second Reading of the Reform Bill*, vol. 1, London: Roake and Varty, 1832, pp. 6–7.

17   Walter Conser, *Church and Confession: Conservative Theologians in Germany, England, and America, 1815–1866*, Macon, GA: Mercer University Press, 1984, p. 100.

18   Kenneth Locke, *The Church in Anglican Theology*, London: Routledge, 2016, pp. 29–43; Eric Evans, *Britain Before the Reform Act: Politics and Society 1815–1832*, London: Routledge, 2014, pp. 10–50.

proceeded from an act of disseminating imperiality, declared against the sovereignty of the Roman Church and initiated as early as the fifteenth century, the process set in motion in Great Britain around 1830 can be compared with the one that took place under the First Empire: the establishment of state control not only over the Church but also over a plurality of religious institutions, which were then protected by freedom of conscience. The French imperial state that developed after the Egyptian Expedition had also been a mechanism of both secularization and the development of mining. But this was done by establishing public ownership of underground resources, and building a regime of concessions. The legal organization of mining property that the First Empire put in place made the right to mining dependent on sovereign right. This right was 'reserved by the state as a whole, represented by the sovereign, to dispose of underground property as public property, independent of the private ownership of the land that conceals it, and to dispose of it for the greatest advantage of society'.[19] This principle founded a sovereignty that was not only territorial but also subterranean. The sovereign state was from then on master and possessor of the subsoils.

Three provisions governed this principle's operation. The public authority would grant concessions to the people best positioned to draw value from the subsoil. It would also supervise mining in keeping with public order, ensuring the conservation of the soil and the security of the mine workers. Finally, it would collect taxes and levy tribute on the products obtained from the exploitation of these subsoils. The principle of state ownership was thus a way of guaranteeing the profitability of underground resources through a system of concessions by which the wealth produced could be taxed, and mining regulated. The administration of the subsoils answered to a triple demand of profitability, control, and tax revenue. It allowed the state to ensure that powerful financial companies could dig more deeply beneath the earth than the owners of the land, who lacked sufficient investment capacity. Only large companies could effectuate the passage from artisanal mining close to the surface to industrial systems that required deeper excavation. The principle of sovereignty of the mining law declared by the French Revolution

---

19 Héron de Villefosse, *De La Richesse minérale*, cited in Lionel Latty, 'La Loi du 21 avril 1810 et le Conseil Général des Mines avant 1866. Les procès-verbaux des séances', *Documents pour l'Histoire des Techniques* 16, December 2018, p. 18.

and instituted under the First Empire was simple: ownership of the soil does not imply ownership of what lies beneath it, which is reserved for the state. The exploitation of coal mines could thus not be carried out without prior authorization.

The real administration of subsoils by a concession regime began to be precariously established only in the eighteenth century. Starting in 1744, an edict attempted to suppress a freedom that landowners had enjoyed until then: that of digging on their land. After 1744, the edict prescribed technical measures to assure the safety of underground mining. State reason fixed the reasoning for underground excavations; this was an embryonic form of a mining rationality. If the principle of concessions had forerunners, its application was more fragile. Resistance to the edict of 1744 was strong and widespread. If all the mines in the kingdom – coal and metal – were in principle to be placed under the regime of permissions, the monarchy would never be able to apply the law across all its territories. It was only with the Revolution and especially under the First Empire that mining law was established effectively and durably.[20] This gave the state control over who had access to what was beneath the ground, who could explore and exploit what was under their feet. This concession regime was born during the Revolution.

The 1791 law put the mines at the disposal of the nation. The Revolution affirmed the principle of exploitation by concession against the 'arbitrariness' of private ownership of subsoils. Later, the Committee of Public Safety expressed a desire to review and rectify all laws on mining. In 1801, the Directorate reduced from six to two months the waiting period granted to landowners to decide whether or not to exploit the mineral resources under their land. But it was only under the First Empire that the law would become stabilized, after four years of debates in which the emperor himself took part. With the law of 1810, the government became responsible for selecting the person most likely to exploit the subsoil successfully. But, by also increasing opportunities to request concessions, the law promoted free enterprise, while reassuring landowners. It allowed the state to invest direct capital to assure the profitability and productivity of soil and subsoil. The law set out a mechanism for dividing agricultural properties on the surface, and established a monopoly of state property under the ground. By founding a

---

20   See Latty, 'La Loi du 21 avril 1810', pp. 17–29.

principle of 'useful exploitation', it posed the question of scientific competence. In order for there to be 'grounds to request a concession', a deposit of mineral strata had to be identified that could ensure 'certainty of useful exploitation'. A geological analysis had to show that the subsoil was rich enough to be mined, and that the quality of the minerals and the accessibility and constitution of the strata would allow for extraction. The Conseil Général des Mines had the task of expressing scientific opinion prior to granting permission for mining. Two laws acted in concert: the secularization of Church goods of 2 November 1789, and the mining law of 28 July 1791. Through them, two phenomena overlapped: the creation of the modern nation-state and the exploitation of the subsoils. The imperial order of secularization thus deployed state sovereignty even into the entrails of the subterranean worlds; it manifested as a descent underground.

From secularization to steam power

The secularization of Church goods by European states determined the birth of the fossil economy in the British Empire, as well as its introduction by the state in the context of catch-up industrialization, of which Bonapartism is one model. These processes are indissociable from the metamorphoses of an imperiality, which – since the Reformation, the colonization of the Americas, and the transatlantic slave trade – had been concretized only in the possession of *colonies*. It was through colonial possessions that the European states affirmed and materialized their imperial sovereignty and entered into rivalry on the international field. Without Great Britain's involvement at the heart of a world economy organized around mercantilism, colonization, and the slave trade, and its ability to control this economy for its profit, industrialization would likely never have occurred. Since the fifteenth century, the slave production deployed in the plantations of the Caribbean and the Americas had led to massive deforestation, which is part of the history of climatic upheaval.[21] But accounting for the emergence and proliferation of industrial capitalism requires us to

---

21 See Donna Haraway, 'Anthropocene, Capitalocene, Plantationocene, Chthulucene: Making Kin', *Environmental Humanities* 6, no. 1, 2015, pp. 159–65.

understand the ways in which colonialism itself was transformed beginning in the eighteenth century.

Up to now, we have analysed the multiple consequences of the Egyptian Expedition for the construction of the French Empire by following the trajectories of its spread in Europe and Africa. To the extent that the expedition is incomprehensible outside of competition with the British Empire, it should also be understood in the broader geopolitics of the French Empire's desire to catch up economically with its British rival, while using military conquest to break the sources of its commercial strength. This geopolitics is what historians, in reference to Franco-British rivalry in India, call the Great Game.

To what extent did this geopolitics participate in the expansion of the fossil economy, through the intermediary of imperialism? How did the Egyptian Expedition, by participating in the escalation of violence between the British and French empires, contribute to establishing the geopolitical order that presided over the generalization of coal and oil extraction in the former provinces of the Ottoman Empire? How did the expedition, in seeking to break British commerce in India by controlling the Mediterranean, lead the British Empire to adopt the strategy of maintaining the territorial sovereignty of the Ottoman Empire, and so contribute to the generalization of fossil fuel extraction to Asia and Africa? To what extent did the secularization of empire, that order that appeared when the French Republic professed its pseudo-Islam during the Egyptian Expedition, contribute to establishing the geopolitical equilibrium responsible for global warming?

Revisiting the Egyptian Expedition

The *Description de l'Égypte*, written during the expedition, described a country located 'at the centre of the ancient continent, between the Mediterranean and the Indian Ocean', which is 'the natural storehouse of the trade of the Indies'.[22] In other words, in the eyes of French imperialism, Egypt was a strategic point of contact, located at the crossroads of Europe, Africa, and Asia, and so appeared as the beating heart of global

---

22 Napoleon Bonaparte, *Campagnes d'Égypte et de Syrie*, Paris: Éditions de l'Imprimerie Nationale, 1998, p. 49.

trade.[23] During the Revolution it became a nerve centre for geostrategic reasons: it could make it possible, if not to conquer India, then at least to block access to it by British trade. The invasion of Egypt was thus an act of war declared at once against the Mamluks and the British Empire.

Its stated goal was to restore civilization and prosperity by setting up projects of irrigation and canalization.[24] The French presence was posed as one simple step in a transition, whose purpose was to help Egypt become an independent nation and modern state: it would reconstruct Alexandria and make it among the most powerful places in Africa and in the world, augmenting its population and fertilizing the countryside with canals, in order to 'give the land over to agriculture' thanks to the water of the Nile. France promised wealth to Egypt.

In reality, coming after the Haitian Revolution, the goal of the project of establishing a new colony in Egypt was to replace Saint-Domingue, the most lucrative plantation colony in the Western slave economy. Sugar and cotton would no longer be produced in the Americas, but between Asia and Africa.[25] After the Revolution had taken the initiative of liberating the slaves, the whole colonial economy hoped to regenerate itself by relocating Caribbean cotton production to Egypt. The imperial economy that France intended to deploy in Africa was still agricultural, and the energy it was to be based on was hydraulic. The plan was to build a system of irrigation in order to fertilize Egyptian soils. The Revolutionary economy in Egypt thus proposed to replace the colonial products of Saint-Domingue by shifting the American plantation economy to Africa and Asia. The empire set out on a route opposite to that of Christopher Columbus.

The empire's agricultural project created the possibility of a French conquest of India, to counter the British Empire. Once France was 'master of Egypt', it would also become master of 'Hindustan'.[26] The imperiality it claimed to deploy was an *empire of emancipation*, resting on the idea that the peoples of Hindustan were eager to 'throw off the yoke' of their Mughal masters, who had 'oppressed them' for too long.[27] This empire was conceived of as a global network, a place of meeting

---

23   Ibid., p. 89.
24   Ibid., p. 94.
25   Ibid., pp. 94–5.
26   Ibid.
27   Ibid., p. 95.

and emigration but also of the spread of civilization to Africa via Egypt. The imperial administration would regenerate the country's greatness, gradually conferring on it independence and perhaps even global leadership. By the association of Egypt and France, Africa itself could be 'civilized': colonized by Egypt in the name of Western culture.[28] As we have seen, imperial France claimed to bring back the dead and restore great nations through wealth, art, and industry.

The idea of an empire of Africa and the Orient was the closing thought of the *Description de l'Égypte*. The legacy Bonaparte left in Egypt was an administration oriented towards 'modernization' under the direction of Mehmed Ali (Muhammad Ali).[29] The Saint-Simonians would play a central role in this industrial sequel to the Egyptian Expedition. While contributing to training engineers, they formulated a neocolonial politics *avant la lettre*, based on an embryonic principle of self-determination. The strategy of supporting Arab nationalist uprisings against the Ottoman Empire, deployed without success by Bonaparte after the failure of his pseudo-Islamic politics, here took the form of association.[30]

Association and the Arab nation

In Egypt, Saint-Simonianism declared that governing non-Europeans was the only way to prepare them for their coming independence, in the form of a nation-state that was *politically independent* but allied with Western economic interests. Observing the way of life of the Egyptian people, Enfantin saw harbingers of an Arab nationality to come, one that was summoned into existence by freeing itself from the Ottoman yoke. 'I have said that shared misery and unanimous hatred for the Turks were cause and sign of Arab nationality,' Enfantin wrote, 'but I sense that it was by the unification of power established by Mehmed Ali on the ruins of the government of the Beys that this nationality has been formed, and that it has developed through the progressive admission of

---

28   Ibid.

29   Khaled Fahmy, *All the Pasha's Men: Mehmed Ali, his Army and the Making of Modern Egypt*, Cairo: American University in Cairo Press, 1997, pp. 1–18, 306–18. While he analyses the relations between Ali and the British Empire in detail, as well as internal politics, Fahmy does not consider the relations between Ali and the French Empire.

30   Henry Laurens, *L'Expédition d'Égypte (1798–1801)*, Paris: Seuil, 1997, pp. 256–7.

the natives to military and administrative roles.' 'It is equally good to observe', the Supreme Father continued, 'in this people . . . whose base is Mahometan, a phenomenon of religious tolerance of which no Christian people, I believe, could cite a similar example.' This was because 'for centuries, Muslims, Christians, and Jews have lived here with much greater understanding than have Christian sects in our civilized countries; one could say that the Egyptians, noble inheritors of the ancient priests of Memphis, took from the Qur'an only a disdain for idolaters and a love for those who believe the unity of God'. The tolerance of Islam was read as a harbinger of a modern Arab nation to come, of which Egypt would be the centre in North Africa. According to Enfantin, this announced the need for Egypt to enter into a Mediterranean system dominated by European industry, and to take a leading role in Africa and the Near East as a modern and Arab Great Power.

'Egypt is undeniably, of all the Muslim countries, the one most susceptible to communion with Western civilization; and it is also, of all the Mahometan peoples, the Egyptians who possesses the most genuine love of fatherland', Enfantin assured.[31] This praise of Egypt should be seen as an anticipation of a crucial aspect of the expansion of imperialism in the Arab world. Enfantin, like the British governors of Egypt after him, such as Lord Cromer, doubted that the Egyptian Arabs were capable of governing themselves. The precise role of colonial tutelage was to make them sovereign by 'civilizing' them. Even after his disappointment with the politics of modernization set in action by Mehmed Ali, Enfantin continued to see this as a necessary step in the formation of an Egyptian nation, allied with the industrial development propelled by European virility. He formulated the idea of a governed and associated sovereignty. The project of political independence within economic dependence on Europe, characteristic of what would become neocolonialism after independence, was, in reality, at the heart of imperialism, even before its deployment on the African continent and in the Middle East. The history of neocolonial ideology begins with this Saint-Simonian mission of civilization, which claimed to lead peoples towards self-determination within the framework of a politics of association.

Imperial association was a project of uniting local sovereigns who were more or less independent but all governable by Western powers. In

---

31   Prosper Enfantin, *Oeuvres d'Enfantin*, vol. X, Paris: E. Dentu, 1872, p. 203.

the economy of this project, the Saint-Simonians designated Mehmed Ali as Napoleon's Arab and Muslim successor, his 'executor'. After Bonaparte had 'marked Egypt with his powerful finger', Enfantin declared, Ali had 'taken hold of it to ensure the destiny Napoleon's pointing finger had prepared for it'.[32] In Egypt, the Saint-Simonians allied themselves with the French engineers and soldiers who had remained behind after the expedition. The most enthusiastic of these was Ferdinand de Lesseps, vice-consul of Ali's government between 1833 and 1837, and the organizer of the Suez Canal project. If, along with British India, the Egypt of Ali and the Saint-Simonians was one of the laboratories for future imperialism in the Middle East and Asia, the first colonial site where the project of association was established was Algeria. It was in Algeria that the 'universal association of men' became a *colonial* association, and that the project of abolishing 'the exploitation of man by man' transformed into the exploitation of colonized man by colonizing man.

Association and steam power in Algeria

In Algeria, the Saint-Simonians planned industrial projects similar to the ones they had planned for Egypt, but which they had been able to implement only partially: industrialization, but also developing the sciences and arts while emancipating women and improving the material conditions of the indigenous population. The association not only of sexes and classes but also of races was theorized as the goal of a new industrial project, of which Algeria would be the site for testing and experimentation. From 1839 on, Enfantin had himself appointed a member of the scientific commission for ethnographic exploration of the Algerian population. In order definitively to win the war against the Muslims of Algeria, the Saint-Simonian leader assured the French military, it would be necessary to invent an imperialism different from the one that had exterminated the indigenous peoples of the Americas and reduced Blacks to slavery through the slave trade. The stated goal was for colonization to become economically fruitful.

---

32 Prosper Enfantin, *Oeuvres de Saint-Simon et d'Enfantin*, vol. X, Paris: E. Dentu, 1866, p. 19.

Algiers will continue to bury thousands of Frenchmen and millions of francs, because we ought not to want to colonize as we did in the era where we seized a country inhabited by cannibals; as we colonized when we conducted the Black slave trade, when we reduced vanquished enemies to slavery, when we exterminated them like heretics, in a word, when we ignored the necessity that we be associated with them.[33]

Defeating the Muslims in Algeria meant colonizing without exterminating or converting. The colonial association of races was secular, liberal, and abolitionist. The task of secularizing empire was to pursue European colonialism while abolishing slavery, the effect of a convergence between imperial secularization and White abolitionism. The idea of association was the formula of a new colonial project positioned in opposition to slavery, a colonization of Africa that would negate the negation of man.

This post-slavery Saint-Simonian colonialism claimed to convert indigenous subjects to industrial development, no longer to Christianity. Never completely put into practice, this project stemmed from a critique of military violence that never questioned the legitimacy of colonialism itself. By inventing more subtle methods of occupation, the imperial critique of the Christian violence of 'fanatical' colonialism intended to convert war into a general process of 'pacification'. This Saint-Simonian transition from one imperialism to another began in 1830. 'This era of 1830', Enfantin wrote, 'has been fertile with newness for France', due to the crisis in the colonial slave plantations of the Americas. 'The crisis of enfranchisement would of necessity be felt in our colonial possessions; the enfranchisement of slaves, the abolition of the slave trade, the recognition of emancipated republics in the Americas were its consequences.'[34] The Saint-Simonian identified the crisis of colonialism in the Americas with the beginning of European imperialism in Asia and Africa. Thus 'all the peoples of Europe, satisfied with having made a long truce to the war they had been fighting for more than twenty years, felt an irresistible need for expansion, and turned their eyes to the Orient'; 'this was the focal point of all European diplomacy'. Enfantin related that France had

---

33 Prosper Enfantin, *Correspondance politique, 1835–1840*, Paris: Au Bureau du Journal Le Crédit, 1849, p. 176.

34 Prosper Enfantin, *Le Colonisation de l'Algérie*, Paris: Bertrand, 1843, p. 458.

not wanted to stay 'behind'; it wanted to 'see and to know what was to be done', and to 'establish steam-powered navigation on the Mediterranean'.[35]

Enfantin wrote his description of the spirit of the age in order to call on France to support colonization. Imperialism, founded on the combustion of coal and the steam engine, should no longer be warlike. 'It is our peaceful power that should show itself as strong, while now it appears in extreme weakness', Enfantin wrote. This should be the case 'first in Algeria, and also in the Orient and on the seas, where we encounter not English artillery, but something still more formidable: the stunning commerce of the English and the Americans'. Enfantin encouraged the creation of a Ministry of the Colonies, with its own navy separate from the Ministry of War. It was 'precisely because the ministry of the navy is and should be military that there is need for a ministry of colonies to organize our production and commercial power, our peaceful power over the seas'.[36] The keystone of this project based on steam navigation was a gesture born in Egypt: building an industrial imperialism based on the combustion of coal. According to Enfantin, where Napoleon had two ministries of war, one interior and the other exterior, 'in an industrial age like ours' there should be 'two industrial ministries'. But a Ministry of the Colonies was needed, to guide the governance of colonial possessions from the metropole. Because 'above all, it is not only a matter of industrial specialization; it is a matter of governing, and this word embraces war, justice, religion, education, public works, the police, and civil administration; all these things fall outside of the Ministry of Commerce'. The Ministry of the Colonies would thus be a government of the colonies, which would 'one day' embrace 'at its breast those men who have pacified and colonized Algeria, those who accomplished the so difficult work of abolishing the slave trade and freeing the Blacks'. 'It will also embrace those who, in the Orient, will have given us the role we ought to have, as a civilizing influence.' Those, also, 'who will have opened up for the commerce of the entire world those new routes' that were 'the Suez isthmus, the Dardanelles, and the isthmus of Panama. Finally, those who will have accomplished for maritime commerce what France began with its railway networks; that is to say, those who will have drawn the great routes of steam communication that will follow

---

35   Ibid., p. 459.
36   Ibid., p. 498.

our trade.'[37] 'All these men, who will have accomplished great things, will emerge from and depend directly on the Ministry of Colonies,' Enfantin concluded. The colonial war that would pacify the indigenous populations would be conducted against the coarseness of nature. The great men of empire 'who tend to rise in our day are the ones who best know how to wage war on nature and submit it to man', and who 'place in the common domain that most powerful weapon of wealth, steam power'.[38]

The charismatic leader of the Saint-Simonians addressed himself to the colonists and the French imperial state in the following terms: 'Let us prove that we have heard and understood the voice that rises above all others and cries out to France, to the world: Peace and labour!' 'Let us organize peace, organize labour; this will colonize Algeria and save France', by delivering it from 'men of war'.[39] France's salvation was industry, not war, which should be subordinated to peaceful and economic development. This prophetism was self-fulfilling, because it was itself an actor in the empire's expansion. Enfantin called on scholars to work for the empire by creating a practical and imperial philosophy. 'Let the philosophers' who had overturned 'the altar of the God of armies employ all their science to draft the blueprints for the temple of the God of labour'. He called on 'warriors, so strong to discipline men who must fight men' to use 'all their strength to discipline those men who must triumph over nature!'[40] Theology became the declaration of secularization by the empire, answering to a principle of election that put God literally at its service. According to this principle, God must elect a man to accomplish the great work of pacification through the new global empire. Later, in 1858, Enfantin would declare the French the world's leading people, and elect Napoleon III to the title of global sovereign.[41]

The system of the Mediterranean

This imperiality of steam power – secular, liberal, and abolitionist – was fed by a project known as the system of the Mediterranean. A vast project of pacification, it was based on the idea of a union of agriculture

37   Ibid., pp. 499–500.
38   Ibid., pp. 500–1.
39   Ibid., p. 502.
40   Ibid., pp. 502–3.
41   Ibid., p. xii.

and industry. Industry would take the place of war. Civilizing Africa and
the Orient implied submitting agriculture to credit and associating it
with the banking networks that underpinned the fossil industry and its
coal mines. Unlike the old wars, what was needed was to deploy the
peaceful force of 'industrial credit'.[42] Imperial peace would thereby free
itself from the monopoly of the vertical sovereignty of the state, obliging
it to become associated with the banks in order to live. The living organism would no longer be the state, which would become only one organ
of a greater entity: the circuit opened by steam engines and railways.
What made this circuit constitutive of peaceful industry was, indeed, a
divine attribute: self-creation. Industry, because it is permanent creation, instinctively repels war. The one 'who creates cannot be reconciled
with the one who kills'. The alternative was formulated thus: industry or
death. What war prevented was the *fertilization of the earth* by industry.
This is why the banks had to become sovereign through the spread of
credit. Financial support for the exploitation of land and of underground
fossil energies would now be at the heart of a new imperial system. The
bankers would reign as masters, and another alternative was formulated: credit or misery.[43]

According to Chevalier, a Saint-Simonian close to Enfantin in the
1830s and a major French industrialist under the Second Empire, the
domination of industry by credit was the keystone of a worldwide and
decisive peace that would conjure away war. This 'definitive peace', he
wrote, 'should be based on association between the Orient and the West'.
It could take place only by ceasing to be political and military, integrating the Orient into an industrial system governed by the West. This
empire would be the fruit not of one nation or man jealously electing
itself to rule the others, since 'each people', Chevalier declared, 'and each
class has its own proper genius, its own particular destiny'. Peaceful
association implied that each people contributed to the global market,
occupying 'in the workshop, the laboratory, and the temple, the place
assigned to them by nature'. In this way, 'the humanitarian project is at
once singular and multiple'.[44] Association implied that non-European

---

42   Michel Chevalier, *Système de la Méditerranée*, Paris, 1832, pp. 7–9.
43   Ibid., p. 9. Chevalier declared: 'Suppress credit, and there will be nothing but
ruin and misery for this immense army of industrialists who for fifty years have come up
from the earth to fertilize and beautify it, and among whom the bankers are chief.'
44   Ibid., p. 24.

people offered primary materials to the European peoples, who in turn would provide capital, engineering, and technical knowledge. Under this condition, peoples could be unified within a gigantic industrial system-become-a-world.

According to Chevalier and the Saint-Simonians, the advent of this system would do nothing less than resolve the greatest conflict that had driven all of human history. 'The most colossal struggle, the most general and most rooted, to ever make the earth resound with the tumult of battle is the one between the Orient and the West.'[45] The new imperiality would end this struggle by imposing peace. But it was merely the historical translation of a more fundamental conflict between two metaphysical forces: 'the most stunning manifestation of a war that has gone on for six thousand years between *spirit* and *matter, spiritualism* and *sensualism*.' It was this struggle that industry would bring to an end, by dissolving all dualisms; out of it, the Mediterranean was called on to 'become the nuptial bed of the Orient and the West'. This project of union was the foundation of an imperialism whose communication routes would unify the continents of the Mediterranean: Europe, Africa, and Asia. The unity of the empire would no longer be military, but would be woven by communication networks. 'The introduction of railways on the continent on a large scale, and of steam ships on the seas, will be not only an industrial but also a political revolution', Chevalier declared.[46] Imperial industry overturned the distinction between economic and political: technoscience was in itself political revolution, and would now take its place. Through these technical inventions, as well as the telegraph, it would 'become simple to govern the greater part of the continents bordering the Mediterranean with the same unity and instantaneity that now exists in France'.[47] Railways would thus open the way to a rule that would be freed from meteorological conditions and climate constraints, more than canals and rivers ever could. But Chevalier also prophesied future developments in the fossil economy and combustion. 'Whatever marvels steam power is already bringing forth under men's fingers, it is still inexperienced in its operations and applications, whether to railways or to navigation.' Chevalier did not

---

45   Ibid., p. 29.
46   Ibid., p. 38.
47   Ibid.

give in to amazement, noting that only a minor part, 'four to five per cent of the caloric force of the consumed combustible' was utilized by steam engines, 'complicated devices whose weight makes them highly inconvenient'.[48]

What scientific progress should aim for was to network continents with a system of communication whose connections were a series of ports. Railways would play a crucial role. From North Africa to the Ottoman Empire and passing through Russia, the system would connect railways and waterways. Thus, the idea of cutting through the Suez and Panama isthmuses was conceived of within the economy of a system of rule.[49] Mediterranean agriculture would be 'made to flourish' by 'numerous irrigation and drainage canals', and 'mineral riches' would be exploited 'following a great coordinated plan'. But the submission of the agricultural economy to the banks was the condition for the new imperial system.

'Suppose, lastly,' wrote Chevalier, 'a vast system of banks pouring a salutary chyle into all the veins of this body with its all-consuming activity, its innumerable articulations.' Capital appeared as a circulation of blood. The task of the banks was to circulate blood and cerebral information throughout the body in a vast web. An association of the globe through the emergence of a vast circuit of banking and financial networks, whose strong arms were communications networks and railways: this was the organism that would unify the Mediterranean world. This circulation of human and mercantile flux was the life of the imperial body. It irrigated continents, and multiplied connections between them. To form this new political body implied converting the military budget into infrastructural and technical spending. It required establishing not military colonization, but a Mediterranean confederation based on a system of communication networks composed of railways, steam ships, and canals.

---

48   Ibid., pp. 38–9.
49   Ibid., p. 50.

The French Empire's fossil Orientalism: from Algeria to Indochina

For the Saint-Simonians, the colonization of Algeria fitted into the larger frame of this project of ruling the Mediterranean. But Algeria in the nineteenth century was a limit case of industrial imperialism. From 1834, the call was made to explore Algerian subsoils in search of coal. Pierre Genty de Bussy, the civil intendant of the regency of Algiers – with no declared connection to Saint-Simonianism – made this the sine qua non for the construction of a steam-powered navy controlling the Mediterranean, in the image of the British Empire in India. If 'we wish to have a powerful steam navy,' he wrote, 'we should begin by studying and developing the resources and fuels offered by mines located near this sea'.[50] The call to exploration was doubled by a call to establish agricultural banks in the colonies, on the model of the Edinburgh banks.[51] In this way, the economy described in the Saint-Simonian system of the Mediterranean was to be concretely realized in Algeria. De Bussy's work contains many observations on Arab and Kabyle tribes' practices of charcoal and iron extraction, and a systematic exploration of Algerian soils and subsoils was conducted at the start of 1840, with plans to begin extraction.

These writings testify to the existence of a fossil Orientalism since the 'age of coal'. The French army used a steamboat named the *Sphinx* during the conquest of Algiers in 1830. A typical embodiment of fossil Orientalism, the steamboat was also used a few years later to steal the Luxor Obelisks from Egypt so that they could be reinstalled in the heart of Paris, the Place de la Concorde. As such, steam power was central to warfare and thus vital to expansion towards the so-called Orient, including what was then called the Far East; and the many poems comparing the steam machine to a god involve comparisons with oriental gods such as Afer or the *jinns* of the *One Thousand and One Nights*.

But the fossil economy was marginal in colonized Algeria, where agrarian capitalism dominated the economy. The colonial state

---

50   Pierre Genty de Bussy, *De l'Établissement des français dans la régence d'Alger et des moyens d'en assuere la prospérité*, Algiers: Imprimerie du gouvernement, 1834, p. 135.

51   Ibid., p. 144.

organized the expropriation of indigenous land and its exploitation by European settlers. For this reason, the racial division between Arabs and Amazigh populations (the so-called Berbers) was embedded in a form of ecological knowledge that was used by French scientists to justify the exploitation of indigenous land. As Diana K. Davis famously argued, the racialized figure of the 'Arab nomad' is part of a larger ecological myth regarding North African land.[52] French colonial scientists argued that North Africa was forested under the Roman Empire. Agriculture had thus developed, but the Arab Conquest of North Africa transformed it into a semi-deserted land. The nomadic mode of life was accused of deforesting the landscape by ruining the Roman agrarian system. This racial trope was deployed even in geological treatises, as former Saint-Simonian Henri Fournel argued in *Richesse minérale de l'Algérie*.[53] Beyond Algeria, the divide between the Arab nomad and the settled Kabyle anticipated the way in which Arabs and non-Arabs would later be divided along racial lines by the British Empire in the so-called Middle East, including places such as Mesopotamia – now Iraq – where oil was abundant.[54] This racial divide belonged to the broader ecology of Orientalism. Orientalists participated in expropriating land by accusing Arabs of deforesting nature and recreating an endless desert. And they explored the underground by calling indigenous metaphysics of land and subsoils 'superstitious' and 'unproductive'.

In Algeria, racism not only participated in dispossession: by aiming to 'protect nature' from an ecologically disastrous 'Arab nomadism', it presented settler colonialism as nothing less than the resurrection of nature via the restoration of Roman imperiality. The imperiality of French colonialism was thus central to the narrative of ecological resurrection. By means of its neo-Roman language, the French Empire could deploy its colonial ecology only by positing itself as the successor of Rome. The racialization of Islam thus stands at the centre of the

52   Diana K. Davis, *Resurrecting the Granary of Rome: Environmental History and French Colonial Expansion in North Africa*, Athens: Ohio University Press, 2007, pp. 3, 135–40.

53   Henri Fournel, *Richesse minérale de l'Algérie*, vol. 1, Paris: Imprimerie nationale, 1849, p. 90.

54   See Diana K. Davis, 'Introduction', in Diana K. Davis and Edmund Burke, *Environmental Imaginaries of the Middle East and North Africa*, Athens: Ohio University Press, 2011, pp. 1–22. On Iraq specifically, see Samira Haj, *The Making of Iraq, 1900–1963: Capital, Power, Ideology*, Albany: State University of New York Press, 1997.

settler-colonial economy of dispossession. French colonialism constantly opposed the *homo islamicus* and the *homo economicus* by arguing that Islam, as a set of institutions, was incompatible with the requirements of capitalism: economic development and agricultural growth.[55]

There was an eco-racial complex at the heart of French colonial institutions in Algeria. The racialization of Arabs participated in the environmental transformation of land by legitimizing French land expropriation as well as extractive practices. While fossil fuels did not play a central role in the colonial economy, extraction of underground resources was nonetheless deployed in Algeria. Geological exploration and mining were mostly conducted to collect phosphate, which was mainly used as a fertilizer for agriculture along with bones.[56] Former Saint-Simonian engineers such as Fournel, or those close to their networks, such as geologist Jean-Baptiste Élie de Beaumont, would play a crucial role in exploring the Algerian subsoil for the benefit of France.

The call to exploration answered a commercial need, but also a military one: forming a steam-powered French navy that would be able to compete with the English navy, because it would no longer be dependent on England to supply it with coal and iron.[57] According to a French navy lieutenant, the 'principal goal' should be the 'near-unlimited growth' of a steam-powered navy, of which 'iron and coal are the body and soul'.[58] It is thus not surprising that, after large-scale colonial coal mining failed in Algeria, exploratory mining in Tonkin (now in northern Vietnam) was first of all a response to the need for fuel for the French army's steam ships. The colonization of Asia responded to the French Empire's energetic needs, which the colonization of Algeria had not been able to satisfy.

The conquest of French Cochinchina occurred between 1858 and 1866, under the Second Empire. Conducted by the navy, it was a direct

---

55 Muriam Haleh Davis, *Markets of Civilization: Islam and Racial Capitalism in Algeria*, Durham, NC: Duke University Press, 2022, pp. 2, 19–43.

56 Émile Cardon, *Manuel d'agriculture pratique algérienne*, Paris: Bureaux de la Revue du Monde Colonial, 1862, pp. 87–8; Jean-Baptiste Élie de Beaumont, *Étude sur l'utilité agricole et sur les gisements géologiques du phosphore*, Paris: Bouchard-Huzard, 1857, pp. 4–5, 59, 105; Fournel, *Richesse minérale de l'Algérie*, vol. 1, p. 187.

57 *Considérations sur les marines à voiles et à vapeur de France et d'Angleterre par un lieutenant de vaisseau*, Paris: Chez Aymor, 1844, pp. 30–2.

58 Ibid., p. 30.

product of French naval imperialism.[59] The navy governed the penin-
sula until the establishment of a civil government in Cochinchina in
May 1879. The military's need for supplies led metropolitan interests to
invest in Tonkin coal for economic profit. The result was coal mining on
a massive scale.[60] The need to create a fleet with global reach launched
the French Empire on the path of coal extraction in Indochina.
Competition between business interests and military needs played a key
role in the take-off of this imperialism. But at the heart of this competition was the state apparatus, which determined its structure and condition of possibility. Beginning in 1884, Republican networks competed
over coal, engaging important figures of the Third Republic and their
entourages.[61] Imperial secularization, turned colonial laïcisme, constituted the shared ideology of these competing groups. The Alliance
Française, founded that same year, would spread the secular ideal of
Republic overseas. In the eyes of the Republicans, the order of secularization justified colonization, as the triumph of scientific progress over
religious traditions. It is thus not enough to say that the establishment of
secular schools and the extension of the French colonial empire were
the shared and simultaneous projects of the Third Republic.[62] More
precisely, the imperialism that unfolded in step with laïcisation was
founded on the extraction and combustion of coal. Ferry's politics,
whether sending Admiral Courbet's squadron into the Gulf of Tonkin,
negotiating with the pope, or addressing the educators of the Republic,
were inspired at once by the Saint-Simonians and Edgar Quinet and by
a desire to regenerate France after its defeat by Germany. Against the
backdrop of this latter conflict, the Third Republic's colonial project in
fact responded to the same demand as the Egyptian Expedition: to
compete with the British Empire in India.

---

59 Pierre Brocheux and Daniel Hémery, Indochine: la colonisation ambiguë 1858–
1954, Paris: La Découverte, 2001, pp. 29–36.
60 Association des Mines du Tonkin, 'L'Industrie minérale en Indochine', p. 60. In
1913, 500,000 tons of coal were produced.
61 Brocheux and Hémery, Indochine, p. 41. Dupuis, close to the Gambettists and
Governor Freycinet, was in competition with Bavier-Chaffour, the nephew of Jules
Ferry. Paul Bert, a fervent anticlerical Republican and patron of normal schools, would
end his life as governor of Indochina.
62 Jean-Marie Mayeur, Les Débuts de la IIIè République, Paris: Seuil, 1973, pp.
132–3.

British hegemony and speed

The story that begins with the French Revolution's expedition to Egypt, in which Volney and Bonaparte are key actors, is not strictly a French story. What motivated the expedition was a desire to compete with the British Empire, whose capitalist economy was by far the most developed. The Revolution did indeed envision the military and imperialist project of an invasion of India by Revolutionary France.[63] Talleyrand described it in 1798 in a note to the Directory. The conquest of Egypt would prepare for the conquest of India via Suez. The idea of a French colonization of India, although it would be abandoned, thus served to give force of conviction to the Egyptian Expedition.

The inter-imperial war between France and England at the start of the nineteenth century inspired mutual defiance. The French military was convinced that England wanted Egypt; and Wellesley, then British governor in India, persuaded the British East India Company that the French coveted India. As unrealistic as the latter might seem, it was not far from Napoleon's wish to 'truly destroy England' by seizing Egypt.[64] Despite the failure of this dream, a desire to threaten the Indian trade persisted on the French side. If Wellesley himself was not convinced that the Egyptian Expedition represented a real menace to British India, he strategically made Bonaparte his alibi. The presence of French troops in Egypt could easily become a threat to the British presence in India. His power of conviction inspired a fear that would contribute to the East India Company's gradual transformation into a colonial actor integrated into the British state apparatus. By passing off an unlikely invasion of India by Bonaparte as a real menace to the company, Wellesley invented a diplomatic tool to force imperialist conquest as a solution, against the will of both the British government and the company. After 1798, the Egyptian Expedition allowed Wellesley to legitimate an offensive policy of declaring war on Indian sovereigns. The mechanism was simple: they were accused of being allies of Revolutionary France, and plotting against the British Empire.[65] If

---

63   François-Charles Roux, *L'Angleterre, l'Isthme de Suez et L'Égypte au XVIIIè siècle*, Paris: Plon, 1922, pp. 347–9.

64   Napoleon Bonaparte to the Directory, 16 August 1779, cited in ibid., p. 355.

65   Here I am following the account in Edward Ingram, *Commitment to Empire: Prophecies of the Great Game in Asia, 1979–1800*, Oxford: Clarendon Press, 1981, pp. 115–95.

Wellesley made Bonaparte and the expedition an alibi to satisfy his own ambitions and desire for conquest, it seems that Henry Dundas, the secretary of state for war, really feared an invasion of India by French troops. Thus, the expedition contributed to destroying the equilibrium of powers in India.[66]

By seeming to pose a threat to the British Empire, the Egyptian Expedition pushed the British state to engage further in the process of colonizing India, deploying a geostrategy organized around a fierce protection of its possessions from potential rivals. The inter-imperialist rivalry with France shows that the British state was directly implicated in the colonization of India well before 1858, as its ambiguous relation to the East India Company – a state within the state, an imperium within the empire – attests. This is not to say that the East India Company switched from mercantile trade to military colonization under the effect of the expedition. Its commercial activities cannot be separated from the British state and the parliamentary debates prompted by the sovereignty of this *imperium in imperio*, this empire within the empire.[67] It was, in fact, the imperial British state, not the company itself, that, after 1800, systematically organized mineral and geological exploration in India, playing a primary role in the process that prepared for the extraction of coal in India.[68] British capitalism had to be at once imperial and military in order to become fossil.

It was in 1823 that the first British steam ship navigated Indian rivers.[69] The initiative was private at first: the idea of using the boats came not from the colonial power, but from entrepreneurs in Calcutta and their sponsors in London. As a joint stock company, the East India

---

66   Laurens, *L'Expédition d'Égypte*, pp. 48, 250–5.

67   On this point see Sudipta Sen, *A Distant Sovereignty: National Imperialism and the Origins of British India*, New York: Routledge, 2002, pp. 1–29. Sen maintains that, far from limiting itself to purely commercial activities, the company developed its own sovereignty, a *statehood* in the form of indirect government, from the last two decades of the eighteenth century. His study of parliamentary debates shows that while relations between the composite British nation-state and the company were unstable, the latter's administration was accountable to the king and to Parliament.

68   Deepak Kumar, *Science and the Raj: A Study of British India*, Oxford: Oxford University Press, 2006, pp. 33–4.

69   Saptal Sangwan, 'Technology and Imperialism in the Indian Context: The Case of Steamboats, 1819–1839', in Teresa Meade and Mark Walker, eds, *Science, Medicine and Cultural Imperialism*, New York: St Martin's Press, 1991, pp. 62–3.

Company initially had strong reservations about introducing these vessels. Its directors were reluctant to make an investment without the assurance of drawing significant profits. But pressure on the company from Anglo-Indian merchants and their sympathizers in England led Lord Bentinck, governor general of India since 1828, to take interest in how the vessels might be used most effectively. State reason would then make steam power a key mechanism in defending the empire.

In the context of a war of conquest, the speed of steam ships made it possible to mobilize a large number of troops more quickly from one end of the country to the other, decisively improving the British Empire's stability on the Indian subcontinent. Steam power became the lungs of the imperiality of power, the contemporary condition of world domination. Its supporters declared this in the clearest of terms: 'Steam vessels might carry with them the same advantage in a political point view which the Romans derived from their admirable military roads.'[70] Governor Bentinck integrated them into the very body of the British Empire, as 'a component part of our national force'. The coloniality of steam power appeared in the political promotion of this now-imperial energy source. 'In no part of the world will the power of steam have produced a greater multiplication of the existing means of national wealth and strength as it will in India.'[71] From now on, not only the wealth of the empire but also the maintenance of its political power would depend on steam. The military use of steam ships in the First Anglo-Burmese War, of 1824–6, convinced the company to introduce them in the British Empire. Although poorly planned, the war was won thanks to these fossil vessels, through their unique advantage: speed. This allowed them to attack and block the enemy, as well as to withdraw rapidly. The British victory opened the route to the Far East, and these same ships then allowed the empire to win the Opium War against China.

Neither surplus value nor the interests of the capitalist class are sufficient to explain the British Empire's massive use of steam power. It was the logic of military colonization and the geostrategic protection of routes to India that led to the multiplication of steam ships on the

---

70   *The Friend of India*, 8 June 1839, cited in Sangwan, 'Technology and Imperialism', p. 63.

71   Lord Bentinck, cited in ibid.

waters of the Indian subcontinent. Imperial war and capitalism were part of the same military–fossil complex, irreducible to any supposedly intrinsic logic of capitalism. The steam engine was an instrument of naval and imperial war before it became part of the workings of the empire's economic production. Any analysis that leaves the state on the margins of its explanation of global warming will not be able to account for this.[72]

If an alliance of economic and military interests led the British Empire to take the decision during the 1820s to use coal for its naval fleet, it was for an eminently strategic reason. The deciding factor was the superior mobility and speed of steam ships in war. This is not to say that the imperialist use of steam power caused the use of steam engines in English textile production. But what wove these two processes of fossilization together was the liberal administrative state's intervention as a power that exercised a monopoly on legitimate violence through its armies, and regulated social violence through law.

How inter-imperial rivalry led to global warming

For steam power to become the slave of fossil imperialism, it still needed to work its way into the bowels of the state. Without the permanent wars between European colonial states, without the network of imperial institutions founded on the monopoly of violence, the world economy could never have embraced capitalism and brought about climate upheaval.

By following this hypothesis, I try to offer a synoptic vision of the connections that linked the nineteenth-century secularization of empire to the exploitation of coal. The point of departure for my analysis is the British Empire. As we have seen, from the sixteenth century onwards, the state policy of expropriating agricultural lands and subsoils was part of the same movement as the monarchy's secularization of Church

---

72 Malm, 'Who Lit This Fire?' pp. 222–3. Because he works from an a priori concept of fossil capitalism, Malm tends, in my view, to minimize the importance of *military* events and inter-imperial rivalry in the East India Company's transition to the use of steam power to drive its vessels. On military rivalry and the importance of techniques of what he calls 'risk management', see Barak, *Powering Empire*, pp. 4–5, 20–1.

goods. This point of departure provides a clue to the links that formed between the secularization of Church goods, the imperiality of the monarchical state's increasing autonomy from Rome, and the extraction of coal, which was then still for domestic use. Imperial secularization belongs to the initial conditions of the emergence of fossil capitalism in Great Britain. It determined the way that lands and subsoils were appropriated by the British imperial state in the sixteenth century and then redistributed on the market, where they could be appropriated by private capital. This first moment, in some sense, constitutes a matrix whose analytical role is to explain the role of the secularization of the imperial state in the emergence of fossil capitalism after 1820. But, in my view, the exposure of the links between secularization, empire, and coal in the sixteenth century was merely a sort of anticipation. Their importance would be demonstrated only later, when the process of industrialization accelerated in the nineteenth century. The secularization of the imperial state was a long-term process that contributed to pushing British textile production into a fossil economy based on steam engines and the burning of coal.

The Reform Bill of 1832 constitutes a key moment in British political history, in that it liberalized the state apparatus. As we have seen, the reforms that secularized the Empire's politico-religious system and established religious pluralism were initiated after 1812 and accelerated in 1828, before stabilizing around 1830. These reforms were in no way marginal. They transformed the very structure of the state and the Church by opening Parliament to non-Anglican religious minorities, in a profoundly Christian British society. The British state could become a modern administrative apparatus only by emancipating its institutions from their religious dependence on the Anglican doctrine of the established Church. While there was neither a privatization of Anglicanism nor a separation of Church and state, the state was secularized by ratifying the dissociation between participation in public life and membership in the established Church. The model of secularization deployed here was constituted by the drive to constitute a Christianity expanded beyond the limits of official Anglicanism, and thus cannot be viewed as the absence of religion in the public sphere. If this distinguishes it from the model of French secularization as effected by Bonaparte, it can still be seen as the birth certificate of a bureaucratic state comparable to the one established in France after the Revolution. The dynamic of state control over the established Church, inaugurated by the Anglican Reformation, was, in a sense, continued into the nineteenth century, with the tendency for state control to become *unilateral*. While the established Church was not separated from the state, the state abolished the constraints that Anglican dogma and ecclesiastical authorities had exercised on its legislative and institutional functioning. From this point of view, the 1820s marked the emergence of a secular state in England. Despite major differences, in its generic form this regime shared characteristics with that of France, which can therefore be seen, following Marx, as an ideal type of modern capitalist state.[73]

Despite the connections between Church and state, the latter became independent of the authority of the established Church, which entered into a relation of subordination. Without ever challenging the ecclesiastical *establishment*, this state autonomy coexisted with the emancipation of religious minorities. The British model articulated the state's secular sovereignty over the established Church with a new type of religious pluralism, as the French model had done.

What Marx said of the Bonapartist state can thus be extended into a theory of imperial secularization. To the extent that the Bonapartist state seems an ideal type, should not its model of imperial secularization, in principle, teach us about the mechanisms that connected secularism and capitalism in Europe? To answer this question requires an assessment of the centrality of an institution like the civil code in world history. If, according to Hegel, this Napoleonic institution constituted the beating heart of the modern rule of law, this was because it acted as such across history. It became the paradigm of all modern and secular law, and the code was imposed as the only legitimate form of juridical

---

73   See Fernando Coronil, *The Magical State: Nature, Money, and Modernity in Venezuela*, Chicago: University of Chicago Press, 1997, pp. 222–4. According to Coronil, the hypothesis of Bonapartism as the model for the modern capitalist state needs to be modified, because it does not work in the case of rentier states such as Venezuela. In these 'peripheral' states, the modern state is not deployed to the benefit of society, which is subjugated to the interests of the petrol state. Coronil proposes the idea of a rentier Bonapartism opposed to a classic Bonapartism. To the extent that my analysis primarily concerns fossil states in Europe, it is limited to the European triarchy. From this point of view, the paradigmatic status of the French imperial state can be maintained up to a certain point, even though my comparative study also takes account of variations from this French model, particularly in terms of secularization in its relation to the state ownership of the subsoil.

rationality. The codification of the Sharia and its transformation into family law followed the model of the civil code in the Ottoman Empire, as well as in Egypt.

If this state – the product of imperial secularization – can be seen as the epitome of the modern capitalist state, can it also be viewed as the model *par excellence* of the *fossil* state in its relation to secularization? My historical exposition responds to this question by showing, first, that the *secular* sovereignty of the imperial state is a sovereignty that is at once territorial and *subterranean*. As such, the First Empire extended the principle of state ownership to the subsoil, setting off an exploitation of resources based on the concession system. While state ownership of subsoils is not universal, it is at the heart of systems for exploiting underground resources in other countries, both European and non-European. The Saudi monarchy and the Republic of China, for example, declare underground resources to be state property.[74]

The emergence of the Napoleonic principle of subterranean sovereignty in Europe should be connected to the emergence of modern geology, as well as to new ways of relating to the subterranean, whose exploration was rationalized by the translation of a sort of disenchantment of the underground world into 'European consciousness'.[75] This disenchantment was expressed in the progressive dissolution of the idea, still widespread in the eighteenth century, that the subsoils were populated by demons and infernal creatures, and in the birth of an exploratory rationality. This shift, linked to the emergence of geological science, brought with it a systematization and rationalization of practices of underground exploration. It secularized human relations to the earth and to non-human beings, while disenchanting the underground

---

74   See Barak, *Powering Empire*, p. 222. Article 14 of the Saudi basic law of government declares: 'All natural resources that God has deposited underground, above ground, in territorial waters or within the land and sea domains under the authority of the State, together with revenues of these resources, shall be the property of the State, as provided by the Law.' Article 3 of Mineral Resources' Law of the People's Republic of China firmly declares that 'mineral resources belong to the state. State ownership of mineral resources, either near the earth's surface or underground, shall not change with the alteration of ownership or right to the use of the land which the mineral resources are attached to.'

75   On the connected emergence of a new geological science and a new relation to the subsoils in the nineteenth-century Ottoman Empire, see Barak, *Powering Empire*, pp. 396–7.

world. In this way, the secularization of the sciences that explored underground worlds was articulated with the institutional rules that governed their exploitation.

Nonetheless, the imperiality of these dynamics of secularization are only fully revealed within an international and geopolitical horizon. Returning to the Egyptian Expedition, the matrix of imperial secularization and this book's point of departure, I have tried to resituate this event within the more comprehensive frame of the inter-imperial rivalries that gave it meaning. If the Egyptian Expedition, along with British colonization in India, marked the start of a new type of colonialism, this was because, at the end of the eighteenth century, the geopolitical order that had existed for two centuries was shaken from top to bottom by a series of events. These were marked by the military weakening of the Ottoman Empire and the development of Russian and European military powers. This overturned relations of power in a region that since the end of the sixteenth century had been dominated by three Muslim empires: the Ottoman Empire, the Safavid Empire, and the Mughal Empire.[76] Their destabilization, which overturned the equilibrium of powers, marked the birth of the so-called Eastern Question.

Between 1709 and 1739, the Ottomans won several battles against Russia and other Central European powers, which seemed to show their military superiority. But, during the period of peace between 1730 and 1774, a change in relations of power began, which manifested in three successive Ottoman losses to Russia. The imperial history that we have analysed by beginning from the Egyptian Expedition can be understood as a consequence of these defeats in 1774, 1792, and 1812.[77] Volney's *Considerations*, predicting the disintegration of the Ottoman Empire (which would be consummated only after the First World War), were written after the second of these defeats. Inspired by these predictions, the project of a French expedition in Egypt was intended as a response to the weakening of the Ottoman Empire and to British influence in India. Meanwhile, at the end of the eighteenth century British imperial geopolitics began to cast its gaze on the north-west border of India. Its ambition was, first of all, to maintain the territorial integrity of

---

76   Wael Hallaq, *Shari'a: Theory, Practice, Transformations*, Cambridge: Cambridge University Press, 2000, pp. 396–7.

77   Ibid.

Afghanistan and Persia, in order to secure India's western border against the threat of a Russian Empire emerging victorious from its confrontation with the Ottoman Empire. After 1800, this diplomatic and military strategy was also explicitly conceived against France. This led in 1809 to a treaty of alliance between Great Britain and Persia, which aimed to make the latter into a sort of buffer state.

These inter-imperial rivalries explain in part the military decision to employ steam ships. After a first attempt in 1824, the East India Company's new charter generalized the use of steam navigation during the 1830s. The route linking India to England became the keystone of the British Empire. A system of bases for refuelling coal was organized along the route. It was precisely because the Ottoman Empire was situated at a nerve centre, and because Russia appeared as a potential threat in India and Asia, that many of the British argued for maintaining the integrity of the Sublime Porte. Without the mediation of the Ottoman Empire, the colonial exploitation of India itself would prove impossible. Beginning in the 1820s, the British Empire consequently made the Ottoman Empire a strategic ally, to guarantee navigation routes and the transport of coal between England and India. The Ottomans, while conducting policies of reform and centralization, also carried out their own coal-mining activities.[78]

When, following Volney's prophecies, European imperialism in the nineteenth century sought to deploy itself over the wreckage of the Ottoman Empire, practices of coal mining developed within the empire itself. At the same time, a crucial sequence began in the history of the Muslim world and what would become the Middle East: the era of Ottoman modernizing reforms known as the Tanzimat.[79] These were, first of all, in answer to the need to reform the Ottoman military system, and they were then generalized to law and the economy.[80] They began in 1826 with Sultan Mahmoud II's abolition of the Janissary corps, a military order initially composed of European slaves. This abolition gave the

78 On Barak, 'Outsourcing: Energy and Empire in the Age of Coal, 1820–1911', *International Journal of Middle East Studies* 47, 2015, pp. 425–45.

79 According to Barak, the invention of the Middle East as a region could only take place once this system of navigation was stabilized. The word *Middle* thus refers to the space located *between* Great Britain and India. Barak, *Powering Empire*, pp. 3, 138; and Barak, 'Outsourcing', p. 426.

80 Hallaq, *Sharī'a*, p. 398.

central government increased power, from both a political and military point of view. But it also had an economic impact, in that the Janissaries were a source of economic protectionism that shielded the empire from external competition.[81] This first reform cleared the way for the establishment of economic liberalism, to meet the demands of the European powers, as well as the pressures from European capital. Some years later, it led to two treaties whose goal was to open the Ottoman Empire's populations and markets to European exploitation. The first was the Treaty of Balta Liman, passed in 1838 between the Sublime Porte and England. It confirmed the privileges enshrined in the capitulations, and definitively suppressed any form of monopoly that might protect Ottoman manufacturers from European competition. In 1839, the Edict of Gülhane went a step further. In effect, it obliged the empire to make payments to Great Britain, Austria, Prussia, and Russia in exchange for their aid against assertions of autonomy by the Egyptian modernizer Mehmet Ali. The decree abolished all 'indigenous' obstacles to economic development, making European culture, science, and capital the ultimate models for change. It led to the elimination of all forms of protectionism, opening direct access to raw materials. Protectionism had meant, in effect, that sellers of raw materials had first to sell them to guilds, at prices that were controlled and fixed, most often by the government with confirmation from a Muslim judge (*qadi*). The gradual elimination of this system and the connected rise in the price of raw materials led to the bankrupting of the guilds during the first half of the nineteenth century, and then to their elimination shortly after.[82] The goal of the Edict of Gülhane was not only to open Ottoman markets to European capital, but also to confer equality to all subjects of the empire regardless of their religion. According to Wael Hallaq, its function was to seek support from segments of the Ottoman population who could serve as intermediaries to the profit of European powers. With access to raw materials and the sultan's cooperation assured, the dismemberment of the empire became superfluous. The solution of maintaining the empire's sovereignty thus appealed to the European powers for several reasons. Notably, it avoided the conflicts that might arise from inter-European disagreements over the partition of the empire. Thus the 1839 treaty

---

81   Ibid.
82   Ibid., pp. 399–400.

stabilized a solution, which would maintain a diplomatic order that only the First World War would undo. But the condition for maintaining Ottoman sovereignty was nothing less than the empire's subjugation to external pressures, turning it into a semi-colonized state through a form of rule that was not military but economic and cultural.

The secularization of the Ottoman Empire was another aspect of the Edict of Gülhane and the pressure exercised by the European powers. In 1840, a modern-style penal code based on Islamic principles was drafted on the model of the French civil code. This was followed by a commercial code in 1850. Rashid Pasha, Ottoman ambassador to London and Paris, was one of the artisans of these reforms between 1840 and 1860.[83] At the end of the Crimean War of 1853–6, the Ottomans found themselves indebted to France and Great Britain, leading to new concessions in 1856 via the Humayun Edict. These concessions accelerated the dynamic of secularization. A representative government on the European model conferred formal rights to non-Europeans, and rejected any mention of the Qur'an or Sharia. This reform, far from being a simple effect of European pressure, also corresponded to a strategy of neutralizing nationalist sentiments by integrating them into the Ottoman Empire. The 1858 land law required peasants to register themselves, to ensure the payment of taxes to the central government while eliminating intermediary powers. The result of the land code was to tie peasants to their lands, and the Ministry of Agriculture, established in 1846, forced the Bedouins to become sedentary. One effect of these modernizing reforms was to establish a landowning class that competed with the religious elite. While the families who benefited from these reforms were mainly of a secular orientation, the religious elites were also able to profit by integrating themselves into the workings of the secular state bureaucracy. The reforms also contributed to a centralization of state power that unfolded alongside the shrinking of the empire's territory.[84]

For the first time in the history of Islamic civilization, the state took charge of the system of autonomous funding of religious institutions known in Arabic as *waqf* (*vakif* in Turkish, *habous* in North Africa). As Wael Hallaq's work on the history of Islamic law shows, this complex system of financing was based mainly on an initial charitable donation,

83 Ibid., pp. 405–6.
84 Ibid., pp. 408–10.

which Muslims made as a way of returning wealth to God by allowing the construction of centres of religious study, which most often consisted of a mosque and a madrasa. According to Islamic tradition, the ownership that resulted from this initial donation was inalienable and could not be appropriated by any human authority. What took place after 1839 with the reform of the legal system in the Ottoman Empire was nothing less than a state appropriation of these religious properties, stripped from their owners, whose autonomy and financial independence tradition had guaranteed. The secularization of the properties and the institutions that depended on them, and the bureaucratization of their members as state employees, constituted a first step in the formalization of the whole of the legal profession after 1839.[85] This system, based on waged employment, evidently implied a challenge to the independence of Muslim legal institutions. The integration of previously autonomous religious institutions into the body of the centralized state was connected to the drive to codify the Sharia, which did not function on the model of a civil code or even of law in the modern sense of the term. Recurring at the heart of these reforms, we see the central phenomenon of codifying the 'Sharia' on the model of the civil code, whose implementation in Algeria we studied earlier. While carrying out these reforms, granting equal rights to religious minorities, and adopting an abstract concept of equality, the Ottoman Empire opened its markets to free competition and dissolved all protectionism and intermediary bodies. The Ottoman imperial state was secularized and centralized at the same time that it became an *abstract structure*, independent of the persons who governed.[86]

If we follow Hallaq's analysis, these transformations of Muslim law can be seen as so many constants of secularization processes in the Muslim worlds. The secularization of the Ottoman Empire thus resulted from the progressive opening of its markets to European competition, but also from the extraction and circulation of coal as a fossil fuel.[87] Secularization, in this sense, was contemporary with the empire's integration into a globalized system of extraction and combustion, well before the oil began to be extracted in the region. The secularization of

---

85   Ibid., pp. 401–3.

86   Barak, *Powering Empire*, p. 207.

87   Barak, 'Outsourcing', pp. 429–31.

institutions, through the codification of the Sharia in the Ottoman Empire or the reform of the Anglican Church in the British Empire, was an integral part of the mechanisms that organized the exploitation and combustion of coal in the nineteenth century. It would be misleading to oppose an Ottoman model based on a supposedly enforced unity of state and Sharia to a European and British liberal model based on the separation of state and churches.[88] On the contrary, analysis of the 1832 Reform Bill and the Napoleonic system of recognized *cultes* shows that on both the European and Ottoman sides secularization was a reinforcement of state control over religious institutions. For this reason, analysis of imperial secularization cannot be limited to Europe. It participated significantly in transforming Islamic tradition from the inside, and shifting the very meaning of some of its central concepts. Islamism is a late offshoot of this process of Islamic tradition's becoming-state, provoked by imperial secularization. This does not, in any case, mean that the Ottomans were suddenly stripped of all power. On the contrary, Istanbul and Cairo sought to exploit their own subsoils following a logic constitutive of modernity's reverberation outside of Europe: as a way of becoming independent of Europe and resisting its yoke by following its model precisely. Because the officers of the Ottoman Empire thought of coal as the condition of possibility for the progress and ascent of the world's most developed nations, such as Great Britain, France, or Germany, they made its extraction and combustion so many sine qua non conditions for development policy.[89] The events that shook the Middle East and North Africa from the start of the nineteenth century, well before the 'age of oil', are therefore part of the history of climate change. The Treaty of Balta Liman was decisive for the fossil economy to the extent that it inaugurated the Ottoman Empire's integration into a world system dominated by Europe.[90]

---

88   This is what Barak suggests; see ibid., p. 233.
89   Barak, *Powering Empire*, p. 209.
90   Resat Kasaba, 'Open-Door Treaties: China and the Ottoman Empire Compared', *New Perspectives on Turkey* 1, 1992, pp. 73–4.

The role of violence in the history of the oil economy

The navigation routes that linked Great Britain and India by way of the Ottoman Empire were part of the conditions of possibility for the emergence of oil. In effect, without the European powers' implementation of imperial policies of control and guardianship over the Ottoman Empire, European private companies would never have been able to discover oil deposits in the subsoil of what was then Mesopotamia. The geopolitical system born with the Egyptian Expedition and the weakening of the Ottoman Empire was thus constitutive of the fossil economy. The age of coal is inseparable from the Eastern Question: to study one necessarily contributes to understanding the other. As consequences of the Ottoman Empire's military defeats after the end of the eighteenth century, the Egyptian Expedition and the colonization of Algeria contributed to the geopolitical birth of a region, and they cannot be separated from the system of exploiting coal and, later, oil and gas. These events attest to the central role played by inter-imperial rivalries in the genesis of a fossil industry that, for this reason, has always been more than a simple economy. The history of coal in the Ottoman Empire contributed to preparing the age of oil, as it would unfold in the Middle East. Following the thread of the Eastern Question, we can trace back to the 1820s the history of the inter-imperial logics that, following the fall of the Ottoman Empire after the First World War, would draw the borders of the Middle East along the lines of the presence of oil.[91]

How, then, to understand the emergence of the oil economy from these inter-imperial dynamics? According to Timothy Mitchell, it was not simply European companies' discovery of oil deposits in Mesopotamia that led the British economy to convert to the generalized use of oil. These rival companies tried not to increase but rather to limit the extraction of oil, until they could assure protection of their own exclusive monopoly. These monopoly practices served to capture a lucrative market and limit competition from other companies, thanks to state support.[92] In this way, the companies learned to identify their own interests with the imperial needs of the state. As a result, the convergence of strategic interests between the British state and the oil

---

91   Malm, 'Who Lit This Fire?', pp. 222–3.
92   Mitchell, *Carbon Democracy*, pp. 54–65.

companies played a key and decisive role in the *generalization* of an economy founded on oil extraction.

The oil economy did not lead to the end of the age of coal; the history of energy is a coexistence by accumulation that never implies the replacement of one type of fossil exploitation by another.[93] As the oil economy itself was made possible by the exploitation of coal, the geopolitical organization based on maintaining the integrity of the Ottoman Empire, together with the set of secularizing reforms, were so many conditions of possibility for its arrival. The set of pressures exercised in the name of protecting the Christian minorities of the Orient from the Islamic yoke played a role in this process, and throughout the nineteenth century prepared the slow dismantling that led to the implosion of the Ottoman Empire. The massive extraction of oil and gas in the Middle East and Africa established during the twentieth century was written a hundred years before, at the heart of what is called the age of coal: it was in the nineteenth century that the geopolitical conditions of the oil economy unfolded, in tandem with that of the Eastern Question and its ties to the coal economy.

Coal is thus more than a simple fossil fuel, a natural entity whose economic exploitation industrialism merely organized. For this reason, global warming cannot be analysed merely as an effect of burning coal. It is the result of a system of powers in struggle, which, articulating itself around coal, goes beyond the limits of the economic, and whose imperiality is inextricably political, cultural, and theological.

The fossil state and its relations with class struggle

The mechanisms of the fossil state thus cannot be reduced to the simple effects of class struggle. The state is not, as a now-discredited vulgar Marxism once declared, the instrument of bourgeois domination of the working class. Workers' capacity for resistance depended on a vulnerability of systems of production that was implied by the very materiality of coal. What we call democracy refers centrally to the set of social rights which, beginning with the right to vote, the labouring classes extracted from capitalists and the state, thanks to the relations of power created by their unions and political organization. This institution is enmeshed

---

93 Barak, *Powering Empire*, p. 10.

with the exploitation of coal, since it was only by sabotaging production processes connected to the use of coal that workers were able to extort these rights and to democratize politics. Oil was adopted precisely because it allowed states to short-circuit forms of workers' resistance based on coal, thanks to the fluidity that makes its use less vulnerable to techniques of workers' sabotage.[94]

The Reform Bills were a fruit of this history, as the result of the state being forced to impose itself as a third party and mediator between working class and bourgeoisie, between exploited and exploiters.[95] It was class struggle that forced the state to become more than a simple defender of the bourgeoisie: or more precisely, it was the relations of power created by workers' insurrections. The fossil state is a deaf machine that digests whatever opposes it, by translating it into a regime of rights and a logic that calls for an extension of regulatory practices. If industrialization and empire are connected, if there is no *primacy* of fossil capital over fossil imperialism but, rather, an interdependence, such that the two are merely analytically distinct but never truly separable, this is precisely because it was the secularization of the state that wove the threads between them. One therefore needs to further inquire into the fossil state's subterranean sovereignty to understand how fossil capitalism emerged in Europe and was generalized beyond the West.

---

94   Mitchell, *Carbon Democracy*, pp. 1–38.
95   Barak, *Powering Empire*, p. 116.

5

Gospels of the Reich: The Eastern Question and the Jewish Question

We have seen the crucial role that inter-imperial rivalries played in the birth of the fossil economy, and how the various military and industrial upheavals that led to climate change were directly related to the weakening international position of the Ottoman Empire after the end of the eighteenth century. A sequence of events in the period 1827–30 marked the acceleration of this process. Directly connected to the intensification of inter-imperial rivalry throughout the nineteenth century, they began to threaten that the war between the powers of Europe and Asia might be imported into Europe itself.[1] In an article titled 'Russia and the Western Powers', originally published on 5 August 1853, Marx wrote: 'The *Western* powers, on the other hand, *inconsistent*, pusillanimous, suspecting each other, commence by encouraging the Sultan to resist the Czar, from fear of the encroachments of Russia, and terminate by compelling the former to yield, from *fear* of a *general war giving rise to a general revolution*.'[2] The potential generalization of the war due to the rupture of diplomatic equilibrium between the great powers opened a discursive space within which Marx prophesied the possible generalization of the Revolution. Because Marx was a thinker of conjuncture, he

---

1   Eric Hobsbawn, *The Age of Capital: 1848–1875*, London: Scribner, 1975, p. 95.
2   Karl Marx, *The Eastern Question: A Reprint of Letters Written 1853–1856 Dealing with the Events of the Crimean War*, London: Swan Sonnenschein & Co., 1897, pp. 74–5. Emphasis added.

tried to read the potential for an *internationalization* of war and diplomatic crisis into the core of the so-called Eastern Question.[3] The Crimean War was probably the first moment in this internationalization of war, before the First World War of 1914–18. While global war was at the core of the fossil global economy, prophecies such as Marx's proliferated.

This chapter examines the way that latent imperial prophecies became reactivated during this period, continuing throughout the so-called age of coal. In formulating these prophecies, a large number of European Christians allowed themselves to dream of a Europe cleansed of Islam and Muslims, as they reactivated the language of the Crusades in a rapidly changing world. From the 1830s on, the hypothesis of a coming dissolution of the Ottoman Empire let Western Europe declare itself *Christian civilization*, in opposition to *Islamic fanaticism*, while at the same time hoping to seize the throne of the old Eastern Roman Empire, on which the Ottomans still sat. As the Ottomans suffered repeated losses to Russia, imperial and diplomatic evangelicalism increasingly mobilized the rights of man as an instrument by which to eradicate all traces of Islam within Europe. The idea of a European Christian civilization was constructed through a project of exterminating Muslims; it would later be mobilized, under the Third Reich, against another people who since the eighteenth century had been defined as Oriental and Semitic: the Jews. The drive to liberate Christian, non-Jewish, and non-Muslim peoples – men and women of Europe, the Orient, and Africa – from the Islamic yoke was a project that Christians and secular figures shared, communing together in a single imperial gesture. Western revolutionaries and Christians called for the oppression of the oppressors, and used the Muslim and the Jew to symbolize the oppressor who was to be oppressed. Their discourse lauded a union of Christian peoples against the common enemy, beyond confessional differences. The Westernization of Christianity that they developed presupposed the racial Orientalization of Islam and Judaism. Christianity became White, and was, from then on, identified with the Aryan race, while Jews and Muslims were racially defined as Semites. In Germany and elsewhere,

---

3 On the nineteenth (and early twentieth) century as the proliferation of interconnected 'Questions' – Eastern, Jewish, German, etc. – see Holly Case, *The Age of Questions*, Princeton, NJ: Princeton University Press, 2018.

racial Orientalism thus functioned to *Aryanize* Christianity, and it was accompanied by the subordination of Oriental Orthodox Christianity to Western Christianity. This Orientalism had a clear imperial vocation, since the method it offered to advance the common destiny of Christian peoples against the Jews and Muslims was the conquest of the world by Western Europe. This chapter examines a crucial aspect of the racial history of secularization, in connection with the development of fossil empires. It argues that the age of coal was inseparable from the invention of the Aryan race and the model of White supremacy that resulted from it.

The analysis that follows situates the history of rivalry between fossil empires in the frame of the mutations that Protestant tradition underwent in the nineteenth century. Imperial secularization as it operated in England, alongside industrialization, was dependent on these mutations. Evangelicalism played a crucial role. Far from any decline or supposed privatization of religion, the British Empire's policies of secularization were informed by evangelical language. It contributed to the nationalization of Protestantism, and so to the creation of an expanded Christianity beyond the confessional limits of Anglicanism.[4]

I propose here to analyse these theologico-political dimensions of secularization primarily by comparing British and German imperialism. In these two countries, the nationalization of Protestantism was at the heart of secularization. It led German nationalism towards a pan-Germanic orientation that would be radicalized by National Socialism.[5] Of these internal mutations of Protestant culture, the birth and development of evangelicalism is in some sense the most striking and indexical. Evangelicalism was imperial in that it participated fully in the geopolitical upheavals that affected the Ottoman Empire throughout the nineteenth century.

4   J. P. Parry, 'Nonconformity, Clericalism and "Englishness": The United Kingdom', in Christopher Clark and Wolfram Kaiser, eds, *Culture Wars: Secular–Catholic Conflict in Nineteenth-Century Europe*, Cambridge: Cambridge University Press, 2003, pp. 152–80. Parry shows that, without abolishing the establishment, the British state attempted to democratize the Anglican Church along a parliamentary model. This reform responded to the ideal of a free church within a free state. Rather than separating the Anglican Church from the state, the British Empire would constitute Protestantism as a sort of national culture that defined proper *Englishness*.

5   W. O. Henderson, *Studies in German Colonial History*, London: Routledge, 2006 (1962), pp. 120–2.

I begin by returning to colonial India and Algeria, and show that the French policy of non-conversion of indigenous subjects to Christianity, deployed as a Bonapartist legacy in Algeria, reappeared in India in a distinct form, especially after 1857. This comparison will lead us to the central role played in the British fossil empire by evangelicalism, whose German model will be presented next. By retracing this history, I examine how the model of secularization deployed by Prussia and then by the German Empire contributed to creating the racial ideologies and political expansionism of the Third Reich.

Imperial secularization between India and Algeria

To what extent did fossil colonialism, as deployed by the British in India, proclaim the order of secularization? To answer this question, we will compare certain aspects of the British colonization of India in the nineteenth century with the French colonization of Algeria.[6] Contrary to what is often claimed by historians of British colonialism, it was neither the repression of the Sepoy Rebellion in 1857 nor that of the Morant Bay Rebellion in Jamaica in 1863 that led to the invention of indirect rule. The historian Sudipta Sen has shown that the British East India Company set up a form of indirect government as early as the eighteenth century.[7] But, by causing a crisis in the imperial liberalism based on the reform of indigenous traditions, the two rebellions tipped British colonial policy towards a model the French Empire had implemented earlier in Algeria: annexing India to the British imperium by declaring Queen Victoria its empress. The British East India Company's power was thus transferred to the Crown in August 1858. British colonialism in India was incorporated into the body of the state in the name of respect for

---

6 Colonized India and Algeria were each integrated into the body of the empire itself. They thus constitute two *imperial colonies par excellence*. India and Algeria acted as laboratories from which the spread of colonialism in Africa and the Middle East can be examined.

7 Compare Sudipta Sen, *A Distant Sovereignty: National Imperialism and the Origins of British India*, New York: Routledge, and Mahmood Mamdani, *Citizen and Subject: Contemporary Africa and the Legacy of Late Colonialism*, Princeton, NJ: Princeton University Press, 2018 (1993). Throughout his book, Mamdani assumes that 1857 marked the start of indirect government in India. Sen demonstrates, on the contrary, that this type of government emerged as early as the end of the eighteenth century.

freedom of religion, as we can see in the Queen's official proclamation: 'We declare it to be our royal will and pleasure that none be in anywise favoured, none molested or disquieted, by reason of their religious faith or observances, but that all shall alike enjoy the equal and impartial protection of the law.' Every colonial authority subject to the empire was to 'abstain from all interference with the religious belief or worship of any of our subjects', at the risk of provoking the monarch's 'highest displeasure'.[8] Like the French state in Algeria, it was in the name of the grand principle of religious freedom that the British imperial state integrated India into its sovereign body. But this empire of religious tolerance unfolded only by racializing religious traditions and people who were increasingly held to be inconvertible. Henry Sumner Maine is generally recognized as a leader of the post-reformist imperialism that was based on upholding tradition, in the name of public order and the supposed immobility of custom. His trajectory attests to what we saw earlier in our study of certain writings from the Bureaux Arabes and military colonization in Algeria: the imperial production of fanaticism as evidence of the enemy's inconvertibility played a key role in the formation of colonial racism. Maine was at the origin of the official reading that saw the 1857 insurrection as an effect of the 'terrified fanaticism' of profoundly religious Indians. The liberals, in his view, had committed a major error by ignoring the importance of tradition and wagering that caste and religion would lose their authority as India was progressively modernized.[9] Worried that secular or Christian missionaries would provoke insurrection among radicalized Muslims and Hindus, the colonial government took an ethnographic turn.

Between 1830 and 1870, France followed a similar trajectory in Algeria, based on a military–ethnographic complex whose first stones were laid during the war against the insurrection led by Emir Abd el-Kader. The beating heart of these techniques was an order to secularize colonial war: the call to secularize education, which would penetrate native society without awakening sleeping fanaticism. Between 1830 and 1852, the colonial army strictly forbade missionary activity to

---

8   Queen Victoria, cited in Cyril Henry Philips, Hira Lal Singh, and Bishwa Nath Pandey, eds, *The Evolution of India and Pakistan, 1858 to 1947: Selected Documents*, London: Oxford University Press, 1962, p. 11.

9   Henry Sumner Maine, 'India', in Thomas Humphry Ward, ed., *The Reign of Queen Victoria: A Survey of Fifty Years of Progress*, London: Smith, Elder, & Co., 1887, p. 474.

Muslims, and colonial institutions substituted secular education for direct conversion to Christianity. The French government's control over Islam and Catholicism in Algeria generalized a colonial policy of controlling religions.[10] By inventing a Muslim *culte*, which it attempted to organize as a vertical and governable structure, on the model of the so-called Israelite *culte*, imperial secularism situated itself at the heart of colonialism. By first forbidding and then limiting Christian proselytism, the colonial order forced Catholicism to conduct its mission through social works. What was invented in Algeria was a policy of *indirect conversion*, mediated by *secular education*.

As we have seen, the theme of Muslim violence not only played a crucial role in the context of colonial Algeria and the French Empire. It was also at the heart of the imperial discourse and colonial techniques of the British Empire. The Muslims of India were defined as supporters of slavery; their law was understood as despotic domination of women by the institution of polygamy. For their part, the Hindus were represented as authentic natives who had been subjugated by the Islamic conquest. Women and Hindus were thus victims of the Muslim yoke. Colonial reason feminized Hindus, while understanding Islam as essentially masculine. According to Robert Orme, the Hindu was the 'most effeminate inhabitant of the globe'.[11] This feminization corresponded to the construction of Islam as a virile, because conquering, religion. The polytheist Hindus appeared as feminine to the extent that they were defined as the ideal prey of the conquering Muslims from the north. In the speeches of scholars and the empire, an assumed constitutive weakness of their race made them vulnerable to the supposedly congenital and intrinsic violence of Islamic monotheism. Imperial reason explained polytheistic men as beings who were constrained to live within the narrow limits of a traditional world they could see only as ancestral and immobile. Like the Muslims, therefore, they should be freed from the violence of their tradition – which the empire occupied itself with doing, up until 1857.

From 1820 to 1857, until the Sepoy Rebellion, this imperial will to liberation dominated colonial reform policies and missionary projects.[12]

---

10   Oissila Saaïdia, *Algérie coloniale: musulmans et chrétiens: le contrôle de l'état (1830–1914)*, Paris: Éditions du CNRS, 2015, pp. 17–19.

11   Robert Orme, cited in Timothy Metcalf, *Ideologies of the Raj*, Cambridge: Cambridge University Press, 1995, p. 9.

12   Ibid., p. 28.

Imperial liberalism's principal enemy was slavery, which it defined as 'endogenous' or 'Islamic'. In both its evangelical and secular forms, this liberalism associated slavery with the religious submission of the indigenous population to the authority of tradition. The empire could define these subjects – whom it would force into agricultural labour and work in the mines for miserable wages – as inferior races only by reconstructing their religions and traditions. Colonial subjects were racialized through the objectivization of their religions. An influential text, *The History of British India*, written by none other than the father of the philosopher John Stuart Mill, deployed its criticism of 'priestcraft' and the arbitrary rule of religion to demonstrate the supposed inferiority of Indian civilization. Mill judged the caste system to be degrading, not because it deployed a form of hierarchical subordination, but because the founding laws of India from which it was generated emanated from a supposedly divine authority. He wrote, in Volney's footsteps, that India was dominated by a 'system of priestcraft, built upon the most enormous, irrational, and tormenting superstition, that ever harassed and degraded any portion of mankind'. Slavery had developed from the rule of priests; but, more than this, Mill decried their mental slavery, declaring that the natives' spirits were chained still more intolerably than their bodies. Through a combination of despotism and priestcraft, the Hindus had become, physically and morally, 'the most enslaved portion of the human race'.[13]

This critique of the religious subjection of the Indian peoples played a major role in colonial liberalism, which aimed to abolish the suffering inflicted by traditional ritual practices, judged by its utilitarian reason as useless and therefore cruel. This reason drew limits around suffering, distinguishing useful inflictions from arbitrary ones. Indigenous religion and the sacrifices it imposed became models of a cruelty that was now judged by the principle of utility rather than in divine terms. Cruelty designated practices of self-inflicted pain that reason deemed to be absurd and senseless, because they had no use. Confronted with suffering that it qualified as absurd and superstitious, the empire legitimated its own violence as an inevitable fact and necessary means to secure the prosperity of all.

13 James Mill, *The History of British India*, vol. 1, London: Baldwin, Craddock, & Joy, 1817, p. 452.

The imperial traditionalism that Henry Maine is often credited with founding was one legacy of the theme of inconvertibility. Colonial administrations could not introduce any large-scale conversion of the indigenous population, under pain of awakening fanaticism and revolt. In this principle, both British colonialism in India and the French Empire in Algeria retained Bonaparte's lesson from Egypt: stop attempting a large-scale conversion of the infidels, and instead work to transform their own traditions in order to produce their consent. As we have seen, this did not mean that Christian missionary activity had to stop; but it would now need to succeed within a regime that separated the Church and the colonial state. In the aftermath of a local revolt that preceded the 1857 Sepoy Rebellion, Archbishop Wilson declared on 24 July 1854 in Calcutta that it was necessary to secure peace and security in India, and that the British Empire's even-handedness contrasted with 'the fierce tyranny of the Mahomedan for 600 years'.[14] Liberal empire would take the place of Islam and the reign of the Muslim Mughals in Asia, just as Volney had prophesied a secular empire in a Middle East liberated from the Ottomans. Wilson, as a liberal Christian, did not say that the victory over Islam would take place through the indigenous population's direct conversion to Christianity. Like Quinet and the French secular Republicans, the British Christians adopted the plan of realizing the essence of Christianity through secular education. Christian morality would be realized indirectly, through social works and secular colonial education, not directly through preaching. While education would not exclude Christianity, it would not teach it *directly*. The Christianity of the British Empire was defined not by a catechism, but by the Christian morality that it transmitted through the instruction of British *culture*, which supposedly incarnated it in a profane and everyday manner. English literature substituted not for Christianity itself but for direct preaching, by teaching Christian morality in action. Christianity was understood to have been secularized within British culture. Neither missions nor conversions were stopped in the colony, but the rare Indians who converted to Christianity did not escape their community of origin, and remained subject to the customary law that governed their status. Similarly, as we have seen, the rare Algerian

---

14 Wilson, cited in John Pollard Willoughby, *Government of India*, London: Edward Moxon, 1858, p. 38.

Muslims who converted were called *Catholic Muslims* by the colonial administration. The secularization of the empire made complete conversion by the colonized an impossible act, because the indigenous subject was subjugated to a community whose boundaries were fixed by secular colonial law. It was by codifying traditions as separate communities subject to distinct customary laws that the empire founded an *indigénat*. It thereby made conversion suspect and limited.[15]

The British Empire contributed to transforming English Protestantism in the metropole, through a series of imperial circulations.[16] The imperial compromise between missionaries and the colonial government offered a model of secularization for Great Britain itself. A speech by Bishop Whately on 18 January 1858 to the Church Missionary Society in Dublin put it clearly: the policy of separation already applied in India should be applied in England. Whately defended government non-interference in religious affairs, which, according to him, was the policy the East India Company had applied for twenty years.[17] As in Algeria, Christian missions aroused the suspicion of the colonial government, which worried about giving the Indians the impression that the British presence was there to force them to convert to Christianity. Whately himself, as a liberal Protestant, supported this indirect model of missionary activity. He declared that, if Christian missionary activity had been properly distinguished from any relation to the British government, the Sepoy Rebellion would never have happened. What was needed, as the Catholics had done in Africa, was a convergence of viewpoints with the secular colonial government, but in such a way that the missions could claim to act freely. The missionaries should conquer a space of autonomy and religious freedom in the colonies. They should refuse any 'assistance of Government as Government to it, as it will excite the greatest degree of suspicion' among the non-Christian colonized and 'raise the greatest prejudice against Christianity'. If the government 'were even suspected of coming forward to aid missionary efforts by its own power,

15 Gauri Viswanathan, 'Coping with (Civil) Death: The Christian Convert's Rights of Passage in Colonial India', in Gyan Prakash, ed., *After Colonialism: Imperial Histories and Postcolonial Displacements*, Princeton, NJ: Princeton University Press, 1995, pp. 183–210.

16 See Peter van der Veer, *Imperial Encounters: Religion and Modernity in India and Britain*, Princeton, NJ: Princeton University Press, 2001.

17 Willoughby, *Government of India*, p. 39.

it would be suspected of exerting physical force, than which nothing could be more fatal to the cause'. The demands of colonizing India thus required a model of separation between mission and state. 'I say', Whately went on, that forced conversion by the use of violence 'would be disastrous in any state of society'; but it would 'be more peculiarly disastrous in such a country as India, for this reason: that it is impossible to take away the religion of the Hindoo by main force'.[18]

To avoid raising suspicion, therefore, the missions should not receive state funding. In a word, the framework of the colonial mission should be liberalized. What would be created in the colonies would thus be nothing less than a reform of Christianity itself, the solution to the crucial problem of its future in the industrial world. What the empire would create in India would be the keystone for any reform of the Church in a Protestant country: a union of Protestant confessions within an expanded Church, the *Broad* Church. This union of churches would come together through imperial mediation, as a mechanism of pacifying the different confessions within Christianity. Love would become the principle of a Christian unity, beyond the different divisions of the *Protestant family*. Whately wrote that it was necessary to reject the doctrine according to which 'Christian men are not to co-operate for anything till they agree in everything.'[19] Christian colonial cooperation would be a sort of common liturgy without a unifying doctrine, a ritual shared by Christians of different confessions.

What Whately described was an architecture for a liberalization of Protestant tradition – which, unlike Catholicism, is multiconfessional. This liberalization required a policy of unification between confessions in Prussia, England, and North America. It was contemporary with the emergence of new confessional currents, centred on the evangelical movement that was established against an official Protestantism it considered routine and too narrowly rationalist.[20] This movement, which brought together multiple confessions and members of numerous churches, was influenced by the German Enlightenment and its biblical criticism. Around 1870, it began to formulate liberal theologies

18 Whately, cited in ibid.
19 Ibid., pp. 38–9.
20 Jean Baubérot and Séverine Mathieu, *Religion, modernité et culture au Royaume-Uni et en France*, Paris: Seuil, 2002, p. 50.

of the kingdom of God that preached the reign of love, according to which the essence of Christianity was no longer the transcendence of the trinitarian God, but a simple morality that called on everyone to love their neighbour. The kingdom of God became the realization of this love between men.[21] The essence of God ceased to be metaphysical, and became purely moral. Since God had become the love of man, the fulfilment of his kingdom would necessarily take place in this world. God would henceforth stand *among men*, drawing close to us in order to make himself present. This was an intuition formulated by Hegel, beginning with his *Phenomenology of Spirit*, as the keystone of what he called absolute knowledge.[22]

This doctrine was the fruit of a labour of reform, a decisive component of which was the Anglican Church's response to historical criticism of the Bible.[23] The Broad Church movement within the Anglican Church emerged from a desire to accommodate Christianity to new times and to the advances of biblical criticism and scholarly Orientalism. The historicization of the Bible by philology and Orientalism thus played a crucial role in the internal transformation of Christianity, for which evangelicalism was the evidence.[24] This transformation was accompanied by doctrinal change: the doctrine of expiation, the pardoning of sins by God in Christ, became less central than the incarnation of God in Christ, which would now be the heart of Christianity. Between 1890 and 1940, this would become the orthodox Anglican position, but, at the start of the nineteenth century, it was the evangelical current that formed the continuum between Anglicans and nonconformists, their overlapping consensus. Social Christianity called for the development of fraternities or *brotherhoods*. While atheism fell under freedom of belief, society should preserve Christian values, because the social effects of atheism could not yet be judged.

Evangelicalism made doctrinal differences secondary, unifying all Christians around a practical communion – a common liturgy and morality, shared rituals and values – beyond differences in beliefs.

---

21   J. M. Mayeur et al., eds, *Histoire du christianisme: libéralisme, industrialisation, expansion européenne*, vol. 11, Paris: Desclée, 1995, p. 400.

22   See note 1 in the Prologue.

23   Baubérot and Matthieu, *Religion, modernité et culture*, p. 201.

24   The celebrated Orientalist Robertson Smith himself belonged to the Scottish evangelical Free Church.

Christianity could then become the cultural heritage of the industrial West, recoded as the source of its civilization and morals. The imperial Anglicanism of the nineteenth century was dominated by evangelicalism: its doctrine declared that God had given the greatest empire in the world as a gift to England.[25] The union of state and Church was the condition for the advent of a global empire, generalizing to the entire globe what the Roman Empire had been to the Mediterranean. Nineteenth-century religious reforms coexisted with this new imperial politics. It was Anglican evangelicals who fought for the abolition of slavery in the empire. During the 1830s, Thomas Fowell Buxton proposed a programme to eradicate what he saw as endogenous slavery in Africa. His plan called for the development of agriculture in the African interior, as an alternate activity to tribal war. The alliance of Bible and plough would thus 'regenerate Africa'. An expedition he organized to Niger in 1841 was a failure, but it contributed to defining a new imperial idea that proclaimed the necessary redemption of Africa. The expedition showed the key role that evangelicalism played in the emergence of the new type of imperial project whose history we are writing, designed to be deployed in Africa as a project of freeing slaves. The evangelicals declared that Africa could only be saved after slavery had been abolished by trade and Christianity.[26] The goal of the empire, therefore, according to many Anglicans, was to abolish slavery. But this imperial Anglicanism was not only deployed in Africa: its other target was Jerusalem. While not all Christians supported missionary activity in Palestine, as the Tractarian movement's opposition demonstrates, evangelical Anglicans supported the project enthusiastically. The restoration of Jews to the Holy Land seemed to them a sign of the imminent return of Christ in glory. Evangelicalism made the British Empire an actor of divine providence, prompting evangelical networks in Prussia and England to form diplomatic alliances based on shared Protestantism. A result of this history was the Anglo-German alliance in the Middle East. As we will see, it contributed to the deployment of a humanitarian politics based on protecting the rights of Christian minorities in the

---

25   Stewart J. Brown, 'Anglicanism in the British Empire, 1819–1910', in Rowan Strong, ed., *The Oxford History of Anglicanism*, vol. 3, Oxford: Oxford University Press, 2017, pp. 45–68.

26   Ibid., p. 47.

Middle East in the name of religious freedom, as well as White abolitionism in Africa. In order to grasp the unfolding and importance of
this imperial evangelicalism, we need to return to its German model.

Evangelical Union in search of an empire

In many respects, Germany was at the heart of the theological mutations
that accompanied the development of the fossil economy in the British
Empire. Through the influence of biblical criticism and scholarly theology, Germany played a crucial role in the spread and internationalization of evangelicalism in the Anglophone countries.[27] To understand the
relations between empire and secularization in the British Empire
through the prism of the centrality of evangelicalism will therefore
require us to examine its German matrix and model of secularization.
Here we move from an analysis of the energetic foundations of the
English liberal state and the French Empire to a historical critique of the
secularization of the Reich, the German Empire. This will extend our
comparative analysis of forms of imperial secularization into the nineteenth century.

The model of secularization at the heart of nineteenth-century
German culture is in many respects comparable to the British model. It
was based on a nationalization of Protestantism, and developed through
a series of church reforms that took place after 1817. These reforms had
the function of establishing a new religious community, beyond differences in confessions. They translated Protestant language into the

---

27   On the influence of the pietist German Orientalist and theologian August
Gottreu Tholuck on Anglophone evangelical networks, see Hughes Oliphant Old, *The
Reading and Preaching of the Scriptures in the Worship of the Christian Church*, vol. 6, *The
Modern Age, 1789–1889*, Cambridge: William B. Eerdmans Publishing, 2006, pp.
117–18. The involvement of Tholuck, as well as Christian von Bunsen – another German
Orientalist discussed in this chapter – in international evangelical networks has been
shown. See Nicholas Railton, *No North Sea: The Anglo-German Evangelical Network in
the Middle of the Nineteenth Century*, Leiden: Brill, 1999, pp. 144–5, 171. Tholuck taught
Henry Boyton Smith and George Prentiss, who would become professors of church
history at the Union Theological Seminary in New York, along with the Princeton
evangelical pastor Reverend Charles Hodge. Among other figures of German biblical
criticism, Tholuck profoundly influenced his Scottish and American students, who went
on to exercise leadership in their churches.

language of 'national genius'.[28] The language of German nationalism was forged in the Prussian Union of Churches.[29] Germany was not a state before it became, around 1870, a new empire, a Reich. It was a union of multiple principalities, known as the Holy Roman Empire of the German Nation. This imperial unity corresponded to a religious unity that was broken by the Reformation. The unity of Christendom became fragmented and gave way to a proliferation of Christian confessions, what German historians describe with the concept of confessionalization. By provoking a new politico-religious hostility, this process of fragmentation played a key role in the formation of modern states and the secularization of Europe.

Determining how *secularization* took place in the context of this empire requires us to grasp the way in which Protestant culture was *politicized* in the German public sphere.[30] The German nineteenth century can be characterized as a second 'confessional moment', which continued and reprised the great confessional moment of the *first modernity*.[31] Secularization and confessionalism were connected in

---

28 Imperial German nationalism should be traced not to a restoration of the religious but to a new concept of religion. Religion became a component of national culture and a foundation of the collective identity of a people. It incarnated profane realities such as *nation* and *civilization*, whose essence could be deciphered from the history of the people.

29 J. F. G. Goeters and Rudolph Mau, *Die Geschichte der Evangelischen Kirche der Union*, vol. 1, Leipzig: Evangelische Verlagsanhalt, 1992.

30 See Philippe Büttgen, 'Qu'est-ce qu'une culture confessionnelle? Essai d'historiographie (1998–2008)', in Philippe Büttgen and Christophe Duhamelle, eds, *Religion ou confession? Un bilan franco-allemand sur l'époque moderne (XVIè–XVIIIè siècles)*, Paris: Éditions de la MSH, 2010, pp. 430–1.

31 For a presentation of this hypothesis, see Olaf Blaschke, 'Germany in the Age of the Culture Wars', in S. Müller and C. Torp, *Imperial Germany Revisited: Continuing Debates and New Perspectives*, New York: Berghahn Books, 2011, pp. 125–40. See especially p. 133: 'The confessional age took place alongside the age of secularization and nationalism', Blaschke writes. 'The culture wars were an expression of a secular age but also of a confessional age.' According to Blaschke, the interdependence of nationalism and religion in the empire was one result. I agree with the correctives that Büttgen makes to this thesis in 'Qu'est-ce qu'une culture confessionnelle', p. 433. He proposes that we see in the contemporary permanence of the confessional not an age but the formation of new confessional cultures. But the grammar that constituted the newness of the language acts defining this new confessionality remains to be determined. The period was not a confessionalization identical to what took place during the Reformation. The hypothesis of a second confessional moment is not opposed to the model of secularization, but adds complexity to the idea and its articulation. See Olaf Blaschke, ed., *Konfessionen im*

Germany. The Kulturkampf under Bismarck, a period of anticatholicism and identification of Protestant culture with national identity, shows the intrinsic ties between secularization and confessionalization. The evangelical Protestant awakening and the development of anticatholicism and antisemitism in Germany are both evidence of the confessionalism that structured the German nineteenth century.

In its German Protestant form, imperial secularization was characterized neither by the separation of the religious and political nor by a decline of religion, reduced to an individual and private belief, but rather by the emergence of new forms, as numerous as they were unprecedented, of *politicizing the religious*. At the heart of these processes was the invention of a *cultural Christianity* whose premises can be traced back to the Classical Age: the construction of *Christianity* as a category to designate an essence shared by all Christian confessions.[32] What the nineteenth century did, therefore, was not to secularize Christianity, but to invent a new Christianity. Before the Classical Age, speaking of *Christianity* had no meaning. During the first modernity, it was theology that gave meaning to discourse on Christianity. Afterwards, passing through eighteenth-century biblical criticism and throughout the nineteenth century, speech about Christianity took place in a *historical manner*, on the margins of theology and sometimes *against it*.

The Union of Protestant Churches belongs to this process, and corresponds to what the historian Olaf Blaschke describes as a second moment of confessionalization. This consisted in resolving the problem of confessional multiplicity within Prussian Protestantism by attempting to create unity through a politically instituted rite. This reform, the idea of which can already be found in Leibniz, was initiated in Prussia by King Friedrich Wilhelm III in 1817. In my opinion, its expression and institution were the premises of the model of German secularization whose imperiality is examined in the following pages. The reform came out of a desire for national unity and progress, in the name of which the king of Prussia ordered the different confessional churches to

---

Konflikt: Deutschland zwischen 1800 und 1970: Ein zweites konfessionelles Zeitalter, Göttingen: Vandenhoeck & Ruprecht, 2002.

  32   See the analyses by Thomas Kaufmann, *Dreissigjähriger Krieg und Westfälischer Friede: Kirchengeschichtliche Studien zur Lutherischen Konfessionskulture*, Tübingen: Mohr Siebeck, 1998, pp. 83–8 and pp. 8, 125, 141.

unite. This did not mean that they had to profess the same dogma or doctrine: what the monarchy wanted was for believers to practise the same liturgy, the same rite, despite differences in belief. In wanting to unify Lutheran and Reformed confessions into a single Protestant union, the monarchy formalized ritual by dissociating liturgy from belief. By the intermediary of its professions of faith, Prussia invented a mode of ritualization that took priority over belief. By dissociating belief and practice, secularization engendered the dynamic of the nationalization of Protestantism.

This church reform was evangelical to the extent that it sought to rediscover the original spirit of the Gospel and the Reformation, *beneath the divisions* between Lutherans and Calvinist Reformed. One consequence of evangelicalism was to constitute a national Protestantism, a *nationalization* that should be understood as an effect of secularization. The concept of the nation was translated into a religious vocabulary, reconfiguring Christianity within a national frame. From there, the uses and grammar of the concept of religion were transformed. Religion became the expression of a profane identity, which was that of the nation, whose criteria were inseparably linguistic, ethnic, and racial. Church reform secularized Prussia to the extent that it contributed to establishing a *national-Protestant culture* at the very heart of state ritual. The Reformation was reclaimed as a historical heritage, and Hegel recognized it as the origin of the modern age.[33] Schelling gave this same story a nationalist interpretation, arguing that since the Reformation had been born on German territory, Germany was *elected* to the title of empire and thus called to rule the modern world.[34] This Schellingian narrative, formulated alongside the policy of Church Union during the reign of Friedrich Wilhelm IV, sets us on the track of the imperiality of secularization in its German version. The writings of one of Schelling's disciples, Constantin Frantz, attest to the becoming-imperial of German philosophy. In Frantz's writings, the Prussian model of secularization reveals part of its imperiality, giving birth to the idea of a German federalism under whose hegemony Europe was called to

---

33 Philippe Büttgen, 'Hegel à Augsbourg: Confession et commémoration', *Revue germanique internationale, Théologies politiques du Vormärz* 8, 2008, pp. 33–53.

34 Alexandra Roux, 'Schelling et l'État: Quel "ciel sur la terre"?' *Revue philosophique de Louvain* 101, no. 3, 2003, pp. 456–78.

establish itself as a federal and super-state empire.[35] The imperiality of German secularization thus went beyond the limits of colonialism, strictly speaking.

Constantin Frantz was perhaps the first German federalist to defend this project.[36] In his writings, the Christian unity of the nation became the unity of a federal empire. Frantz did not transfer the religious from the Church to the secular state. He brought the Church back to its social imperiality through a metapolitical federalism that he put in opposition to the centralized nation-state. This German federalism was conceived of as the resurrection of the Holy Roman Empire, reborn in a new form. Frantz's Germany was the centre from which Europe would be unified by a cultural Christianity. This culturalized Christianity would no longer call itself religion or confession, but *Christian civilization*. European civilization exceeded confessions, as it did nationalities. This broad and supra-confessional conception of Christianity was at the heart of the idea of European civilization that Frantz defended. It was the foundation of an imperial identity that justified a German hegemony spreading out continuously from Eastern Europe. The German federal idea was a *metapolitics of the nation*. 'Germany has never been a "state", and will never become one unless it ceases to be Germany.' It was thus necessary to 'look beyond the boundary of statehood and imagine a community of a quite different kind destined to accomplish far greater tasks', because Germany was an 'international entity', something metapolitical.[37]

This metapolitics was derived from Schelling's speculative philosophy, but it was also Wagnerian by affinity.[38] Wagner himself saw Frantz as his political alter ego: Frantz's federal imperiality was the political project that answered to his artistic work. For Wagner, revolutionary art was post-statist; it tended towards the destruction of the state. A letter

35 Constantin Frantz, *Schelling's positive Philosophie*, Darmstadt: Scientia Verlag Aalen, 1968 (1879), pp. 293–304.

36 Constantin Frantz (1817–1891) was a German diplomat who opposed Bismarck and the construction of a German nation-state in the name of a European federalism centred on Germany. His writings influenced German reactionary thinking and were reactivated by a certain number of Nazi ideologues.

37 Frantz, cited in Leon Poliakov, *The Aryan Myth: A History of Racist and Nationalist Ideas in Europe*, trans. Edmund Howard, Falmer: University of Sussex Press, 1974, p. 306.

38 Frantz, *Schelling's positive Philosophie*, pp. 293–304.

Frantz wrote to Wagner, honoured by their relation and Wagner's esteem for him, was an imperial prophecy. It described Germans as the chosen people, who 'represent the heart of a wholly new system of peoples', 'the motor of progress'. Germans were 'the chosen people of the Christian era, as the Jews were during the prechristian era'. The 'Messiah has already planted his empire in German hearts', Frantz wrote. His empire was trinitarian: 'The Holy Roman Empire was its first form, followed by the Empire of the Son and, now today, that of the Holy Spirit.'[39]

This spirit of the empire was international federalism. This was the third universal Christianity, which would be fulfilled by federated Germany as the empire of the Holy Spirit. Frantz elaborated this German election in the words of an imperial prophetic tradition turned dialectical philosophy of history, and articulated around the Reformation. It was precisely because Germany had caused the confessional fragmentation of medieval Christendom that it would now cause the reconciliation of Christianity's internal division within a new Christianity. Confessionalization had made Germany the empire of the secular; here, the Reformation became the birth certificate of the modern German nation.[40]

Because this empire could not take the same form as the old medieval empire, because it had instead to exist within European federalism, the empire was spirit: the resurrection of the dead empire, the Son himself, through European rule. Imperial federalism took the place of the Holy Roman Empire, sublating it by transfiguring it. It was an *idea*, the idea of a post-statist Germany whose double body would be both nation and empire. This national and imperial duality announced the surpassing of the state. Germany had to become a community of a wholly different type from the state in order to win its legitimate hegemony, to fulfil the destiny to which it was called by political geography. Frantz's Reich was the political body that would incarnate secularity, which would unify confessional divisions in a Euro-Christian union. This imperial union of confessions would take place beyond and against the nation-state. It would exceed the bounds of the state, but would realize the purpose of

---

39   Letter from Frantz to Wagner, 26 January 1866, in Constantin Frantz, *Briefe*, Wiesbaden: Steiner, 1974, p. 41. Wagner paid homage to Constantin Frantz in 1867, in a text titled *German Art and German Politics*.

40   Ibid., p. 297.

secularism: to transcend confessions and make them exist peacefully. This evangelical imperiality was *one* ideological mechanism of European federalism.

To follow the trajectories of this philosophical imperiality of German secularization will require us to look beyond the writings of Hegel, Schelling, or Frantz, to see how it was articulated with the geopolitical questions of the day. To do this, we need to resituate the history of the relations between the Reich and the nationalization of Protestantism in the international context of the Eastern Question. My method here is to analyse the way that certain actors in the Prussian Union of Churches intervened, through Orientalist writings or diplomatic functions, in debates on the future of Europe and the Ottoman Empire. We will see how this seemingly minor literature was connected to an overlooked episode from the diplomatic history of the age of coal: the Anglo-Prussian alliance in Palestine. The British idea of a new evangelical empire, based on a Protestant theology of liberating Christian and Jewish minorities in the Orient and civilizing Africa through the Bible and agriculture, was formulated concurrently with the emergence and development of the fossil economy. In order to examine and make sense of this interdependence, we will turn to the history of the Ottoman Empire after the end of the eighteenth century. The theologico-political upheavals that structured secularization can be understood as effects of this empire's decline, by resituating them within a broader geopolitical frame.

The Ottoman Empire at the heart of German geopolitics

Works published in German between 1827 and 1830 on the Eastern Question helped to establish the idea of the Ottoman Empire's unavoidable dissolution in European public opinion. At the end of the 1820s, two political events dominated diplomatic relations between the European powers: Russia, England, and the Ottoman Empire. The first was the emergence of demands for national independence among the Greek and Slavic peoples of Eastern Europe. While the origins of Greek nationalism date from the end of the eighteenth century, it was after 1826 that it was projected on the international scene. As the question of Greek independence was connected to the policies of the Ottoman Empire, the outbreak of Russo-Turkish conflict in 1827 increased its urgency. The second event was the Turkish defeat in 1827 and the reforms that resulted from it. These put the Ottoman Empire on the path to massive structural changes, which would have a decisive importance in leading the Empire to integration into a world system and opening it to competition from European capital.[41]

The German texts contemporary to these two events are characterized by the defence of the Greek cause and the Russian Empire, in the name of the unity of European civilization. A celebrated book by the Austrian Orientalist Joseph von Hammer-Purgstall and a founding work of Turcology, the *History of the Ottoman Empire*, belongs to this array of texts. It opened with a dedication to the Russian emperor. Hammer-Purgstall paid allegiance to the Russian sovereign as the ruler of an empire which had succeeded, more than all the other European powers, in penetrating to the heart of the Ottoman Empire. Volney had made this same act of allegiance when he supported the Russian imperial title in Eastern Europe and the Orient. Like Volney, Hammer-Purgstall did not address himself to the Russian power as such, but as a *European* power. He paid homage to a power that, while respecting the equilibrium of powers constitutive of the modern diplomatic game, appeared as the *potential incarnation* of a concept of Europe founded on the idea of a shared political destiny. This idea of Europe coincided with a civilizing mission, a shared cosmopolitanism destined to be realized through international agreements. Hammer-Purgstall did not defend the colonial interests of any particular power but rather the common imperiality of the European powers, a project of civilization destined to unify national powers despite their territorial borders. This imperiality exceeded its multiple territorializations by determinate nations, because it could not be reduced to any particular imperial interest.

Hammer-Purgstall's text was far from isolated. German-language writings on the Ottoman Empire were the privileged sites of enunciation for a concept of Europe understood as the ideal imperiality of the West. The 1827 war between Russia and Turkey appeared as 'a combat for humanity against barbarism, for universal human education against

---

41   Wael Hallaq, *Sharīʿa: Theory, Practice, Transformations*, Cambridge: Cambridge University Press, 2000, pp. 396–420.

fanaticism and the will to destruction'.[42] Europe's imperiality was expressed as a defence of humanity and the rule of goodness that 'is destined to dominate the world'. This prophecy was certified by Orientalist science, since whoever 'knows the Turks and the regions they inhabit will know how sclerotic all has become', 'how fanaticism combines with a lack of all feeling, taken to its highest point'.[43] If this empire of fanaticism were destroyed, the one that took its place would have a claim to effective *Weltherrschaft*: world domination. Volney's prophetic intuition was reborn in the heart of Central Europe, Mitteleuropa. The possibility of a pure and simple disappearance of the Ottoman Empire made its territories the potential site from which a new world rule might be established. And, so, the outlines were drawn of an imperiality whose features were variable, insofar as it exceeded the multiplicity of national imperialisms.

This imperiality declared its fraternity with the Greek people seeking to win their political autonomy against barbarism. 'Our gaze', the Orientalist Johannes von Müller wrote, 'is turned with attention and anxiety towards the Orient, and for our brothers, the Greeks, we wish ardently for an end to the atrocity of the crimes that Turkish tyranny has committed for too long'.[44] This politics of fraternity between Western and Eastern Europe was the underside of a common rejection of an Islam that *exceeded* fraternal community. The hope for an ultimate integration of the peoples of the East into a Europe united by a shared project of civilization governed discussions of the Ottoman Empire. The probability of Turkish defeat engendered a territorial extension of the concept of Europe, cosmopolitanizing Christianity beyond confessional differences. This process was imperial to the extent that the Turks were designated as Germany's natural and eternal enemies.[45]

---

42   Die Expedition des europäischen Aufsehers, *Der gegenwärtig regierende Sultan der Türkei, Mahmud II und seine Umgebung: Ein biographisched Charaktergemälde: Nebst einigen Betrachtungen über den jetzigen Krieg*, Leipzig, 1829, p. v. This text is an anonymous biography of the then-reigning Ottoman Sultan, Mahmud II, a reformer who abolished the Janissary corps in 1826.

43   Ibid.

44   Johannes von Müller, *Die Posaune des heiligen Kriegs aus dem Munde Mohammed Sohns Abdallah des Propheten*, Leipzig: Gleditsch, 1806, preface, p. iii. This is a translation of a work by a marginal tenth-century Muslim jurist named Al-Kodouri. The preface is written by Müller.

45   Ibid.

In its writings, Orientalism was closely interested in what it thought of as Islamic law. Its writings, particularly those that dealt with the law of war and peace, served to demonstrate the innate incompatibility between Islamic law and the rights of man, the foundation of European international law and diplomatic order. Johannes von Müller, in particular, worked by surreptitiously passing off *one* text by *one* Muslim jurist as *the* doctrine of orthodox Muslims concerning war and the legitimate use of violence. A marginal text thus came to represent 'the international law of Islam', expressing the way that every Islamic state conducted itself with non-Muslim powers. 'Islamic law' was thus reduced to a right to bloody conquest and the enslavement of anyone who refused to convert. The imperial humanitarianism born from the defence of human rights and freedom against the Ottoman Empire implicitly included a key theme: the idea that slavery was consubstantial with Islamic culture.

With Islamic law presented as a theocratic law that could never be *universalizable*, secular law based on an abstract idea of humanity would now authorize Europe to exercise a new imperial title. The more imminent the definitive death of the Ottoman Empire seemed to be, the more European states were led to speak a genocidal language that called not just for the subjugation of Muslims but for their extermination. *Vernichtung* signified the pure and simple annihilation of the Muslim, described as 'the enemy of all rights of Man'.[46] Were one single Muslim to remain in Europe, the whole conquering spirit of Islam would reign there. To act 'with wisdom' implied recognizing 'that the spirit of Mohammed is not yet dead and that, as long as even one of his faithful remains alive, this spirit will yearn without rest to rule the infidels'.[47] The interpretations of the Qur'an that circulated in the same period reduced it to Ottoman law.[48] The Qur'an was presented as the political constitution of a liberticidal empire.[49] 'Nothing in the world has more influence on humanity than religion': this paradigm found its confirmation in the

46   Ibid., pp. iii–iv.
47   Ibid., p. iv. Knowledge of 'Islamic law' of war and peace would thus be a contribution to 'the knowledge of our relation to Mahometism'.
48   According to Müller, Turkish law was indeed based on the Qur'an. Alexander Müller, *Der Koran uund die Osmanen im Jahre 1826*, Leipzig: Baumgärtner's Buchhandlung, 1827, p. vi.
49   Ibid., pp. iv–v. This reading of the Qur'an as Ottoman civil code relied on a paradigm that saw religions as so many foundations of social life, a paradigm Islam was said to incarnate.

Qur'an.[50] The Qur'an was, 'especially for the Turkish people, the central point of their knowledge, their efforts, and their actions'.[51] The Shahada was a profession of faith, the Muslim state a church, the *mufti* a bishop; Muslim scholars were secular priests, and dervishes monks.[52] This reading of the Qur'an called for the capture of Istanbul as the Russo-British alliance's contribution to the global expansion of European civilization. 'By its fortunate location, this capital could become, alongside London, Europe's greatest centre of activity'.[53] For Istanbul to become Europe would make it Constantinople again: the former centre of the Eastern Roman Empire would have become one of the centres of a new European Empire. Thus, 'once the Turks have been deported from Constantinople, why could it not become the central point for an independent Greek State that would replace war with the Ottomans'?[54]

This victory of Hellenic Europe over the Oriental civilization of Islam would resolve a conflict of civilizations and represent the victory of Enlightenment over obscurantism, for the good of humanity and ethical politics.[55] The death of the Ottoman Empire would also mean the destruction of the states of North Africa, which would then participate in the birth of the New World announced by Napoleon, Washington, Franklin, and Simon Bolivar, and heralded by the abolition of slavery. In deploying itself against slavery, the free world would thus push anything foreign to it outside of its borders.

From now on, empire would signify the rule on Earth of the rights of man. Islam was defined as the law of God and fanaticism. It was no longer only the Antichrist, or the negation of the Christian God and the Trinity: it had become the oppressor *par excellence*. And imperiality declared that the oppressors should be oppressed. From the 1840s on, the German Reich appropriated the imperial title that Germanophone liberals and Christians had attributed to the Russian or British empires. In seeking to found a German Empire whose heart would be Central Europe, pan-Germanism, and then Nazism, were its inheritors. Before we demonstrate this, we will examine how evangelicalism came to be

---

50   Ibid., p. 29.
51   Ibid., pp. 29–30.
52   Ibid., pp. 23, 35, 36.
53   Ibid., pp. 145–6.
54   Ibid., p. 244.
55   Ibid., p. 245.

the carrier of this imperiality, variable and without fixed territory, through which the biblical theme of the kingdom of God had been translated into the rule of freedom on Earth. We can trace one part of this history, beginning in the 1840s, by examining the network of diplomatic alliances between the British Empire and Wilhelmine Prussia.

This network shared a desire to reunify Christianity, not through a return to Rome but through a *new* union of all Christians. Its moment belongs to what historians call the Evangelical Awakening, a movement of spiritual rebirth that passed through the Protestant countries, starting in the eighteenth century but exploding at the start of the nineteenth. In 1830s England it was characterized by several factors: a desire to integrate dissidents and Christians into an expanded Christianity exceeding the narrow limits of the Anglican Church; the introduction of sentiment into individual and collective piety; a critique of the aridity of Enlightenment rationality; and an engagement in the public sphere. Diplomatic alliances between England and Prussia played a determining role in consolidating evangelical networks on an international level. After 1840, they would also lay some of the foundations for the European presence in Palestine.

How imperial evangelicalism was disseminated in Palestine

The church reform of the Evangelical Union became internationalized during the 1840s through its advocacy for a Protestant presence in Palestine, at the time an Ottoman province. This internationalization presupposed an alliance with the British Empire. Christian von Bunsen, a pastor, Orientalist, and Prussian diplomat, was a first-rank figure in this missionary project. Not only did he originate the idea, he worked to realize it through diplomatic negotiations.[56] *The Constitution of the Church of the Future*, a work Bunsen wrote for Gladstone's attention, was the manifesto of an international Protestant Union that would be created through diplomatic activity, and oriented towards building Europe as the *rule of Christ on Earth*. From within Protestantism, the imperiality of evangelicalism gave the project a super-confessional dimension.

---

56   Paul Merkley, *The Politics of Christian Zionism 1891–1948*, London: Routledge, 1995, pp. 13–14, 60. Bunsen would find his most decisive ally in Lord Ashley Cooper, Earl of Shaftesbury.

Here, the Prussian Protestant Union was simply the territorialization of a universal evangelical ambition.

For Bunsen, Christianity was not a confession. It was the religion of the West – that is to say, of the sovereign, White, and autonomous subject for whom Christ was the Revelation. He identified Christianity with piety as opposed to dogma, a source of separation and disunity among Christians, and redefined it as God's ultimate revelation to the White European races, which only the Germans were in a position to truly incarnate. Germany was called to rule the world *spiritually*, as the carrier of a Christian universalism whose historical origins could be found in the Reformation and the Germanic world. Because Christianity was integrated into the economy of a teleological history of civilizations, all culminating at this point, Protestant Germany was called *to an imperial task*. Germany's entitlement to world rule was based on its capacity to fulfil Christianity on Earth – in Hegel's words, to *secularize* it. According to Bunsen, German world domination (*Weltherrschaft*) was thus the fulfilment of God's will on Earth, which called for an evangelical domination of the world.

The form this empire would take was federal rather than military. Its imperiality would be enacted through a diplomatic hegemony that would draw strategic support from international alliances with England and the other Protestant powers, in order to bring about their union. Bunsen was a pacifist and animated by a deep sentiment of European fraternity. A sympathizer of the Italian national movement, he aspired to 'the regeneration of Germany in a spirit not of international competition, but of European peace and freedom'.[57] What he described was a sort of *ecclesiastical and imperial metapolitics*. The kingdom of Christ on Earth would no longer be a universal monarchy; its imperiality would be incarnated at the heart of international diplomatic alliances. Empire, here, meant an evangelical restoration of the universal vocation of the Gospel. Bunsen wanted to extend the Evangelical Union of Christians to Europe, and then to the world: to unify the peoples of Europe in a Christianity now become the civilization of the free world.

This great confederation of churches was materialized through the articulation of a diplomatic strategy, starting with persistently encouraging the king of Prussia to intervene in the conflicts troubling Eastern

---

57 Henri Martin, 'Notice sur la vie et les oeuvres de Christian von Bunsen', in Christian von Bunsen, *Dieu dans l'histoire*, Paris: Didier, 1868, p. xxi.

Europe and Asia. Bunsen hoped to establish a German sphere of influence in the Middle East, through a Protestant alliance based on evangelical networks. This attempt at Christian diplomacy ended in failure, because the king of Prussia was committed to rigorous neutrality. Bunsen was forced to find a diplomatic solution for his imperial ambitions. Queen Victoria herself supported Bunsen's candidacy as ambassador to London. He negotiated directly with Palmerston and Sir Robert Peel to bring the Palestinian project before the British Parliament.[58] Despite his own scepticism, Palmerston defended the project due to the popularity of the evangelical movement in England. The alliance began in 1841 with the aim of installing a Protestant archbishop in Jerusalem. Discussions took place with the British government, in which Gladstone was a minister, and the members of the official Anglican Church, the *established Church*. These would lead to the nomination of a Protestant bishop in Palestine, charged with offering protection to the Christian Arab minorities and converting them to Protestantism. Government support was directly linked to a British desire to compete with France and Russia by implanting and organizing a Protestant community. First and foremost, it was a strategic intrusion into the Ottoman Empire, starting from Palestine.[59] This approach was an extension of the classical strategies that had used Oriental Christian minorities as a way to apply pressure to the Ottoman Empire, whose Islam was seen as the foundation of religious intolerance. The mission corresponded to the British Empire's interests in the Middle East, as they had been configured since the Great Game: if Britain lost control of the Ottoman Empire, its access routes to India, the heart of its empire, would be threatened, particularly by Russia. But there was no organized Protestant minority that England could rely on to compete with Catholicism and the Orthodox Church, and so make it a rival to France and Russia, respectively. England would thus have to break the diplomatic equilibrium, which would provoke an international and inter-imperial war. France, in its negotiations with the Ottoman Empire, had established itself as the protector of Catholic

58 *Christian Observer* 68, p. 772; *Christian Rememberancer* (London) 56, 1868, p. 60; Will Adam, *Legal Flexibility and the Mission of the Church*, London: Routledge, 2011, p. 152.

59 Charlotte van der Leest, 'Conversion and Conflict in Palestine: The Missions of the Church Missionary Society and the Protestant Bishop Samuel Gobat', PhD thesis, Université de Leyde, 2008, pp. 53–60.

minorities in Ottoman territories, and Russia operated similarly with the Orthodox minorities. It was thus necessary to form a Protestant community in the Middle East as a support against England's French and Russian rivals. In return, organizing a Protestant minority in Palestine would allow Prussia to preserve its political neutrality regarding the Eastern Question, while still building a first sphere of influence in the Ottoman Empire.

By allowing England to make itself the protector of the Protestants of the Orient, the mission fitted into the geopolitics engendered by the British struggle against Napoleonic imperialism. It used a custom-made diplomatic argument to strengthen its influence in Ottoman affairs, in order to maintain its territorial integrity and so protect the routes to India, while still respecting the equilibrium of powers and international law. In 1850, a mandate by the sultan officially recognized Protestantism as a religion of the Ottoman Empire. This mandate came after a series of acts that granted recognition to Christian minorities in the empire who were distant from their home church. By pushing for reforms to open the Ottoman Empire to the liberal values of religious tolerance as dictated by Europe, the Anglo-Prussian alliance put itself at the very heart of the Eastern Question.

Conversions of Arab Christians to Evangelical Protestantism began to take place in 1847. The francophone Swiss bishop Samuel Gobat was charged with these conversions. Between 1841 and 1847, the target community had been another supposedly Oriental religious minority: the Jews of Jerusalem. The goal was to follow through on attempts to restore and convert Jews in Palestine.[60] The first bishop of the Protestant Church of Palestine was Michael Salomon Alexander, a Jew who had converted to Anglicanism.[61] The mission to the Jews, and Alexander's nomination, was intended to cause a restoration of the Jews as a *nation* in the Middle East. Their eventual conversion was not excluded, but it was subordinate to another task: a Jewish renaissance, which was needed for the advent of the kingdom of God on Earth. Officially declaring its mission as strictly spiritual was a political choice. In a diplomatic

---

60   Ibid., pp. 58–9.

61   Salomon Alexander officiated in Palestine for only four years, between 1841 and 1845. His mission's main target was the Jewish population, and he worked directly with the London Society for Promoting Christianity Amongst the Jews.

frame, arguing for the protection of religious minorities was, first of all, tactical: it worked to make the rights of man the dominant language in negotiations and to impose a model of religious tolerance and pluralism onto an Ottoman Empire that was defined as fanatical, while introducing the logic of confessionalization to the conflicts in the Middle East.

The year 1886 marked the end of this Protestant Anglo-Prussian alliance in Palestine, which proved unable to resist its own becoming-colonial.[62] The development of German colonialism and inter-imperial rivalry marked the end of the cooperation. Once Germany abandoned diplomatic neutrality on the Eastern Question, and the German Empire's pretentions to rule Mitteleuropa began to be realized, the Protestant pact became impossible. The hour of rivalry between oil companies and the Berlin–Baghdad railway had arrived.[63] In the meantime, Germany had constituted itself as an empire after 1870, and then as a colonial empire over the following decade.[64] In the following sections, I show how imperial secularization contributed to founding its colonial ideology, as well as to the intra-European expansionism of the Third Reich.

The project of German rule in Central Europe

One of the sources of German expansionist geopolitics was the economist Friedrich List. A study of his texts attests to the links between German geopolitics in the context of the Eastern Question and the geopolitics of fossil fuels. List's book *The National System of Political Economy* developed a theory of the conditions of state industrialization. It was strongly influenced by Henry Carey, one of the founders of American protectionism, to whom List had become close during his visit to the United States.[65] He popularized the American idea of the state as a vector and protector of industrialization, and attempted a critique of the dominant theories of free trade. In his book, the fossil

---

62   This project of international Protestant union was based on English geopolitical hegemony, not on political equality between the two states. Prussia remained subordinate to England, which was able to impose an Anglican bishop.

63   Timothy Mitchell, *Carbon Democracy: Political Power in the Age of Oil*, London: Verso, 2011, pp. 54–8, 74, 103. For a reading of these passages, see the preceding chapter.

64   Henderson, *Studies in German Colonial History*, pp. 1–10.

65   Mitchell, *Carbon Democracy*, pp. 126–7.

state appeared as an economic agent administering energy resources. List's *National System* set out a theory not only of German industrial imperialism, but of what we could call a Union of European fossil states. In service of catching up with capitalist Britain by rapid industrialization, List articulated two projects he saw as interdependent: a Union of European countries, and the colonization of the world. The domination of Central Europe by Germany was the condition for the development of a capitalism based on the extraction of fossil fuels and resources in the 'tricontinental' world: America, Asia, and Africa. List also promoted the project of a customs union between the German states and Austria, which came to fruition in 1834 under the name of Zollverein. The project was framed by a systematic theory that evaluated the historical becoming of civilizations as a function of their economy. The commercial and customs union was conceived of as a necessary first moment in the creation of an economic union between equally developed nations to counter British hegemony. These economic and political unions were steps in a socio-economic equalization of nations that could only be gradual, and would eventually lead to perpetual peace.

This union of the countries of Europe was a decisive step in the formation of a fossil internationalism. This union would rival the United States and Russia. In the *National System*, only the powers of the continent were united. England could not be a decisive agent in its creation, but it would *be invited to join* after it had been dethroned by the United States from its hegemonic position in global capitalism. The project of a European union was meant to revive the peace of the French Empire, which had been defeated by its own belligerence. According to List, Napoleon Bonaparte had been the military precursor of a union that could only be viable in economic form. List announced the true empire of Europe, which would be a peaceful, economic, and federal union. According to List, Napoleon's goal had been laudable: to compete with England by creating a vast European continental union. But, because this first European empire was founded on conquest, it had failed and given rise to generalized apprehension.[66] The empire had been less a model of European union than a threat of division between the weak

---

66 On Napoleon as the precursor of a mixed economy, both agricultural and manufacturing, see Friedrich List, *The National System of Political Economy*, London: Longmans, Green, & Co., 1885, p. 331.

and strong countries of the European continent. For this reason, List wrote, 'an alliance of the Continental nations can only have a good result if France is wise enough to avoid the errors of Napoleon' and ceases to speak 'of the Mediterranean Sea as of a French lake'.[67] France would have to set aside certain of its imperialist claims. And Germany, in List's eyes, was the only country in a position to avoid Napoleon's errors and realize the true empire of Europe. France, sooner or later, would need to accept and submit.

For List, Germany's election to the imperial title was justified by its geographical position: at the centre of the world, between Orient and Occident. Germany was Mitteleuropa: the centre of Europe and the Europe of the centre; middle Europe and in the middle of two worlds. A new European politics would proceed from an initial unification of Central Europe, uniting not just the eastern and western poles of the continent but the Orient and the West themselves. Europe could therefore unite only on the condition that Central Europe was unified, on the ruins of the Ottoman Empire. Only Germany could accomplish this, List declared, through an extension of the customs union. As Mitteleuropa was Germany's legitimate sphere of influence, Europe depended on the unification of the countries of the North under German domination. But this 'closer union of the continent of Europe' encountered an obstacle: Central Europe had to play a political role corresponding to its geographical position. The appropriate role for the centre was to be

> a mediator between the east and west of the continent, on all questions of arrangement of territory, of the principle of their constitutions, of national independence and power, for which it is qualified by its geographical position, by its federal constitution, which removes all fear of aggression from the minds of neighbouring nations, by its religious toleration and cosmopolitical tendencies, and finally by its civilization.[68]

With its neighbouring countries, Germany should constitute 'a powerful commercial and political whole', beyond existing monarchical, dynastic, and aristocratic interests. In this way, 'Germany could secure

---

67   Ibid., pp. 338–9.
68   Ibid., p. 332.

long-lasting peace for the continent of Europe', forming 'the central point of a durable Continental alliance'.[69]

This alliance of European nations would subjugate the world and establish peace through a federal order. While defending the peace had been the traditional and medieval function of empire in its Roman and Christian conception, this new empire was no longer theological. It was no longer a sacred empire representing Christ on Earth, but a *profane empire colonizing lands*. The empire of Europe would be secular and liberal, founded on religious tolerance rather than conversion, on federalism rather than conquest or war. If in the metropole this secular imperiality was economic, outside of the continent it would become colonial. It declared the great European nations' right to possess colonies, and announced an explosion of imperialism, against the dual monopoly of France and England.

From fossil colonialism to the religion of the Reich

South America first appeared, in List's text, as the chosen land for Germany to colonize, by sending diplomats, doctors, merchants, and naturalists, but also by purchasing land. According to List, this should be settled 'with German colonists – companies for commerce and navigation, whose objective should be to open new markets for German manufacturers in those countries, and to establish steamship lines' as well as 'mining companies, who should devote German knowledge and industry to winning those countries' great mineral wealth'.[70]

The empire of Europe was set in motion by extractive reason, the logic of a fossil expansion. The colonialism it would set in action *materialized* the imperial idea of European union. What the united European states required 'can be expressed in one word', List wrote. That word was *energy*: the use of coal as fuel to turn the wheels of steam engines and so to support a network of communication routes.[71]

Europe's imperiality founded the right of every European nation to exploit the surface and underground natural riches of the world. The model was the British Empire in India. The exploitation of India would

---

69   Ibid.
70   Ibid., p. 347.
71   Ibid., p. 349.

be joined by a 'dissolution of the Turkish Empire', thanks to which 'a great portion of Africa and the west and middle of Asia' – that is, the Middle East – 'will become productive'. The horizon for the union of fossil imperialisms was the unity of a global empire subjugating the South to the North. Texas would colonize Mexico, while 'orderly governments' would colonize South America and 'promote the yield of the immense productive capacity of these tropical countries'.[72] Steam navigation and the extension of railroads to the 'torrid zone' by the countries of the 'temperate zone' would be the infrastructure of this new imperial order.[73]

South American independence was compared with the coming dissolution of the Ottoman Empire, because it had opened 'the most fertile territories of the earth' to industrial domination and energy extraction. List spoke on behalf of these countries, claiming to know their interests. He wrote that they 'now await with longing desire for the civilized nations of the earth to lead them in peaceful concord along the path of the security of law and order, of civilisation and prosperity'. Above all, their demand was 'that manufactured goods should be brought to them, and their own productions taken in exchange'.[74] List thus presented the foundations of global unequal exchange as a result of the dominated countries' own aspirations: the South's for its own soils to be submitted to the superior rationality of the industrial and fossil exploitation of the countries of the North.[75]

In the frame of this imperial and fossil economy, a united Germany and Austria would conduct its colonial and economic politics in the Middle East and the countries of Eastern Europe. These were the simplest to colonize, because by their proximity they did not require a substantial fleet. Germany could and should act in the ruins of the disappearing Ottoman Empire, clearing a path to the East. In doing so, it would show the European powers that it had 'a great national economic interest' in the East. The question posed by the decline and possible destruction of the Ottoman Empire was the question of Europe itself. In List's text and in the European press of the time, Turkey was represented

---

72   Ibid., p. 213.
73   Ibid., pp. 213–14.
74   Ibid., p. 214.
75   Ibid., p. 172.

as the *living dead*: 'Turkey is, like a corpse, which may indeed be held up for a time by the support of the living, but must none the less pass into corruption.'[76] The idea of a slow Ottoman agony contributed to the deployment of a colonial racism that reduced the peoples of Asia to the state of corpses: 'The case is quite the same with the Persians as with the Turks, with the Chinese and Hindoos and all other Asiatic people.' Colonialism understood non-European peoples as already dead, destined for extinction. The Ottoman decline indicated that Europe would sooner or later reduce the whole of supposedly 'mouldering' Asia to a vast European colonial space: that European colonization was the only possible 'regeneration', the only principle of life. Europe would unfold like an empire of the Holy Spirit, whose 'fresh atmosphere' would, in List's words, make Asia fall to dust. In a word, Europe was the breath of life, and the Orient needed merely to give up the natural riches with which its soil was so richly provided.[77]

If in the project of a customs union List presented himself as a precursor of German state capitalism, his work also defended a profoundly colonial idea: European imperialism was the political and military condition for the economic 'pacification' of the world. In effect, his theory can be considered a model for the German Empire and German colonialism. Bismarck's Reich inherited List's Zollverein project, a common market under Prussian hegemony. Similarly, from the end of the nineteenth century, German colonialism was inscribed in the continuation of List's predictions, whose discourse it activated in reality.[78] To the Mitteleuropa described by List, German colonialism in Africa aimed to add a 'Mittelafrika', by connecting Cameroon to its possessions in so-called Oriental Africa by way of the Congo.[79]

List's economic theories also anticipated certain developments in the fossil economy. But it would not be until the next century that the European Coal and Steel Community would fulfil his wishes for

---

76   Ibid., p. 336.

77   Ibid., p. 336.

78   Henderson, *Studies in German Colonial History*, pp. 74–6, 114–15. Henderson notes that as early as 1841, Von Moltke, a Prussian marshal, after a trip to Constantinople, recommended sending German settlers to Palestine.

79   Ibid., pp. 87–112; Thomas Deltombe, Manuel Domergue, and Jacob Tatsitsa, *Kamerun! Une guerre cachée aux origines de la Françafrique (1948–1951)*, Paris: La Découverte/Poche, 2019, p. 60.

hegemony in the continental organization of fossil fuel exploitation. Through it, Europe organized a system of regulating the price and production of fossil fuels in order to protect producers from competition. The European Coal and Steel Community was thus typical of a larger mechanism, described well by Timothy Mitchell, by which coal industries and oil companies strategically avoid competition by soliciting state intervention. State intervention in the fossil economy is far from marginal, as it allows oil companies to guarantee a market and monopoly.[80] From this point of view, List's protectionist theory exceeds the history of ideas, and can be seen as the foundation of an effective economic policy centred on an overlap between state and fossil industry. Imperiality is at the heart of this system, which I call the fossil state. It is principally by aligning with imperial and colonial state interests that industry and oil companies have assured state protection of their markets and monopolies.[81] The imperiality of the state, and its colonialism, has played a first-rank economic role by allowing the formation of lucrative markets for fossil exploitation. That the German colonial empire was a failure in no way prevented it from dealing death in the name of industrial life. Further, its failure led to the Third Reich's policies of intra-European expansion as a way to repair the supposed injustice caused by the loss of its colonies after the defeat in 1918. In doing this, National Socialism reactivated a different face of the German idea of empire from the one List had presented.

This face of empire was first expressed during the first phase of German nationalism. It took shape in reaction to Napoleon's invasion of Prussia, through a discourse intended to make the medieval Germanic Holy Empire rise from its ashes. This nationalism represented the people as possessors of an empire – the *Volk* as a Reich – erecting itself against the French First Empire.[82] From then on, the word Reich would continuously be used to define the structure of the German federal state, from the First to the Third Reich, by way of the Weimar Republic, whose

---

80 Mitchell, *Carbon Democracy*, p. 39. In the British case, Mitchell notes that the absence of cartels led the state in 1947 to set up policies to purchase fossil companies that had been broken by competition.

81 Ibid., pp. 62–5.

82 See John Edward Toews, *Becoming Historical: Cultural Reformation and Public Memory in Early Nineteenth-Century Berlin*, Cambridge: Cambridge University Press, 2004, pp. 30–1.

constitution also declared it an empire: *Das Deutsche Reich ist eine Republik.* The German Empire was a republic because a republic was the simple constitutional form taken by the imperiality of the *Volk.* The Weimar Constitution thus also described itself with another German formula: *Ein Volk, ein Reich.* This federal imperialism gradually transformed into a colonial and then an intra-European imperialism.

The writings of Friedrich Ludwig Jahn and Ernst Moritz Arndt called for a return to Germany's 'natural' borders, based on the linguistic and ethnic identity of the Germanic *Volk.* They considered Alsace, the Rhine valley, the Swiss Alps, the territories of the North Sea, and parts of Denmark as so many natural regions of the great German Empire.[83] In its reference to the medieval Holy Roman Empire, for which the modern notion of national borders had no meaning, nationalism was not performing a point-for-point restoration. It conceived of the nation exclusively as an ethnolinguistic community, and no longer as the terrestrial representative of a Christian universality. A German citizen was, first of all, one for whom German was a language of use but also of origin. The ambiguity and indeterminacy of the purely linguistic criteria would be lifted as Germanity progressively came to exclude Jews. In defining itself as White and Aryan, it excluded Jews from Europe and the nation as Semites and Orientals.

But, at the time, this still-ideal Reich found its model in the medieval history of Central Europe and the Holy Roman Empire, which it used to justify Germany's election to the rank of greatest European power, master of Europe and perhaps of the world.[84] This first, ideal imperiality of the German nation was not the result of a simple return to the past. Arndt and Jahn believed that the German Empire had ceased to exist with the 1648 Treaty of Westphalia, which by dividing the empire on a confessional basis into a multitude of kingdoms had dissolved the unity of the German nation that, in their view, had existed during the medieval era. *Nation* was thus identified with *empire* through a political reading of history. From here, the contemporary restoration of the medieval Holy Roman Empire appeared as the restoration of the nation. The medieval Germanic empire became the index of the reality of a political *unity* that had progressively declined since the seventeenth

---

83   Ibid., p. 31.
84   Ibid.

century and the Treaty of Westphalia. The German nation, it seems, had existed from 843, the date of the Treaty of Verdun, until the Protestant Reformation.

Because the hierarchical structures of this medieval empire contradicted the idea of national unity, the Reich would need to be regenerated and reformed; it should be a German national identity in opposition to Jacobin centralism. It was through a federalism – a *Ständestaat*, a state of states – that the Germanic empire could metamorphize and be reborn from its cinders. The neo-pagan dimension of this nationalism should not be overstated. Arndt and Jahn's imperial nationalism was not opposed to the Protestant Reformation; it reinterpreted it as a national and secular heritage. This was the meaning of the hyphenated term that proliferated during the cultural reforms in 1840s Prussia: Christian-Germanic.[85]

This nationalism was as colonial as it was imperial. It was articulated with a pan-Germanism that made Mitteleuropa the chosen land and natural zone of influence of the Germanic nation. This imperial geography was at the heart of German hegemony, establishing an imperialism internal to Europe. Before the emergence of pan-Germanism, the imperiality of the federal German state was constructed through a colonial relation to the populations of Eastern Europe, which was itself indissociable from the constitutive hostility the defenders of 'European civilization' held towards the Ottoman Empire. The road that led from this first imperial nationalism in the 1810s to the Third Reich was not continuous. It passed through the failure of the colonial empire, as well as the birth of the Pan-German League. The imperial idea was opposed to the chilly tone of Bismarckian diplomacy and its rejection of colonialism. After the 1870s, it thus became a sort of counter-Reich, as militant nationalism turned against an empire whose borders it considered too restrained.

---

85   Ibid., pp. 33–5. This first imperial nationalism was intrinsically linked to the policies of political and religious reform instituted after 1840. It disseminated the ideology of the Kingdom of Prussia through its monarch, Friedrich Wilhelm IV.

Evangelical ultranationalism or the immanence of God to empire

One of the key actors in this counter-Reich was Paul Anton de Lagarde, who came to List's colonial project by starting from the premises of his teacher, Bunsen. Before becoming an inspiration for the Pan-German League, Chamberlain, and National Socialism, Lagarde was, first of all, a respected heir of the German Orientalist tradition. He studied with August Gottreu Tholuck and under the supervision of Christian von Bunsen, before becoming a professor at Göttingen, the sanctum of the discipline since the end of the eighteenth century.[86] A student of Tholuck and Bunsen, he was, in turn, Troeltsch's teacher.[87] Lagarde was anything but a simple theologian, and unlike his teachers did not preach. He was, first and foremost, an Orientalist – which meant, in Germany at least, that his specialization was *biblical criticism.* Throughout his works, a radical antisemitism was fed by a pseudo-scholarly Orientalism. He put these at the service of a German imperialism that unfolded at the heart of a movement of critical historicization of the Bible, in which the concept of *race* played a key role. Orientalism was its decisive mechanism, because this historicization operated by means of a racial conception of the Orient and the Semitic; indeed, Lagarde was an Old Testament specialist. According to him, Jesus had opposed Jewish nationality through the Judaism of his day. To transfigure Christ against established Christianity thus implied repeating Jesus' historical act against Christ himself, by founding an empire that could surpass the stage of Christianity as Christianity had surpassed Judaism.[88]

This surpassing of Christianity by empire was what Lagarde called *evangelicalism.* He defined it as a simultaneously spiritual and national

---

86   See Robert Hanhart, 'Paul Anton de Lagarde und seine Kritik an der Theologie', in Bernd Moeller, ed., *Theologie in Göttingen: Eine Vorlesungsreihe*, Göttingen: Vandenhoeck & Ruprecht, 1987, pp. 271–306. For the biographical details mentioned, see p. 301. On the case of Julius Wellhausen, see Rudolf Smend, 'Wellhausen in Göttingen', in ibid., pp. 306–24.

87   See Ulrich Bart, 'Troeltsch et Kant: *A priori* religieux et philosophie de l'histoire', in Pierre Gisel, ed., *Histoire et théologie chez Ernst Troeltsch*, Geneva: Labor et Fides, 1992, p. 67. Troeltsch inherited the question of the religion of the future – that is, of the modernization of Christianity.

88   Hanhart, 'Paul Anton de Lagarde'. According to Hanhart, Lagarde distinguished between Judaism and Israelism. The first was resistant to Christianity, while the latter was the historical announcement of the Messiah and thus of Christianity.

fervour, situated beyond Christianity and historical religions. Evangelicalism was the national religion that took the place of secularity, that performed a return to the world. It was, so to speak, the final Christian language of the surpassing of Christianity, the name of a provisional heresy that, in the last instance, would restore the Reich of the *Volk*, the empire of the nation, by dissolving Christ himself. The borders of national religion thus conformed to its practical meaning: a natural or civil religion irreducible to confession. This national civil religion valued piety over belief. For Germans, what was important was no longer to be 'believing but pious'. What they needed was *Frömmigkeit*, a subjective piety totally devoted to the state. With this ultranationalist profession of faith, Lagarde inscribed himself in the purest tradition of national Protestantism, which had been institutionalized in Prussia during the reign of Friedrich Wilhelm IV in 1840, and in which his teachers, the Orientalists Tholuck and Bunsen, had been noted leaders.

Lagarde's gesture performed an anthropological reduction of God to man and of heaven to Earth, an identification of theology with history that was radical, total, and thus without remainder. God became the empire, and the divine was identified with the people, sanctified by their piety. From here, theology would be reduced to historical knowledge of an originary Christianity; it would be dissolved within the union of Orientalism and biblical criticism, the historical criticism of sacred texts. Religion was thus defined as an experience and sentiment of perfection that revealed itself within history. Throughout this history, religion had been menaced by two enemies: the Jesuitical spirit of Christianity, and the Jews.[89] Jewish and Christian theology would thus need to be dissolved in a religion of the future, which for Lagarde was opposed to all transcendence. The matrix of his thought was an imperial project of secularization, formulated as a *new national religion* and directed against German liberal Protestantism. The Prussia of the 1830s, of Leopold von Ranke and Bunsen, was the laboratory for Lagarde's imperialism, which reversed the gesture of religious reform and unification begun by the Evangelical Union of Churches and turned it against Protestantism itself. The unity of the nation now tended to be substituted for the unity of Protestant *religion*. Deconfessionalization was extended beyond the limits of Protestantism, and even of Christianity itself. Lagarde

---

89   Ibid., p. 302.

proclaimed an evangelical doctrine whose master terms were uttered in a neo-biblical language, and deployed against established Protestantism. Through this, he claimed the emergence of a German national religion. Lagarde's anti-Christian turn functioned by de-Christianizing the neo-biblical language of imperiality, taking it beyond the territory of Christianity. He radicalized evangelical reformism beyond and against Christianity. The nation was no longer unified in a communion that had been initiated within the Church, before it radiated through state and society carried by Protestant civility. The nation would now be religion *itself*, and the divine would identified with the dignity of the Reich: in this way, German nationalism reduced God to empire.

Through his new religion, Lagarde presented himself as the founder of pan-Germanism. In his political writings, he explicitly put his Orientalist erudition at the service of his antisemitism and nationalism. This can be seen in his *Profession of Faith for Germany*, first published in 1850 and republished in 1933. The texts that make it up, written for the attention of the Prussian Conservative Party, declared that Judaism was a legacy of the Asiatic and Oriental religions. The so-called *Semitic hypothesis* was at the heart of this new profession of faith: being essentially *Oriental*, Judaism was considered a foreign element within Europe, and a threat to Germany. The Jews were marked as Oriental intruders ceaselessly plotting against the unity of the national body. They were Palestine within the body of a Germany that, while perhaps in theory an empire, was still not a nation, a *Volk*. According to Lagarde, to bring forth the nation would consist of purifying it from traces of the Semitic Orient. He treated Jews not as the faithful of a *religion*, but as members of a foreign nation that menaced the integrity of the German body politic. They constituted a state within the state, a nation within the nation.[90] 'Germany must consist only of German men, and in a German way', Lagarde declared; there could be 'no space for Palestine within it'.[91]

This hypothesis was less an effect of Christianity than of biblical criticism and the historical study of sacred texts. Its model was the definition of the Arabs as a primitive people devoid of history; the Jews appeared as Arabs who were more evolved because they had become sedentary.

90   Ibid., p. 293.
91   Paul Anton de Lagarde, *Bekenntnis zu Deutschland*, Jena: Eugen Diederichs Verlag, 1933, p. 15.

Their law, which Moses invented, was an effect of ancient Egyptian legislation and Arab nomadism. The Jews existed not only in reference to a political community, a nation; according to Lagarde, their existence referred to a homeland said to be located in Palestine. He thus presented the Jewish presence as the presence of Palestine in Germany, rather than of the Jewish religion within a pluriconfessional state. 'For Germany, the result', Lagarde wrote, 'is that the Jews of Germany must either emigrate or become Germans.' 'Friendship is possible with certain Jews on one condition: that they cease to be Jews,' since 'Judeity as such must perish'.[92] This destruction meant not conversion to Christianity, but a theology of national assimilation. Lagarde intended to integrate the Jews into the German nation by disintegrating *Jewish tradition*.

With this, Lagarde defined the conditions for the emergence of a German nation that, to him, still did not exist. By defining what it meant to 'become German', he defined what was required of Jews who lived on German soil. As we have seen, only Jews who *renounced their Jewishness* could remain in Germany. Those who refused to do so should be expelled and installed in colonies in Palestine, their 'country of origin'. What constituted Semitism was not biological race but tradition itself, what we call *religion* or *culture*. This was why, for Lagarde, a sort of conversion was still possible. The injunction to break all ties with their community occupied the place of a condition sine qua non for the Jews' possible humanity. Lagarde's antisemitism was a secularism of integration into the national body through the subsequent dissolution of every community apart from the nation. Lagarde's secular reason made Judaism not a religion but a nation, although without racializing it biologically as his successors would.

Judaism was thus constructed as a politico-religious threat to the integrity of the national body, precisely because it had been communitarianized by Lagarde. The state respected and tolerated freedom of religion, but it could not tolerate a foreign national body proliferating on its territory. In Lagarde's view, churches should be respected and individuals able to choose their confession. Freedom of religion therefore was and must be guaranteed by the state, and as churches were governed by private law, the state could not interfere.[93] But the churches were

---

92   Lagarde cited in Hanhart, 'Paul Anton de Lagarde', p. 293.
93   Lagarde, *Bekenntnis*, p. 66.

tolerated only on the condition that they did not threaten the state. As soon as a community was designated a *nation*, it should be considered a threat. This provision was not a residue of Christianity, but rather the consequence of an authoritarian aspect inseparable from the state's establishment of the principle of tolerance. The limit of tolerance was any threat to public order and the personality of the nation. The latter, which Lagarde conceived on the model of individual personality, could not tolerate being put in danger by a plurality of confessions.

Lagarde's secularism was not a liberal separation of church and state. In no way did it consist in drawing support from Protestantism or any other existing religion; on the contrary, it separated the state from churches and religions in order to engender a process of social secularization that could lead to their decline. His religion of the future presupposed a radical destruction of all existing churches. Lagarde reclaimed neither Luther nor historical Protestantism. He raged against Luther, whom he believed had caused the dissolution of the unity of Christendom, the destruction of the Holy Roman Empire, and the pluralization of confessions. It was necessary to go back further than Luther, but also further than Rome, and even beyond the apostolic Gospels. What was required was not to restore an originary Christianity at the heart of the German nation, but to make of the one and indivisible nation a new religion, a religion of the future that would *surpass* the confessional differences that the Reich still tolerated.[94] This was an anticlerical evangelicalism deployed as religion of the future, which refused all forms of religious diversity – in the name not of some truth or another, but of the unification of the nation.

This anticlerical strategy would be adopted by pan-Germanism, which called for the German Empire to be secularized in order to gain its independence. Its supporters maintained that this was the only way to unify the nation and counter the power of the ultramontane Catholic minority.[95] In this, the pan-Germanists sought the support of a Germanized cultural Protestantism. In their view, the only way that majoritarian Protestantism could be protected was if it was protected by the state. It would necessarily be the loser in a pluriconfessional

---

94   Ibid., p. 70.
95   Michel Korinman, *Deutschland über alles: Le pangermanisme 1890–1945*, Paris: Fayard, 1999, p. 47.

framework, which would favour the vitality of Catholic ultramontan-ism.[96] The pan-Germanists used a classical argument, close to the one used in certain French anticlerical milieux to legitimate the Concordat: the independence of the Catholic Church was a threat to the state and the nation. Pan-Germanism turned to Protestantism for strategic reasons. Not being incarnated in any political institution, as was the Church of Rome, it was compatible with the imperial state and could continue to exist as an institution, a set of established churches. Pan-Germanism thus took root within a specific project of imperial secularization. In the eyes of its supporters, the secularity of the German Empire corresponded to the power of a great nation united by acts of a piety that, following Lagarde, they opposed to institutional religion. This imperial secularism was not reducible to a separation of the state from the Protestant churches. Nonetheless, Lagarde's influence contrib-uted to a permanent alliance between the Pan-Germanist League and the Evangelical Union in Germany, a union of interests that was much more pragmatic than it was religious.

Lagarde's antisemitism was a consequence of his critique of the estab-lished Protestant churches.[97] His secularism fed both his Orientalism and his antisemitism. It was necessary, he declared, to extirpate the residual elements of Judaism from German evangelical culture, in order to regenerate not God or religion, but the human and national essence manifested in evangelicalism. It was not Christianity itself that was to be regenerated, but the nation of which Christianity was the *perverted* spirit, still unconscious of itself. Anticlerical and anti-Christian, Lagarde's antisemitism aimed radically to transform the status quo of the Protestant churches. Retaining the lessons of Ludwig Feuerbach's atheism, or *anthropotheism*, he never articulated a discourse on the essence of God, but only on the essence of the nation, of its race, and above all, its religion. Becoming 'not Christians but Evangelicals' – this credo was the beating heart of the injunction to reform that Lagarde

---

96   Ibid. The text Korinman cites is Anonymous, *Deutschland bei Beginn des 20. Jahrhunderts*, Von eimen Deutschen, Berlin: Militär-Verlag R. Felix, 1900, p. 194.

97   Hanhart, 'Paul Anton de Lagarde', p. 296. While Lagarde certainly meant for Christian confessions to be dissolved in the unity of a national religion, this did *not* mean that the state could disregard religions or fail to guarantee freedom of religion. Beyond this, Lagarde's postconfessional evangelicalism was radicalized in the direction of a sort of post-Christianity.

addressed to German Jews and Christians.[98] Lagarde's colonial secularism was, in fact, an *anti-Christian evangelicalism*.

Lagarde, the Orientalist, agitated for *the formation of a German colonial empire*, employing an organicist and virile philosophy of the national body. 'Men's muscles are strengthened through labour', he wrote; 'the muscles of the nation are strengthened through labour for the nation. One such labour is colonization, and this labour can take place only on the terrain of the world.' The muscular and virile labour that reinforces and regenerates the nation, as labour regenerates the individual human body, was what Lagarde defined as the colonial act. Empire took place on the profane terrain of this world, since it must refuse the illusions of established religion. The German colonial empire was no more and no less than the purpose of the German nation, the justification of its existence. If the empire did not exist, nor would the German nation exist fully; because the nation, by its muscular force, tends irresistibly to empire. According to Lagarde, this empire was nothing but a Germanic state, based, as it was for List, on the domination of Central Europe. The Empire of Middle Europe was Germany defined as Mitteleuropäische Staat. The German colonization of Central Europe was what would allow the advent of the German nation, destined to rule the world. National-imperial identity implied a model of annexing and Germanizing the surrounding territories, strategically relying on the support of Germanophone populations. It was precisely this project that was later translated into the expansionary politics of the Third Reich.

Lagarde considered the true Reich to be the empire of a nation liberated from Christianity and Judaism. Beginning in 1871, he opposed it to Bismarck's contemporary industrialized Reich, which he declared was incapable of founding true national unity. To Lagarde, the colonization of Europe and the world would be the negation of the Protestant by the national, the abolishing of the Christian by the evangelical, and would bring forth the subject through a colonial politics. This imperial-national conception became a determining reference for the Pan-Germanic League, founded in 1891, which saw colonization as necessary to bring about the unity of German-speaking peoples.[99] Pan-Germanism did not only advocate the imperial expansion of Germany; it was also a doctrine

---

98   Lagarde, *Bekenntnis*, p. 70.
99   Korinman, *Deutschland über alles*, pp. 51–2.

according to which it was only by colonization that Germany could become a unified political subject. Colonization was an obligatory passage towards the rebirth of the Reich. Lagarde's colonial politics, taken up by pan-Germanism before it was taken up by National Socialism, was an annexionism that maintained, in particular, that the Germanization of Poland was the necessary preliminary for a progressive extension to the whole of Europe.

If Lagarde rejected Bismarck's policies, this was because he supported the project of unifying two things that in Bismarck's empire were opposed: intra-European imperial policy and overseas colonial policy. He supported German colonial tutelage on the Adriatic Sea and in the Balkans; he was, therefore, the father of both pan-Germanism and the Third Reich's colonial policy only because he transformed the imperial title of unified Germany within Europe into a *German colonial empire*. Paul Anton de Lagarde put Orientalism at the service of secular reason. It was at the heart of his critical and historical erudition, which took the disciplinary form of Orientalism. Nonetheless, a careful examination of his discourse tends to trouble the concept of secular reason itself, putting its definition into question. Lagarde's religion is not private faith but public morality: 'We should be not believers, but pious.'[100] The concept of religion he mobilized was precisely a call to collective piety and not to individual belief; religion designated the soul of the national body. Here, we see the *violently anti-liberal* dimension of Lagarde's anti-Christian secularism. Lagarde rejected the reduction of religion to mere opinion, and called for *a religion of the earth* that was nothing other than a radical form of secularization, the fulfilment of the divine in the body of the nation.[101] He rejected other worlds in the name of a religion of the *presence of God*, here and now, beyond religion. 'We need the presence of God and of the divine, not its past, and this is why it can no longer be a question of Protestantism', 'of Catholicism', or even 'of Christianity'.[102] Anti-Christian evangelicalism led Lagarde to make the presence of God in the flesh of the people into a demand for a neo-pagan piety of Earth and nation.

This should lead us to relativize all claims for the primacy of piety or practice over belief that remain inscribed within the horizon of a secular

---

100 Lagarde, *Bekenntnis*, p. 70.
101 Ibid., p. 62.
102 Ibid.

rationalization of the *religious fact* and the uses of the category of religion. Lagarde's concept of religion expressed a norm that went counter to the liberal reduction of religion to mere belief. Religion as piety is a counter-norm that is no less secular than the other; but it is anti-liberal. The secular reason of Orientalism should therefore be seen as double; and this duality corresponds to two faces of the concept of religion itself.

This is not to say that the ideas of piety or the necessary reunion of body and soul are structurally reactionary. Lagarde's public piety had meaning only because it was meant to strip God of his transcendence and reduce his presence to his incarnation in a *national piety*. Lagarde deployed a national pantheism whose foundation was anti-Christianity and a critique of subjective belief. This radical and anti-liberal secularism descended directly from the secularism of Bruno Bauer, whose *Jewish Question* Marx criticized. It would be mobilized by pan-Germanism in its strategic alliance with nationalized Protestantism, and would find its culmination in the project of colonial domination that the Third Reich inherited from the Pan-Germanic League.[103] Secularization and colonization – the realization of God on Earth and the genocidal racialization of peoples – functioned in tandem, recalling Quinet's writings. This German colonial ideology was a delayed effect of the model of secularization launched in Prussia in 1817. It was a moment of reversal of the logic of nationalizing Protestantism that had been at the heart of the Union of Churches. With Lagarde, evangelicalism literally turned against Christianity itself, as the nation took the place of the Christian God whose assassination it had participated in. Following Schelling, Lagarde claimed Luther's gesture in the Reformation only as a historical act of establishing the German *nation*, radicalizing the evangelical culture introduced by the Union of Churches and the jubilee ceremonies of the Reformation. An evangelical was one who celebrated the Reformation not as a return to Christianity but as an action of the Germanic nation. Evangelicalism was a cultural heritage defined by a history that not only converted the Reformation into Aryan supremacy but substituted it for Christianity itself. Protestant culture should become evangelical to the point of ceasing to be Christian; it should be radicalized to the point of becoming anti-Christian. Evangelicalism

---

103   Anonymous, *Deutschland bie Beginn des 20*, p. 194; Korinman, *Deutschland über alles*, p. 47

became anti-Christian once it established a civil religion whose God was purely *immanent,* in a neo-pagan and neo-Spinozist celebration of the world. The ideologies that Lagarde inspired thus contributed to the emergence of National Socialism.[104]

The invention of the Aryan race and the roots of the Third Reich's antisemitism

Opposing Germanism to Jewish 'Semitism', Lagarde's evangelicalism radicalized a gesture sketched by his teacher, Christian von Bunsen, whose role in the Anglo-Prussian alliance in Palestine we examined earlier. In the lineage of Schlegel's Orientalist philology, Bunsen studied the Indo-European races in order to decipher the origin of the Germanic and 'Aryan race'. Bunsen redefined Whites as the only race perfectly compatible with Christianity, and the Aryans as the only truly Christian race.[105] The act of election by which the Germanic Aryan race was herald of the kingdom of Christ on Earth depended on this racialization. Its

---

104   See Johann Chapoutot, *La Loi du sang: penser et agir en nazi,* Paris: Gallimard, 2014, pp. 25–6, 35–40. In the first chapter of the book, Chapoutot, a historian of Nazism, shows to what extent National Socialist thought deployed a sort of spiritual immanentism against a Jewish materialism that supposedly separates this world from the beyond. In opposing this division between terrestrial and sacred, Nazism declared the sanctity of nature and the world. Chapoutot cites an article published in the SS journal *Das Schwarze Korps* under the title 'Trouble in the Blood – Here Below and Beyond'. It condemned the mistreatment of animals as the effect of a 'mechanical view of the world' based on Judaism and Christianity. This vision, 'which sees the animal only as a machine devoid of sensibility, particularly offends the faith that is proper to our race. For us, God is manifested everywhere in nature, because nature is sacred and we adore in it the revelation of an eternal will'. As Chapoutot rightly notes, anti-monotheism played a crucial role in this thought, rooted in radical naturalism and secularism. Lagarde is, in my view, a link in the transformation of German neo-Spinozist philosophies of the early nineteenth century into fascist themes. This transformation, which is not intrinsically contained in Hegel's or Schelling's philosophy, took place through biblical criticism and Orientalism, as Bunsen and Lagarde's writings attest.

105   Martin, 'Notice', in Bunsen, *Dieu dans l'histoire,* p. xxi. When Renan employed the same theme, he referred to Bunsen's work. Ernest Renan, *Questions contemporaines,* Paris: Michel-Levy Frères, 1868, pp. 348–9: 'M. de Bunsen is correct when he thinks that the successive perfection of Christianity must consist in drawing further and further away from Judaism so that the genius of the Indo-European race will predominate'. The racial dimension of this idea of a Christianity deployed against the Semitic spirit is clear when Renan speaks of Islam (pp. 350–1).

deployment contributed to the Westernization of Christianity by presenting the domination of the Orient as an instrument in the realization of
the kingdom of God on Earth. The imperiality that thereby infiltrated the
evangelical Christian tradition encouraged Protestants, Catholics, and
evangelicals to see the apocalyptic prophecies in the Book of Daniel
being fulfilled by the ongoing dismantlement of the Ottoman Empire.
The double process – the Westernizing of Christianity along with the
Orientalizing of Islam and Judaism – determined the contemporaneous
formation of racial antisemitism. It led evangelical Orientalism to create
the concept of the Aryan race by opposing it to Semites. The evangelicals
thus continuously set up the industrial West and the free world in place
of the abolition of Jewish law and the fulfilment of biblical prophecies.
The likelihood of the Ottoman Empire's imminent demise led them to
formulate a neoprophetism that predicted the destruction of Islam. The
old theme of an Islam-Antichrist destroyed by the imperial messiah and
Christ as emperor was transposed into the victory of *free civilization* in
the Orient, amid rapid industrialization. This discourse was in no way
marginal, and it saturated the history of German antisemitism up to its
genocidal explosion under the Third Reich.

German imperial nationalism, from the Union of Churches to the
Third Reich, was structured by its language. The *imperial* dimension of
this discursive economy can be seen in the fact that the guide, or *Führer*,
presented himself as a man at the head of an empire, the leader of a
Reich. The Third Reich reinvested this language, converting the ancient
prophecies of Germanic emperors to fossil industrialism. If it fulfilled a
prophecy, this was the one that had declared the reign of spirit in the
rule of a final Germanic emperor. In 1488, Frederick III's astrologer,
Johannes Lichtenberger, wrote a politicized Joachemite *Prognosticatio*.
Joachim's third *status* signified 'the universal state of the final emperor'.
The third age of history, the age of spirit, was transposed into a third
state.[106] The emperor-reformer in the fifteenth-century Germanic
prophecy was to chastise the Church, under God's protection, while
pushing back the infidel Turks.[107]

This prophetic theology of empire, which Charles V still subscribed to,
was not redeployed in identical form in the nineteenth century. There were

---

106   Gerbier, *Les Raisons de l'empire*, p. 50.
107   Ibid., p. 51.

crucial differences between the theologies of the medieval Holy Roman Empire and those of the modern Reich. The Holy Roman Empire had not been conceived as an empire of the German *nation*; only the imperial and industrial Reich was, from the nineteenth century to the Third Reich. The nationalization of Protestantism and the emergence of evangelicalism contributed to an imperial secularization that, far from dissolving Christianity, functioned by mutating its language. The political theology of the Reich, inheriting the ideologies of pan-Germanism, identified the divine with the *terrestrial empire of a nation*. The reign of spirit was reduced to the reign of an emperor who would lead the nation to its terrestrial salvation. This implied ruling the world, this world, understood as the *only real world*. It was an empire of the sacredness of the world, a Reich that spoke the language of imperial prophecy, reborn in a new form. This Reich, possessed by a century of regeneration and the submission of the churches to its yoke, defined itself through struggle against what it called Semitism, against the Muslim and the Jew. But the imperiality of the prophecies of the Germanic Holy Roman Empire had to undergo the series of metamorphoses we have examined before it was able to infiltrate a totalitarian state based on an alliance between the military and fossil industry. From then on, the Third Reich was an empire that ruled the world by the *election* of a nation. It would no longer convert Jews to Christianity; and for this very reason it defined them through acts of biological racialization whose unprecedented violence led to extermination.

The New Church, the customs union, and the Reich were all forms that could be taken by the spiritual body of the German state, the metapolitical *Volk* that lay beyond or beneath the state. In List's political economy or Bunsen's Protestant evangelicalism, to construct the German nation never meant merely to found a centralized nation-state. For List, Germany was understood as the centre of a customs union that would extend across the whole of the European continent in a supposedly non-violent, economic and diplomatic, way. Germany thus would become, in one way or another, *all of Europe*. In Bunsen's evangelicalism, the Church was what allowed the *Volk* to exceed the state form, to found a communitarian bond on an infrapolitical level that exceeded the limits of the state. This imperial metapolitics would lead the Reich to elevate the Germanity of the Aryans to a supranational level, in order to fulfil a vocation that, due to its irreducible dignity, was supposedly universal. The universal would thus be incarnated in the particular.

The apocalyptic language of the Book of Daniel, mobilized by industrial colonialism, announced the coming of Christ on Earth and the new millennium. Its prophecies were increasingly deployed as the Ottoman Empire seemed destined to destruction. To be reformulated, the biblical figure of the Jewish law had to be identified with the Orient and with an act of submission to the crushing transcendence of God. The fulfilment of the law by the Gospel, as formulated by the Apostle Paul, was identified with the domination of the Orient by the West. By Orientalizing the biblical theme of the law of God, evangelicalism equated the Ottoman Empire with the biblical figure of the law, so justifying its imperial missions in Palestine and the Arab world. In this way, it was able to make industry the site for the fulfilment of the Gospel. But the Gospel was converted to industrial civilization only by means of race, by the designation of an Orientalized law of God as Semitic: Jewish and Muslim. Protestantism, after nationalism had reconfigured it as the religion of the White race, in a sense gave birth to the space of its own displacement. What displaced Protestantism as nationalized by the policies of the union was nothing other than a neo-pagan religion of the people and its roots, which agitated for the colonial expansion of the German race across the world. Protestantism was thus displaced not by itself, but by the imperial and racial workings through which it had been nationalized, leading to the homicidal madness of the Third Reich.

Hegel's Fourth Reich

The apocalyptic language that structured evangelical diplomacy and the Reich was also the language of the philosophy of history, as magisterially deployed by Hegel. But, as has been repeatedly affirmed since Karl Löwith, the medieval tradition through which nineteenth-century philosophies of history were elaborated is not reducible to the Christian theology of salvation. Nor is the philosophy of history the transposition of Christian sacred history onto the terrain of profane history. There was no simple transformation of the theme of the end of the world into theories of the end of history. The hypothesis of Christian eschatology being secularized in Enlightenment philosophy omits a crucial mediator: imperiality. Medieval Christian eschatology had to give way to a whole *imperial* tradition before it could become the heart of the political theology of the Christian West. This late imperial theology emerged with Dante's *Monarchia* and was formalized in the empire of Charles V, where it then died. It was this theology that Napoleon transformed between Asia and Africa, and that Hegel and the French Republicans inherited. Since the Crusades, its fate had been linked with Islam.

The philosophy of history that took shape in the nineteenth century was thus imperial because it was *neo-Roman* and *neo-biblical*. The idea of progress that ran through this philosophy was imperial and neo-Roman, because it was elaborated on the terrain of the profane history inherited from the pagan authors of the Roman Empire. From the first century after Christ, this had been constructed from the hypothesis of a transfer of the empire from Orient to Occident, the *translatio imperii*.[108] With these two words, the ancients and medievals described the transfer of the imperial title from one empire to its successor. The philosophy of history was neo-biblical, to the extent that its key themes referred to the Torah and the New Testament, even if it transformed their language and subverted their discourse. The imperial tradition this philosophy proceeded from was an effect of the association of the God of the Bible with the paganism of the Roman Empire. This imperial tradition constructed its discourse by drawing from an interpretation of Hebrew apocalyptic writings that was at once Christian and pagan, particularly from the Book of Daniel as read by pro-imperial Christian priests such as Paul Orosius, an apologist for the empire, contemporary of Saint Augustine, and critic of the separation of the city of God and the terrestrial city.[109] In this imperial reading, the four kingdoms described in Daniel's prophecy corresponded to four empires that would succeed each other in history, up to the arrival of the end of time. The Fourth Empire would represent the final historical regime. Mobilizing the German language of the Holy Roman Empire as it was

---

108   Reinhard Gregor Katz, *Translatio imperii: Untersuchungen zu den aramäischen Danielerzählunger und ihrem theologiegeschichtlichen Umfeld*, Neukirchen-Vluyn: Neukirchener Verlag, 1991.

109   Benoît Lacroix, *Oróse et ses idées*, Montreal: Institut d'études médiévales, 1965; Laurie Lefebvre, "Réécrire l'histoire: L'utilisation du matériau suétonien par un historien chrétien, Orose," *Latomus* 72, no. 2, 2013, pp. 492–501. Orose used writing techniques that allowed him to construct continuities between Biblical narrative and the history of the emperors of Rome.

dying under Napoleonic arms, Hegel identified the four steps of history with four Reich.

Teleological and evolutionary philosophies derived from the metamorphoses of imperial Roman tradition become the language of Europe's colonization of the world. Hegel's rationale for the supposed superiority of the West, and his pure and simple exclusion of the whole continent of Africa from humanity, is inseparable from the order to realize religion on Earth. The exclusion of Africa and the Orient from history 'properly speaking' allowed the Trinity not only to be identified with, but also to be tendentially reduced to, an imminent and temporal reality: the West's imperial destiny and its triumph over the rest of the world. Hegel's philosophy of history was thus indissociably prophetic and colonial. As we have seen, it inherited a model that had already structured medieval profane history: the voyage from the Orient to the West. History moved from east to west as the empires of the Orient transferred their power to those of the West. The imperiality of history thus subjected geographical space to the unity of one single and unique time. This time would progressively be occupied by the concept of progress, which is not an effect of secularized eschatology but a legacy of the metaphor of the voyage from east to west that had structured profane history as imperial transfer. Progress became the name of this itinerary, which made geographical poles into two sequences of a history that travelled from east to west. The nineteenth century made this imperial structure into the passage from a supposedly primitive and Oriental confusion of the social and the religious to their Western differentiation into autonomous spheres. Progress was identified with secularization, and a geography of civilizations was established in terms of their supposed religious principles: the Orient, Muslim in its majority, was opposed to a West that was Christian in principle, and secular in its effects. The subject of history ceased to be divine providence and became a new being, human and divine: a social and collective entity irreducible to its individual manifestations. This subject surrounding the circle of history was then named *the human race*. In the form of the spirit of the age or of a humanity beyond men themselves, this abstraction that is more real than individuals seemed to act in the world, making history. This immanent being could now humanize or dehumanize peoples by pronouncing the judgement of God in a new ontological space-time, presented as the only existing reality: *history*. The concept of the secularization of Christianity was an order declared from inside the imperiality of European philosophy.

The European triarchy, or the three secular fossil empires

The Hegelian theory of the secularization of Christianity is not merely a philosophical caprice. Its imperiality puts it in solidarity with the fossil empires that took shape during the age of coal, and with a concurrent idea of Europe. Over the course of this era, the powers of the European continent constructed themselves through mimetic rivalry with England. It was against English commercial hegemony and command of the seas that industrialization was introduced by state-driven reforms in the rival states of France and Germany: both were states that claimed, in competition with one another, the right to found an *empire of the European continent* in order to unify it. The French idea of European Union as formulated by Bonaparte was indissociable from the Mediterranean system put in place through the colonization of Algeria. Germany, for its part, first articulated the idea of a customs union of Germanic countries, and then launched itself into the annexation of Eastern Europe under the Third Reich.

The introduction of the fossil economy in Germany was an intervention at the heart of one of the first attempts to unite the European continent. The imperiality of Germany as a European nation led its geopolitical reason to conceive of Mitteleuropa as its natural zone of deployment. In its colonial form, this was manifested in the project of annexation. When it took the form of economic integration, this imperiality tended to become federalism. It assigned the European countries to a hierarchy, but without being reducible to the internal colonialism exercised by the rich northern states over those in the south of the continent. At times, it declared itself opposed to so-called *exterior* colonialism: Bismarck opposed diplomatic hegemony in Europe to the German colonialist movement. 'My map of Africa lies in Europe' was the maxim that diplomatic reason opposed to German expansionist ideology. For its part, the France of the Third Republic made the colonization of Algeria and Tonkin substitutes for the empire it had lost in Europe after the defeat of 1870. European colonization of Africa and Asia was thus inseparable from the desire to incarnate empire in Europe.

The French Revolution woke the sleeping emperor: since Charles V, there had never been an attempt to unite the European peoples through submission to a single yoke. Nor had defeat ever reverberated so strongly across Europe. If this empire's failure was incontestable, the traces it left were tangible: the secularization of law in the civil code, the plurality of religious *cultes* recognized and financed by the state, the legal institution of private property. These regal institutions were foundational for a simple reason: they let France establish a model of modernization that would then radiate across Europe.

These state reforms were secular because Bonaparte was emperor of the earth, an empire without heaven or God, and carried through these changes while institutionalizing the Revolution. This emperor had to pass through Egypt in order to establish his electoral legitimacy. The imperiality of which Bonaparte was the carrier acted to unite competing European colonialisms. In this way, the imperiality shared by Europe was grafted onto the body of the European states. The First Empire was the assassin of one of the great vestiges of Christendom: the Germanic Holy Roman Empire. This destruction encouraged Hegel to see Napoleon as reason incarnate. The fall of the Holy Roman Empire did indeed give birth to claims for national independence, but it did not mark the end of the idea of empire. Instead, it opened the way for new imperial ideas that would culminate in the deployment of a fossil, and a genocidal, Reich. The racial nationalism born in Germany to counter French imperial domination was not the disappearance but the differential repetition of one face of imperiality.

It is now time for us to analyse the historicity of imperiality, which is marked by the constant repetition of its reincarnation in new forms.

6
A Circle of Returns: Towards
a Critique of Imperiality

It was neither the progressive de-Christianization of Europe nor the persistence of Christianity that brought our world into being. This false alternative prevents us from understanding how secularization developed from the colonial mutations of empire. If this book has attempted to short-circuit the thesis according to which secularization emerged from the Reformation, Christianity, or a process endogenous to Europe, it has also not presented a narrative of secularization as a pure and simple exit from the Christian world. It has tried to describe secularization historically, as the slow birth of one cultural world against the backdrop of another, and to think philosophically about how our modern way of life was born from the entrails of a *determinate* Christian order.[1] This Christian world was none other than *Western* Christendom, which is not the same thing as Christianity itself; it proceeded from the Roman imperialization of the Christian Church and biblical tradition, via the definition of Islam first as Antichrist and then as law. The Christian world from which the secular world of the moderns emerged should be thought of as the becoming of powers that aimed to construct and to unify this world. The powers of the Western-Christian world were two in number: Church and empire. The political, and thus effective, existence of a Christian *world* as a world of laity and clerics was dependent on universal monarchy, and did not pre-exist it. And, because this

---

1   Martin Heidegger, *Nietzsche*, vol. 4, San Francisco: Harper & Row, 1982, p. 100.

monarchy never existed, the Western-Christian world never empirically existed either: it existed only as an indefinite concept and project of unification. Empire was one of the political forms taken by this unification on a global scale. The construction of this world as the only one there is – the secular reality that the command to secularize is meant to call us back to – was one aspect of this imperial attempt at unifying the globe.

What I am calling imperiality has not been identified as an object by political philosophy, where, for the most part, it has remained tributary to a narrative of modernity centred on the appearance of the modern nation-state and, more recently, on governmentality or coloniality. This critique of modernity has a long history, which perhaps began in Europe with Nietzsche before it became increasingly popular after the First World War. Many Muslim or Islamist intellectuals as well as the majority of decolonial authors defend a critique of modernity as such. From their point of view, coloniality and modernity are entangled, if not identical. This was not the position of Edward Said or of Frantz Fanon, who, in this respect, were closer to an anticolonialism that always more or less sought to deploy a modernity proper to the Global South, one that would not only be reducible to Europe's but would surpass it by inventing a new humanism.[2] There is thus a tension between a critique of *all* modernity on the one side and, on the other, a will to indigenize modernity by pluralizing it beyond the West. This conflict between the critique of a colonial modernity and the idea of multiple modernities is internal to decolonial thought. The notion of transmodernity proposed by Enrique Dussel and the concept of *decolonial pluriversalism* are intended to resolve this tension.[3]

In what follows, I want to change the terms of this debate. Beyond the critique of colonial modernity or the idea of multiple modernities, it is the *interdependence* of the development of the territorial nation-state and the *colonial metamorphoses* of the idea of empire that need to be

---

2   The most poignant expression of this idea is to be found in the conclusion of *The Wretched of the Earth*. Certain authors affiliated with the postcolonial current also defend this idea; for example, see Partha Chatterjee, *Our Modernity*, Dakar: Sephis-Codesria, 1997.

3   See Walter Mignolo, *The Darker Side of the Renaissance: Literacy, Territoriality, and Colonization*, Ann Arbor: Michigan University Press, 1995, pp. 118–48, esp. pp. 133–4.

interrogated. While the dominant narrative of modernity clearly varies under the pen of philosophers or historians, it is still possible to describe its broad outlines schematically. Generally speaking, the advent of European modernity is described as the progressive autonomization of European states and the calling into question of the guardianship of the Roman Church and its centralizing tendencies. The majority of historians date this process from the sixteenth century, developing over the following two centuries. Medievalists tend to find its origins at the end of the Middle Ages, starting from the fourteenth century, and it seems evident that Gallicanism became generalized by pursuing an autonomization of kingship that had begun earlier.[4] Protestant princes began to separate themselves from Rome, and national churches were gradually formed, under the exclusive guardianship of secular royal power. The Reformation and the confessional fragmentation of Christendom it engendered are most often described as the determinate cause of this process, of which secularization was an effect. From this point of view, the emergence of the Enlightenment, the eruption and spread of the French Revolution, and then the development of democratic civil societies in the nineteenth century all continued and completed the process of modernization by separating states from churches, which came to fall under private law and were confined to a strictly social role. The developments of science and technical progress would then replace the world of faith, and the twentieth century would bring the process to term in a spectacular regression of faith and religious practice.

This narrative has two central protagonists, the state and the Church. But a third term exists, which is often passed over when the question of the secularity of modern power is posed. This is empire. During the Middle Ages, as we have seen, empire referred to a political form that would incarnate the unity of Christendom by uniting the different Christian kingdoms of the West. A whole generation of historians believed that the proliferation of Protestant churches had made the old imperial dream of Christendom impossible. The dawn of modernity was thus also the twilight of empire. The emergence of competing states that exercised power over a delimited national territory took place against the backdrop of the death of the idea of universal monarchy. The

---

4   Gallicanism was a doctrine which supported the autonomization of the French Catholic Church vis-à-vis the Church of Rome.

integration of kingdoms into a transcendent unity would have been the necessary consequence of the weakening of Rome, since the Catholic Church had been the guardian of the imperial order. The autonomization of states with regard to the Church was thus doubled by the *decline* of empire, which was a political appendage of the rule of the Roman Church. As long as empire and the Roman Church were considered the two faces of Christendom, it was logical that their progressive decline would go hand in hand. In this understanding, modernity was a set of substitutions: substitution of the rights-based territorial state for the empire, and private or individual religious practices for the temporal power of the established Church. Republicanism and the Protestant Reformation were the two sources of modernity, which was transposed to the global level by the substitution of international law, and respect for the national principle, for the old imperial peace, and diplomatic equilibrium between powers for their submission to a universal Christian order that transcended the territory of their sovereignty.

As we will see by reading several key texts of political philosophy, theories of modernity share a common narrative according to which the birth of the modern world was the twilight of the medieval Christian empire.[5] Secularization thus appears as the progressive emergence of the nation-state on the body of the deceased empire. By presupposing this narrative, as I see it, the 'great' philosophical analyses of modernity have tended to pass over two correlated problems: the continuous tension between the nation-state and the mutations of imperial form; and the role that colonization played in these mutations. This chapter questions a certain number of these analyses, and in so doing clarifies some of the philosophical stakes of the theory of imperiality.

The theme of the death of empire secretly inhabits the secularization debate. This allows us to reformulate its terms as follows. To what extent were the philosophies of the modern state that emerged in the Classical

---

5   There are traces of the narrative of the nation-state's emergence from the ruins of empire. One of its first appearances is in Ernest Renan, *What Is a Nation? and Other Political Writings*, New York: Columbia University Press, pp. 261–3. But the best-known and most influential version of this narrative is probably Benedict Anderson, *Imagined Communities: Reflections on the Origin and Spread of Nationalism*, London: Verso, 1983, p. 11. In most cases, this narrative presupposes an opposition between *nation* and *empire*, which the analysis of modern imperialisms refutes by showing a clear, if complex, overlap between the two signifiers.

Age effects of medieval imperial theologies, the theologies of the Holy Roman Empire? The possibility of establishing a series of links between imperial Roman theology, Classical royal theology, and the theology of the sovereignty of the territorial modern state has been the keystone of the debate on secularization since Carl Schmitt's *Political Theology*. By deploying the thesis of the imperiality of power, this chapter does not dissolve the question of the theologico-political; instead, it shifts its stakes by reformulating its terms. This involves a transformation of the Derridean declaration of the globalization of Christianity into an expression of the dissemination through colonization of Roman imperiality, irreducible to Christianity as such. The goal in advancing this concept of imperiality is not to *legitimate* the so-called modern era, nor to affirm constitutive autonomy or fundamental secularity against the hypothesis of a globalized Christianity, as Hans Blumenberg does.[6] Rather, the aim is to theorize the double irreducibility of the imperial to the colonial, and the colonial to the Christian. I begin this analysis with a critical reading of Jacques Derrida's *Faith and Knowledge*, to grasp the difference between imperiality and what Derrida calls 'globalatinization'.

Why the colonial dissemination of imperiality is not the globalatinization of Christianity

The word *religion*, linguists and anthropologists teach us, has nothing universal about it. According to Derrida, its Roman origin testifies to its

---

6 Hans Blumenberg, *The Legitimacy of the Modern Age*, Cambridge, MA: MIT Press, 1985, pp. 73–4. Without following Blumenberg, but agreeing with certain of his intuitions as well as certain of Peterson's and Voegelin's, my approach examines secularization as an order, a *political command* and a reorganization of space, formulated by secular reason. This order, as well as the discourse that expresses it, are inseparable from the imperial and colonial policies of secularization. Carl Schmitt, author of *Nomos of the Earth*, did not make this link himself. See Schmitt, *The Nomos of the Earth in the International Law of the 'Jus Publicum Europaeum'*, New York: Telos Press, 2006. There is something of a schism between Schmitt's *Political Theology* and *Nomos*, in that he never shows how colonization was able to affect, in return, the very structure of the theologico-political complex, and determine the way it was secularized through modern concepts of sovereignty.

fundamental contingency.[7] Because it was universalized alongside and
in tandem with Christian missions and colonial expansions, speaking of
religion, in the last instance, always means speaking as a Christian. To
presuppose the universality of the 'religious', Derrida maintains, following Asad, is to participate in the Christianization of the world that he
names 'globalatinization'.[8] The circulation of the word *religion* in the
world is thus the reverse side of Western hegemony, a domination that
is indissociably Roman and Christian. In other words, imperialism has
never ceased to be Christian, for the simple reason that it is itself
Christianity. We have all therefore become Christian; and all colonization, however profane in appearance, has always been in one way or
another a Christianization. From this perspective, the imposition onto
the world of the code of *religio* is a Christianization of the world,
globalatinization being the spatial dissemination of what Hegel theorized as a progressive secularization of Christianity in time. What was
realized through successive epochs of historical time was globalized
through the colonization of space.[9]

The condition of possibility of this assertion is its relative historical
indeterminacy: we know nothing or almost nothing of the concrete historical forms this hegemony has taken, or how it was constructed. We know
only that it 'has been underway now for centuries', as Derrida writes. Still,
if to speak religion is to speak Latin, it may be that *another* Roman question is at stake, one that cannot be reduced to the question of Christianity.
It may be that the Roman question as it was posed before the emergence
of Christianity is the *imperial question*.[10] The imperial question is not the
question of a form of government distinct from the modern state. It examines the existence of imperial returns that haunted the formation of
Western hegemony as the modern nation-states were constituted. Here is
where the question of imperiality begins – where the empire-form itself

7   Jacques Derrida, 'Faith and Knowledge: The Two Sources of "Religion" at the
Limits of Reason Alone', in *Acts of Religion*, New York: Routledge, 2002, pp. 66–7.
Derrida takes up and renews the theologico-political question as posed by Carl Schmitt
through a critique of the European character of the concept of religion as defined by
Émile Benveniste.

8   Ibid.

9   Ibid. One of the differences between the Derridean concept of globalatinization
and the concept of the secularization of Christianity is that the first designates, at least
in part, an *imperialist* process.

10   Ibid., p. 67.

died, failed, fell into ruin. It was the effective failure of Charles V and then Napoleon in founding an empire in Europe that opened its process of rebirth. What I call *imperiality* is not a uniform concept of empire that can be reduced to a pagan, Jewish, or Christian origin, but the multiplicity of ways in which the defunct Roman Empire inspired ideologies of its rebirth. A multitude of afterlives compose the word empire, as I use it to speak of the West or of colonialism: world domination, the peaceful integration of a plurality of peoples, the continuous transfer of power, political fulfilment of prophecies, messianism, etc.

'*Religion* circulates in the world, one might say, like an *English word* that has been to Rome and taken a detour to the United States', Derrida writes, naming two entities that are not only Christian but also incontestably imperial.[11] So is not the so-called Roman question, beyond the matter of the Latin *language*, a question of the legacies and multiple metamorphoses of an imperial model of world domination? Briefly, is not globalatinization simply an effect of the question of imperiality, in the way it was posed to Europe and the Western world as the keystone of their Roman heritage? Is not the question of *Western* Christianity and its political theology intimately tied to a *double* Roman spectre, within both Church and the empire? Can we understand the birth of the modern state and its mimetic rivalry with the Roman Church without the mediation of the imperium, without writing a critical theory of empire and imperiality?

The question and hegemony of European discourse on *religion* thus leads us to substitute in some sense the question of empire and its colonial reincarnations for the theologico-political question of Christianity and its globalization; or, more precisely, to displace the second question onto the first. This means examining the invention and universalization of the concept of *religion* as the deployment of an imperial tradition, while remaining attentive to the different metamorphoses that have punctuated its trajectory.

We will need to determine to what extent the European colonizations of the world perpetuated – or, on the contrary, departed from – the medieval history of empire when they imposed the code of religion and race – but also of *anti*-religion and race – on the world. The theologico-political dimensions of the colonial states, their exclusive and bloody sacralization, their racial, religious, and identitarian geographies, can be

11   Ibid., p. 66.

read as so many effects of a *colonial metamorphosis* of the idea of empire – of what I call imperiality, whose history unfolds, in the ideology of the actors themselves, in a circle within which spectral effects continually return to haunt the living. This circle is often pictured as a crowd of faces of the living dead, from Marx's vampire to the zombies that inhabited the colonial imaginary. As a result, I do not argue that empire really is a spectre haunting us but rather that imperiality appears in the form of haunting to actors themselves, in the element of the ideologies by which they make sense of their action in the present. Spatial phenomena underlie these feelings of haunting: the dismemberment of the Holy Empire of Christendom and the dissemination of its shreds in both the colonial and the metropolitan.

The emergence of a secular globality beginning in the nineteenth century did not conjure away the resurrections of the empire of Rome and of Christ. Was this because the secularity of globalized space could itself only be spoken, like *religio*, in Latin – as a span of time (*saeculum*)? Starting from this question, several objections to the Derridean theme of the Christianization of the world could be formulated, maintaining the critique of the concept of religion while dissociating it from the hypothesis of globalatinization. This now-classic hypothesis rests on a confusion between the word religion and its uses. What was universalized by imperialism was not only a *word*, like the many other Latin and European words that were translated and reappropriated outside of Europe. From here, what matters is not to identify the origin of the term *religio*, but to analyse its conceptual history and examine its uses, their variations, and above all the effects that discourses on the religion of non-European people have produced on those who articulated them.

By setting aside the mechanisms that produced it, the Derridean reiteration of secularization tends to reduce European colonization to a simple effect of Christianity. Colonial violence, which non-European peoples have suffered since the fifteenth century, tends to be *reduced* to the theologico-political violence of Christianity. In place of an analysis of the *workings* and mechanisms of the colonial machine, we find suspicious the declaration of a ceaseless dissemination of a Christianity, in a direct line from Hegel and the German thinkers. But this discourse, which was at the heart of the philosophical secularism of Feuerbach, Marx, Nietzsche, and Freud, should itself be analysed as a moment in the globalization of the concept of religion.

For the rest, there is nothing that would authorize the declaration that the Roman dimension of imperiality, whose Roman matrix pre-existed Christianity, became confounded with Christianity to the point of being engulfed and dissolved within it. This interpretation is no more legitimate than the one that argues that, since Constantine, Christianity has become confounded with the Roman Empire to the point of constituting one single entity. In a word, my hypothesis consists in maintaining the mutual irreducibility of the Christian to the Roman, so as to grasp the dialectics of their entanglement and opposition throughout Western history.

Imperiality and the critique of governmentality

The blind spot of the theologico-political debate around the concept of secularization is not simply the colonial question but, more precisely, the articulation between imperiality and coloniality. As long as the question of a possible reduction of colonialism to the permanence of empire is not posed philosophically, the terms of the debate will remain incomplete. In my opinion, this question should be substituted for the classical question of the Christian origins or essence of *modernity*. It is authorized by a critical rereading of two fundamental theories of European political philosophy: the theory of governmentality proposed by Michel Foucault in *Security, Territory, Population*, and the theory of imperialism articulated in Hannah Arendt's *The Origins of Totalitarianism*. For Foucault, as for Arendt, modern and contemporary colonialism *presupposed* and *confirmed* the death of empire. 'The Empire is indeed dead,' Foucault declares, suggesting it was colonialism that performed the assassination. It is during a reflection on Europe that Foucault expresses this.[12] Europe is a modern idea: it is no longer Christendom, and no longer oriented towards a terminal Empire. By opening the space of governmentality and thus of modern territoriality, the Classical Age seems to have concluded empire, to have marked its definitive and irreducible death. If governmentality was inaugurated by a decline in the Catholic Church's organizational power and universalist vocation, it also necessarily announced the death of the empire. If modern Europe

---

12   Michel Foucault, *Security, Territory, Population: Lectures at the Collège de France, 1977–1978*, trans. Graham Burchell, New York: Palgrave, 2007, p. 247.

was the diplomatic invention of a regime of mutual recognition by the *raisons d'états* of competing states, it appeared only on the ruins of the imperial unity of European peoples that had existed under the aegis of Rome. After the Europe of the Reformation was established, by proclaiming that the empire sought by Charles V was impossible, there was no longer a shared Christendom whose unity transcended state reason. Thus, the Reformation and the death of empire, confessionalization and territorialization, seem to implicate each other in the dynamics of the establishment of absolutist monarchical power.

Foucault's hypothesis, which I am freely summarizing, presupposes an implicit definition of colonization in which its beginning coincided with the conquest of the Americas. Foucault shares this definition with a whole European historiography of imperialism. The birth of colonialism was the death of the Empire.[13] The colonialism of the Classical Age performed the assassination. According to this hypothesis, the formation of colonies was indissociable from the birth of governmentality. Colonialism was the extension overseas of the competition between sovereigns that raged at the heart of Europe itself. The essentially fragmented space from which governmentality was born was globalized through colonization. Europe's colonial conquests confirmed the constitutive multiplicity of political space, organized as a plurality of *raisons d'états* that were so many forces in conflict. According to Foucault, it was this fragmentation that broke the continuity of the history of the medieval Holy Roman Empire. From then on, the relations of domination – colonial or neocolonial – that Europe holds with the rest of the world, and which constitute it as such, would always exist. Contemporary Europe in some sense perpetuates the death of empire through neocolonialism, which is itself only a function of governmentality.[14]

A similar analysis of colonialism informs Hannah Arendt's *The Origins of Totalitarianism*. She deploys a theory of imperialism that defines it as a

---

13   Ibid., p. 295.

14   For me, then, what is needed is neither to extend the concept of governmentality to the colonies, nor to return to a classical theory of the state that is content to affirm the permanence of its Christian theologico-political sovereignty. The theory of imperiality sketches out another path: grasping how the return of the empire – as the recursion sustaining modern sovereignty – continues to constitute the language of the *state*, while also being articulated with practices of government whose dissemination makes empire impossible. There are thus only imperial *effects* of sovereignty rather than a single authority deploying itself as a totality over a given territory.

strategy of unlimited expansion that proceeds from a more or less consummated mourning of the founding of a unified empire. England was the triumphant modern power because it consummated this generalized mourning of the Roman imperium. Imperialism is understood as a way of taking leave from empire, and so is distinguished from imperial conquest, from the founding of empires. According to Arendt, the history of the British colonial empire attests to this: it was no longer concerned with assimilating a multitude of peoples into a unity that encompassed them all, but, instead, with extending the British nation to the four corners of the globe and governing by respecting popular customs, even if it did so through the intermediary of indigenous authorities instrumentalized through the system of indirect rule. Imperialism, as 'expansion for expansion's sake', is thus distinct from any annexation of territory that leads to its integration into the body politic of a nation that is subsequently defined as an empire.

Despite their differences, Foucault and Arendt both consider empire and imperialism to be not only distinct but *incompatible and contradictory*. But their philosophical formulation of the theme of the death of empire has one exception. For Foucault, the exception to the death of empire is the German Reich. Europe is not an empire because the Europe of nations was an attempt to make Germany forget its imperial dream.[15] Modern Europe was a creation of countries that formed a twentieth-century alliance against a Germany that opposed this order, tragically and desperately. The Third Reich thus seems to be the ultimate form of the resurrection of the sleeping emperor, arriving to counter the Europe of nations and its strategic equilibrium with the project of unity through empire.

But there is another exception. One event, absolutely decisive for the history of modern secularism, seems indeed to have broken the inaugural link between modern governmentality and the death of empire. This event is nothing other than the French Revolution, and its imperial completion by Bonaparte. The Revolution secularized law and state only by seeking to restore the empire, through a process of conquest and annexation that was deployed in Europe, on the continent itself. It thus woke the phantom of the sleeping emperor, and showed that he lived on beyond his death. Never since Charles V had there been an attempt to unite the European peoples by

---

15   Ibid., pp. 304–5.

submitting them to one single yoke. This corresponds to Hannah Arendt's reading in 'Imperialism', the second part of *The Origins of Totalitarianism*.[16] The French Empire marked an unprecedented and profoundly contradictory exception: a colonialist nation that still lived as an empire. If Napoleon had failed to unify Europe in an empire, it was contemporary France's colonial project that had tried to perpetuate the imperial constitution of the nation. French colonial history, in all its singularity, *continues* to deny the assassination of empire by the nation. For Arendt, the exception to the death of the empire is French colonialism: it is not only Napoleon but also and above all the whole of French colonial history that runs counter to the current of modern and contemporary history.[17]

France would thus be the only modern nation that sought to construct an empire by means of imperialism. For Arendt, this singularity was the fruit of a contradiction between an imperialism based on unlimited expansion and an imperial structure that sought to integrate conquered territory into the nation. The Commonwealth was not an empire, and indirect rule was not the *indigénat*. It aimed not to make Africans English, but to make them 'better Africans'. *The empire is the nation, the nation is the empire*: unlike England and all other European nations, this was the impossible equation France attempted to realize. In this framing, the French colonization of Africa and particularly of Algeria appears as the ideal type of an attempted *imperial integration*, in the era of an imperialism that made this integration impossible. As long as the dominant British form provides the model of imperialism, the singularity of French imperialism is ultimately reduced to an association of imperialist elements with imperial resurgences. This contradiction between empire and imperialism produces and presupposes an exclusion that is still more violent and absurd than it is – at least apparently – assimilationist. Its paradigm is the *indigénat*, French nationality distinct from citizenship.

The question that can lead us from a theory of governmentality to a theory of imperiality is the following: How can we understand the paradigmatic status of something that appears, in the dominant theories of colonialism expressed by Foucault and Arendt, as an exception? To what extent is the European imperial exception in truth the rule through which

---

16   Hannah Arendt, *The Origins of Totalitarianism*, New York: Harcourt Brace Jovanovich, 1973, pp. 128–9.
17   Ibid.

colonialism can be understood? As we have said, *the death of empire does not prevent its resurrections*; on the contrary, it inaugurates the history of its incessant cyclical returns. The ambiguous presence of imperiality at the heart of colonial modernity thus seems like a ceaseless ghostly return. It haunted the practices of the first secular states born after the Reformation, and also the post-revolutionary nineteenth century with its imperialism. What seems anachronistic at first sight in fact leads us to a multiple and entangled temporality, a specific modality of the presence of *an imperial past in a colonial present*.[18] It is thus possible to subvert the theme of the death of empire as follows: not only does it not prevent resurrection, but in truth this death itself is what gives the idea of empire its power. This ideological reality of empire after its death is what I call imperiality. Imperiality thus becomes a sort of variable that colonialisms have attempted to define: an *empire* = *x*.

Imperiality's entangled times

It is by beginning from the impossible returns of empire, as they are deployed in the space of ideology, that Europe and modernity can be deciphered as colonial realities. Colonialism, whether colonial or not, military or economic, statist or cultural, functions through the *remembering of a dismembered empire* – metamorphosed, certainly, but still active at the interior of ideology. Imperiality is this cycle by which the dead empire seems to constantly return in vain, at the heart of colonialism and its discourses. European colonialisms can be distinguished only by their particular way of relating to this project, *always thwarted*, of resurrecting global domination. The deployment of imperialism is thus at once a way of summoning and warding off the seeming spectre of the renascent empire. The body of the empire can only be apprehended as simultaneously dead *and* living. The colony is the site from which the

---

18 Arendt tends to understand French imperialism as an exception, as a still *imperial imperialism in the age of the death of empire*. French colonial history thus contradicts the dominant form of colonial imperialism, which was initiated and dominated by the British. This assumption is debatable. Contrary to what Arendt declares, on an ideological level, British imperialism was as imperial as French imperialism. See David Armitage, *The Ideological Origins of the British Empire*, Cambridge: Cambridge University Press, 2000, p. 24.

imperial returns. The irreducible singularity of determinate colonial histories is what must always be envisaged through the mediation of this hypothesis, of a dialectic of the resurrection of empire through colonial formations that constantly render it impossible. The *imperium* is pluralized, and thus is always singularized through competing colonial projects.

The colonialism of nations is what tends to give a value to the variable *empire* = x, while at the same time making empire impossible. By definition, and perhaps by essence, then, it is a constant and permanent failure, a vanity destined to death but always continuing to remain alive. This contradiction is precisely what makes imperial universalism impossible. Once imperialism is stripped of its political form, its cultural and ideological components are only more effective, and accompany its neocolonial afterlives.[19] The imperial return is the beating heart of cultural imperialism, of this imperiality without fixed territory which survived historical decolonization. The extension of the process of decolonization requires a critique of the imperiality of power that spread out across the world with the formation of a world economy and the development of capitalism.

Imperiality is this recursive persistence that continuously haunts states in the form of what Marx calls a spectre.[20] Two spectres thus haunt

---

19   This is the meaning of *neocolonialism*, a notion developed by Kwame Nkrumah in *Neo-colonialism: The Last Stage of Imperialism*, London: Thomas Nelson & Sons, 1965, pp. ix–xii. Nkrumah reversed Lenin's perspective by inverting his title, *Imperialism: The Last Stage of Capitalism*. This extension of the category of imperialism beyond its strictly colonial forms was decisive, and opened the way for postcolonial studies of cultural imperialism, as well as of economic dependency and resource exploitation. Colonialism and neocolonialism are thus both forms of imperialism. For a periodization and historical distinction of different forms of imperialism in terms of phases of capitalist development, see Marc Ferro, *Colonization: A Global History*, London: Routledge: 1997, p. 18. The old type of colonization is linked to the stage of free competition. Colonial Algeria is its last example. The new type of colonization is linked to the monopoly stage theorized by Lenin. This colonization is the fruit of the industrial revolution and finance capital, and dates from 1871. The third type of imperialism is imperialism without colonization, as in the example of the Ottoman Empire and Egypt. In my view, empire designates a variable of which imperialism itself is only one determinate form, which allows us to theorize this final limit case. It can thus be applied to non-colonial forms of imperialism, and allows us to examine the multiplicity of these spectral effects, often called postcolonial or postmetropolitan, to the extent that they ignore imperiality.

20   Derrida famously comments on this double meaning of spectrality in his work on Marx; see Jacques Derrida, *Specters of Marx*, New York: Routledge, 1994, pp. 4–5. In this chapter, I am much more indebted to a critical reassessment of Marx's idea of entangled temporalities than I am to Derrida's hauntology.

Europe, and perhaps the world: revolution – or, for Marx, communism – and imperiality. This formula captures my hypothesis by taking up a Marxian concept from the first sentence of the *Manifesto* to challenge the Foucauldian narrative of the death of empire. If the empire is both dead and alive, the capitalist present appears to be thorned between the two spectres of imperiality and revolution. But while the spectre of revolution haunts the present from the future, imperiality is what the present makes of the past. The latter never was identified as such by Marx, notwithstanding the fact that Bonapartism appeared as the main figure of anachronism in the present. It is historical actors themselves who put on the old costume of empire that dresses most bourgeois revolution and socialist dictatorships. The *return* can thus be distinguished from the *remnant*. The non-linear analysis of an era can be opposed to the analysis of past strata that remain the same despite the passage of time, as residual forms of what no longer exists which haunt the present as mere vestiges. This is how metaphors of ghosts and spectres are still used in most theorizing in colonial and postcolonial studies.

The present is the *active reconstruction* of a past that it has the power to conjure. Without the acts of the present, the past wouldn't exist as *this* newly reconfigured past. The past is thus reconstructed by an era as its relation to itself. Since the past does disappear in the nothingness called time, it only exists through the self-reflection of the present, thus reopening the past as a set of unanswered questions, reinvesting traces as a prophecy looking backwards in the circle of time. It is neither the linearity of progress nor the return of the repressed past but the non-contemporaneity of the *present* that defines the historicity of imperiality. Its seeming spectrality refers to a subtle sense of environment and present tasks, the framing of what is contemporary and a desire to bring back the dead, much more than to any political facts that a historian might analyse by consulting the archives of empires. The imperiality born from the Enlightenment was the claim to the Roman imperial title and the universalism that defines it. It was also the desire to bring back to life Alexander, Caesar, Moses, or 'Mahomet'. None of their spectres came back. Only the unfulfilled desires in the long history of their dissatisfaction. Only imperiality.

If imperiality is ceaselessly fragmenting, it is not the *same empire* that returned through the colonial globalization, in its unprecedented violence, that has taken place since the conquest of the Americas. The circuit of a returning imperiality was opened by the defeat of Charles V's empire, whose function had been to conduct a reform of feudalism through the defence of Parliament and a nobility of virtue.[21] This empire of reform became an empire of revolution through the proclamation of secularization. If the medieval empire had sought to bring a close to historical time, the secular empire intended to open a new era of universal history. The empire was thus transformed by the present, which, by causing its return through the colonies, retrospectively conferred on it a seeming spectral reality, somewhere between the dead and the living.[22] But this seeming spectrality was only a temporal effect of spatial movements: the fragmentation of empire and the dissemination in the colonies as well as their permanent return. The metropolitan spaces of Europe and their alleged centrality are territorializations of these returning circles and ongoing circulations.

The empire of the multiple and the death of the One

How can we situate the concept of imperiality and its secularization in the history of Western empires and their ideologies? What is the difference between the empire of heaven and empires beneath the earth? Empire presented itself first, in the Middle Ages, as a figure of the One, as the ontological unity of the multitude that founds the idea of monarchy. For Dante, it was the name of the sovereignty of the One exercised over the whole of humanity in the name of God and Rome.[23] The argument was simple: the emperor should reign over the world for the well-being of humanity. Humanity, Dante argued, should be governed by a single power, because empire made humanity most resemble God. Dante's emperor was ordained in heaven as most perfect in the order of creation. Taking his authority directly from God, he was designated as God's vicar, without the mediation of the Church. Empire thus meant

21   Laurent Gerbier, *Les Raisons de l'empire*, Paris: Vrin, 2016, p. 43.
22   The literature on zombies in the colonial world is vast. In my view, the zombie is only one face of the reality of empire that haunts the colonies and racism. On Black experience as situated between life and death, see Calvin Warren, *Ontological Terror: Blackness, Nihilism, and Emancipation*, Durham, NC: Duke University Press, 2018, pp. 26–62.
23   Dante, *Monarchy*, Cambridge: Cambridge University Press, 1996, pp. 15–19.

absolute authority in the temporal order. This Christian empire was also the successor of Rome, to the extent that God himself, according to Dante, had willed the Roman Empire.

Dante's argument shows that imperiality proceeded from the theological hypothesis of a *resemblance* between God and man. This supposed resemblance, and the continuity between God and power that it affirms, was at the heart of the theologico-political complex, understood as the possibility of representing divine power on Earth. This task was what Dante reserved for empire, against the absolutist pretentions – thus themselves imperial – of the Roman Church. The theological opposite of imperiality was thus the affirmation of a radical dissimilarity between God and the human, of their incommensurability. For this very reason, the category of monotheism has no rigorous analytical unity and, as much as the concept of religion, it needs to be unpacked if one is to describe the imperial and anti-imperial tendencies of differing declarations of divine unicity.

Historically, imperiality is what remained when the Christian world seemed to give way to a modern world, a trace left by the dismemberment of the empire of Christ, of heaven, and of the One. And its dissemination would give rise to a form of power liberated from the spectres of the One, to an imperial government of the multitude as such. This death of Oneness is perhaps the beating heart of what Foucault has named governmentality. If this hypothesis was to be confirmed, one should redefine governmentality by narrating its birth anew and by reconceptualizing its relation to state sovereignty in non-Foucauldian ways. Behind the historical circle of returns, there would lie a process of governmentalization of the state through the *governmentalization of its imperiality*. It is this interdependence that Foucauldian theory does not allow to be analysed, Foucault having been led by it to dissociate governmentality from state sovereignty. Their articulation through imperiality, as well as the hypothesis of the governmentalization of the imperial state, makes it possible to affirm that the contemporary mechanisms of power are not reducible to effects or images of the One.

The role of Western imperiality in the accumulation of capital

The functioning of those powers that are described as *modern* – the state, the nation, and capital – is inseparable from the colonial mutations of imperiality. While it has been constantly articulated with colonialism, the imperiality that haunted the birth of the modern state and the capitalist economy is irreducible to the simple possession of colonies. This can be seen in the case of the Reich.

'Western particularity' is not the fruit of the spirit of Christianity, or of the scientific rationality that singularly developed in the West. It results from the double process of the fragmentation of the Christian empire of the West and the dissemination of its scraps through the proliferation of colonies. This double process structures the history of what I call imperiality. It was in Europe, and only in Europe, from the fifteenth century on, that the claim to absolute power was territorialized by attempting to materialize it in the creation of colonies. In trying to realize empire in the colonies, Europe fragmented and multiplied its imperiality through colonization. From then on, there was no longer a unified empire but only empires in the plural, which each claimed the imperial title for themselves by being colonial empires in competition with each other.

The history of modernity is the history of the fragmentation of the Christian empire and its colonial dissemination. The ideologies of modernity present this double process under the Christian figures of death and resurrection. They are the surface effects of the colonial process of the fragmentation of Roman imperiality as reformulated by Western Christendom. If the word *empire* still has a meaning today, it is to designate these impossible returns that haunt the sovereignty of nation-states that never cease to claim an absolute power, without limits and without exterior, which leads them to want to take the place of God himself. The goal of the preceding chapters has been to examine the effects of secularization provoked by the colonial dissemination of imperiality during the nineteenth century. They have shown how wars of conquest and evangelization became civilizing missions, all the while claiming to abolish slavery through free labour. Thus, the transformation of Muslim infidels into colonized subjects deployed during the colonization of Algeria should be connected to the transformation of the Black slaves of the Americas into the subaltern labourers of racial capitalism. This double process is linked to the birth of liberal and industrial empires that followed from the colonial dissemination of imperiality throughout the nineteenth century.

Imperiality is the name of the power that subjugated the colonies to the European metropoles, and colonialism itself to the sovereignty of modern states. Existing critiques of colonialism, modernity, or Christianity have not known how to identify the imperiality of state violence that is the beating heart of the processes of capital accumulation. Neither postcolonial criticism and its decolonial transformations nor Marxism ever really accomplished this. The colonies were the site *par excellence* where the imperiality of the European states, born from the ruins of the Western Christian empire, was manifested. The concept of the West thus cannot be reduced to a sort of empirical fact that could be confirmed. No geology, no geographical data can suffice to define the West, if only because it includes at least two continents: Europe and America. The unity of the West corresponds to the unity of the imperiality that haunts nation-states and imperialisms while engendering race. It is not surprising, then, that empire has remained an alternative political form of the capitalist bourgeoisie and a possible model of organization parallel to the formation of modern nation-states. In some sense, the history of German or American federalism can remind us of this. My hypothesis consists in grasping imperiality as the beating heart of the ideologies of capitalist modernity, of territorial nation-states but *also* of forms of government that go beyond sovereignty. The empire-form thus contributed to the birth of the *modern territorial state* and determined its monarchic and absolutist dimensions.[24]

How did the colonial dissemination of imperiality that I situate at the heart of political modernity determine the birth of capitalism? How did the dialectic that connects the impossible returns of empire to the racist massacres perpetrated by colonizers structure what Marx called the primitive accumulation of capital? The answer can be found in the question: by organizing together the pieces of the singular phenomenon that we call today the modern nation-state, by redrawing the skeleton of Leviathan. The dissemination of imperiality through colonialism *contributed to the birth of capitalism* to the extent that imperiality

---

24   The imperial dimension of state centralization is affirmed in *The Civil War in France*. See Karl Marx and Friedrich Engels, *Marx-Engels Werke*, Band 17, Berlin: Dietz Verlag, 1962, p. 336. On the paradigmatic dimension of the Bonapartist state, see my analysis of the concept of the fossil state in Chapter 4 of this book.

sustained the practices of state violence that punctuated the unfolding of this accumulation. Black slavery and the expropriation of peasants, the destruction of life, and the seizure of land were economic realities only as forms of this violence that brought capital forth in blood.[25] Imperiality is what translated the theme of the blood Christ into royal blood and, in Marx's text, made the modern state appear as capital in the form of a vampire.[26] In my opinion, what Marx, Foucault, and Fanon all ignored is that imperiality was at the heart of the dynamics that wove together the appropriation of Church goods, enclosures, and the transatlantic slave trade. The colonial dissemination of imperiality was the keystone of the accumulation from which capitalism was born, the underpinning of the gigantic work of annihilation and expropriation that Marx, in his Hegelian language, described as a negation destined to be negated itself. Under this apparently innocent word, *negation*, hides the phenomenon of violence and destruction.[27]

But imperiality continues to be reborn for a more fundamental reason: its differed reprise in diverse forms is witness to its *irreducible historicity*. This act of rebirth under different faces is the matrix of the processes of *secularization* of institutions. The ongoing return of the imperial event is never an identical repetition. The empire that returns is not a terminal empire, oriented towards the conversion of infidels and the advent of salvation by the divine election of its sovereign. It was another empire that was charged with universalizing civilization, in place of colonial Christianity, to bring about the secular emancipation of peoples as it radiated outwards. The *secular world*, therefore, emerged only through a new process of imperialization, the one by which capital became fossil. The secular might be nothing other than a historical configuration of the earth.

---

25   Karl Marx, *Capital, A Critique of Political Economy*, vol. 1, New York: Penguin, 1992, p. 915. Imperialism made capitalism possible, and is neither an extension of it nor a simple stage. Capitalism was constituted through the imperial circulation of Europe and its colonies, in a permanent and still ongoing process.

26   Gil Anidjar, *Blood: A Critique of Christianity*, New York: Columbia University Press, 2014, pp. 128, 137–40.

27   This work of destruction – the phenomenon of state and racial violence as well as the upheaval of the earth that it provoked – is nonetheless irreducible to the Hegelian logic of the negative. Foucault's gestures – from the history of madness to the critique of 'the repressive hypothesis' in *The History of Sexuality* – were, perhaps, nothing but a contestation of the remains of Hegelian negativity in the analysis of power deployed by Marxism.

Epilogue

The sacrifice of heaven was an effect of the colonial disseminations of a dismembered empire. This empire's colonial rebirths tried to assassinate the God who had been upholding its claim to rule. The desire to represent God on Earth by converting the world to the Christian religion led, so to speak, to inciting the murder of the Father and his heavens. The representative (the empire) dissolved the one it represented (God) through the colonial mechanisms of representation itself. The failure of the Christian empire was the condition for its colonial dissemination, in the form of a spirit who, somewhere between life and death, has never stopped deciding the fate of the living. This process, a gigantic sacrifice of heaven that destroys the earth while promising symbolic or real death to the living beings it dehumanizes or rehumanizes by means of race, gave birth to so-called modernity. Through it, the *empire* of Christ was turned against Christ himself.

The pretention to omnipotence, of which the generalized surveillance of populations is only one of many contemporary phenomena, flowed from this historical dialectic. Everything took place *as if* fossil colonialism had actualized an imperial potentiality whose contingent realization had been *deferred*. Nothing destined Europe to dominate the world. But the emergence of territorial states, of colonialism, and of capital that followed the Reconquista led to a reprise of the imperial project, to its differential repetition. This is why the radical contingency of Europe's colonization of the world must be affirmed. If imperiality was

constitutive of the political fiction of the West, its simultaneous realization and failure in colonialism was in no way a necessary unfolding
governed by a sort of teleology. Only a series of contingencies led to the
emergence of industrial capitalism, and led imperiality to become the
ideological face of the process of accumulation.

This book thus sketches a philosophy of history. It does not address the
structure of historical temporality independently of the events themselves.
By doing this, it contests Hegel's philosophy of history on its strategic terrain.
Rather than seeking a historicity irreducible to Hegelian progress, as Freud
and Nietzsche magisterially did, or attempting to pluck the dialectic itself
from the history of spirit, like Marx and Fanon, this book has redefined
what, according to Hegel, is at the heart of the history of the world: secularization. Secularization, in his account, and in the eyes of his disciples up to
the present day, is a call to return to the world, to the real that we had lost
through the Oriental invention of a single and transcendent God. But the
call to cease fleeing the world assumes that subjects are strangers to it, that
they must be integrated to it willingly or by force. This world – at the heart
of which the colonized are excluded by race, and life on Earth is threatened
with extinction – is presented as the *only* real world, as *this* world in opposition to other worlds of theologies. This world is the secular (*saeculum*), the
world to which secularization is meant to bring us back.

Would there not be a sort of impossible circularity here, in the mesh
of which this ecological and racial history of secularization would
become trapped? How can we theorize secularization without first
examining the reality of the secular to which we are destined by its
process? Does a secular world not need to exist in order for something
to be secularized? The concept of the Secularocene responds to this
famous Heideggerian objection.[1] It shows that the secular is nothing

---

1   Martin Heidegger, *Nietzsche*, vol. 4, San Francisco: Harper & Row, 1982, p. 100:
'In most decisive respects, such talk of "secularization" is a thoughtless deception,
because for there to be "secularization" (*Säkularisierung*), "becoming-worldly"
(*Verweltlichung*), *already implies a secular world*, toward which and in which one is
made worldly. The *saeculum*, the "world" through which something is "secularized" in
the celebrated "secularization", does not exist in itself or in such a way that it can be
realized *simply by stepping out of the Christian world*.' [Translation modified following
Meziane's translation; emphasis added.] By affirming the (onto)logical primacy of the
secular over secularism as a doctrine and of secularization as a process, Asad recovers
and deepens Heidegger's intuition. See Talal Asad, *Formations of the Secular: Christianity,
Islam, Modernity*, Stanford, CA: Stanford University Press, 2003, p. 16. Still, an

other than the earth, in its state of upheaval by the system of its industrial exploitation. Secularization does not at all bring us back to a world that we would have lost by imagining the existence of illusory heavens. As an order by fossil empires, secularization acts on the world and transforms it. Through these empires, the critique of heaven overturns the earth. The Secularocene is the name and effect of this mutation, secularist ontologies being what codified the terrestrial by defining it as *secular* and opposing it to the heavens referred to as so-called *religion*. Secularization is thus the becoming-secular of the earth and the world. Its racial and ecological history is inseparable from the way in which monotheism was rejected as the foundation of a religious violence that the moderns have continually racialized.

It may be that the formulation of this hypothesis will put us on the track of a philosophy that affirms the differences of eras, a theory of the interweaving of epochs. It is aware of the impossibility of subsuming the singularity of epochs under the identity of a single substance, of a great chain of events that would be named *history*. Contesting the dogma of the *irreversibility* of time as well as the illusion of its linearity, it conceives of each so-called epoch as a system of returns to past, future, or merely possible periods. It makes the illusion of presence dissolve through the description of a multiplicity of space-times, of pasts that replay their meaning in a crowd of presents, making possible futures resonate. This work thus calls for another. It makes the still-absent voice of another book resonate beneath this one: another work that doubles its lines by its subterranean presence, a presence irreducible to that of the fossil states of the earth.

---

indeterminacy remains, throughout this book, as to what is signified by the secular. One of the roles of this epilogue is to sketch out a response and to answer Heidegger's objection to the concept of secularization.

Index